Public
Opinion
in America

ALAN D. MONROE

ILLINOIS STATE UNIVERSITY

Public Opinion in America

DODD, MEAD & COMPANY
New York   1975

Contents

List of Figures

List of Tables

Preface

The purpose of this book is two-fold: to summarize and analyze the nature of public opinion in contemporary America and to examine the implications of that nature for the possibility of a functioning democracy. While the first of these objectives is largely—but not entirely—a matter of weighing the evidence provided by a host of scientific studies, the second inevitably involves a sizable injection of the author's own normative values. I will not attempt to define or defend those values at this point, for the reader will soon encounter them. Hopefully, I will have been successful enough in drawing the critical distinction between fact and judgment that the reader will feel free to disagree with questionable conclusions.

One facet which may distinguish this book from some similar efforts is that it presents findings on what Americans are actually thinking about some important current issues. There are some obvious pitfalls here, for there is always the possibility that tomorrow's events will make today's conclusions look foolish. But armed with a belief that there is a basic stability to the public mood, I have taken that risk. At the same time, I have sought to present what seems to me to be the best available documentation for my generalizations, even if those data come from previous decades. While use of the most recent data is desirable when describing the distribution of preferences concerning a current issue, it is a less important criterion when one is seeking to support basic generalizations about the nature of mass behavior. In the latter case, I have sought to illustrate the argument with the clearest and most directly applicable research, whatever its vintage.

While this is a book that deals specifically with *public opinion* and not with political participation and voting behavior, a fair amount of material devoted to the electoral process is included. It is included because elections are the primary channel available for public opinion to influence government. Whether or not elections perform that function adequately is a question considered at length in the book.

Additionally, the inclusion of this material may prove useful in those situations in which both public opinion and voting behavior are included in a single course.

Any writer of a book such as this must necessarily acknowledge many debts. First, this project would have been impossible without the benefit of a generation of researchers whose findings, some of which are cited within, make it possible to justify conclusions about the mass public. I should also acknowledge the assistance of several political candidates and their staff members who gave me the opportunity to conduct and analyze surveys which, whatever their political utility, greatly increased my understanding of the electorate.

Of all of the individuals who have had a hand in my education in political science, four deserve special mention. During my graduate work at Indiana University, Leroy Rieselbach and Elton Jackson exposed me to some of the subject matter that has eventually found its way into this volume. Less direct, but equally important, were the contributions of Charles Hyneman and Charles McCall, who raised the questions of popular democracy that are always the ultimate concerns of the book. Also deserving of mention is Jere Bruner of Oberlin College, who read the entire manuscript with an eye to improving it in both style and substance. The comments of Gerald Pomper, Rutgers University, were helpful too. The reader may well regret that I was too stubborn to take more of their suggestions. My appreciative recognition goes to Alberta Carr for her editorial suggestions and typing skills in preparing the manuscript.

The greatest debt, finally, is owed to the students in my public opinion class at Illinois State University during the last eight semesters. Whether or not their own education in the subject was enhanced by the experience, mine certainly was.

Alan D. Monroe

PART 1

THE STUDY
OF PUBLIC OPINION:
POLITICAL THEORY
AND METHODOLOGY

Opinions and Democratic Theory

1

"The public demands action!"
"The president is ignoring public opinion!"
"Let's talk sense to the American people."
"All power to the people!"

The universality of such rhetoric in today's world testifies to the importance of public approval for political action. Virtually every part of the political spectrum desires the support of the mass public for its demands. Candidates for public office vie in accusing each other of either ignoring the views of the voters—or of slavishly following the public mood. This preoccupation with the role of the average citizen in the political process is not a new one; the public has been alternately damned, praised, and appealed to throughout the history of political discourse. It would be an overstatement to say that the history of political thought is a history of controversy over what we now call "public opinion." But a considerable part of that body of thought has been devoted to argument over questions related to the views of the public.

The fact that persons of differing political persuasions might agree that public support is needed to justify the legitimacy of their positions hardly leads to a harmony of views. It was only a few years ago that the president of the United States asserted that a "silent majority" supported his policies, while his critics simultaneously accused him of ignoring the wishes of the people. Indeed, the intensity of political debate is now heightened, for spokesmen of the Left and Right both seem to be firmly convinced that the "God" of public opinion is on their side. In part their disagreement is a result of the tendency of any serious combatant to believe that all "reasonable" men will agree with his position. However, the disagreement also stems from the variety of meanings attached to terms like "public opinion" and "democracy." These issues will be dealt with in this and later chapters. The point here is that the study of public opinion is highly relevant to political discourse and action, no matter what ideological position one holds, and that the subject is sufficiently complex and problematical to require careful analysis.

DEMOCRACY AS PUBLIC OPINION

In the world of the twentieth century, there is no single political word as popular as "democracy." From Washington to Warsaw, from Cape Town to Copenhagen, governments everywhere proclaim themselves to be "democratic." The key element in the concept of democracy, one which seems common to most uses of the term, is the notion that governments must take into account the wishes of the population and that the root of political power is the people themselves, rather than any authority bestowed by divinity, heredity, or accident of history. Beyond this core of meaning, agreement quickly disappears. There are at least three commonly used methods of defining democracy and these lead to somewhat different conclusions about whether a given political system is democratic.

Democracy as a System of Values.   The term "democracy" is sometimes used to indicate the total character of a society, rather than an attribute of its politics.[1] It is in this vein that writers have argued about the requisites of a "democratic personality" or the importance of a certain type of family life. The key element in this conception is often a concern with equality among individuals. It is on this basis that nations such as the People's Democratic Republic of Korea (North Korea) would defend the name they have taken.

Another value-laden use of "democracy" emphasizes the importance of individual liberties, particularly those of expression. Thus, many would decide whether or not a system is "democratic" on the basis of whether or not there is true freedom of speech and press. Whatever the values employed, this sort of approach leaves much to be desired. Whenever one seeks to judge a total society, rather than just its politics, his task becomes enormous. When one seeks to do this on the basis of normative values, it becomes even more difficult. Thus, the conception of democracy as a "way of life" must be left to social critics, and a more useful approach sought for the purpose of this inquiry.

Democracy as Political Structure.   Political thinkers of a more empirical bent have sought to determine which characteristics of political structure are necessary for a democracy. Nations are evaluated on

[1] An influential example of this approach is John Dewey, *The Public and Its Problems* (New York: Henry Holt, 1927).

the basis of whether or not they have elections, whether political competition is permitted, how egalitarian the basis of legislative representation may be, and so on. One of the best formulations of this type is that of Ranney and Kendall, who specify four "Principles of Democracy":

1. *Popular Sovereignty*—the idea that power is ultimately vested in all of the members of the community.

2. *Political Equality*—the principle that every person theoretically can exercise the same degree of control over public policy.

3. *Majority Rule*—if there is a disagreement over alternatives, that choice which is favored by the greater number should prevail.

4. *Popular Consultation*—the idea that those holding governmental positions will attempt to learn what popular preferences are and act upon them.[2]

There is considerable virtue in such a listing for illuminating some of the practical implications of the concept of democracy. However, there are some limitations to it as a working model. A basic problem is that it can lead to overemphasis on legal frameworks, rather than on political realities. Some nations go to great lengths to insure high rates of electoral participation and yet their elections seem to have little impact on the actions taken by the government. The Soviet Union, for example, customarily achieves a participation rate in elections in excess of 99 percent of the electorate and takes great pains to assure that no fraud can occur. The only aspect that seems to be neglected is that no choice of candidates is offered to the voter. Additionally, there is the possibility that a political system may be democratic at some times on some issues and undemocratic in other instances. For example, a government might respond readily to the desires of voters on domestic economic questions, but completely ignore the public on issues of foreign policy. Or it is conceivable that a political system might be quite democratic at the local level, while remaining much less so in national politics. A reliance on structural aspects will not allow such situations to be easily distinguished. Thus, the definition of democracy in terms of legal structure leaves something to be desired.

Democracy as Political Process. A definition of "democracy" might concentrate on what most people associate with the term: the extent to which government responds to the people. Defining the term in

[2] Austin Ranney and Willmoore Kendall, *Democracy and the American Party System* (New York: Harcourt, Brace, 1956), pp. 43–55. The brief summaries of the principles are this author's. The first four chapters of Ranney and Kendall contain a lucid explication of many of the issues involved in the concept of democracy.

this way avoids the practical problems that appear to pervade alternative definitions. It also emphasizes the role of the public and its opinions. Thus, for the purpose of this book, we will take "democracy" to mean *the extent to which public opinion influences public policy*. In other words, democracy is the correlation between what the people ask for and what they get from the political process. This notion allows us to inquire, for instance, whether the United States is relatively more democratic in domestic affairs than in foreign affairs. In defining democracy in this way, we are not ruling out the questions posed by the concept of democracy as a characteristic of governmental structure. Rather, we are excluding them from the definition and turning them into questions for study. In Chapter 14, for instance, we will concentrate on the issue of whether the institution of elections does indeed act as a medium of communication between the public and those who make decisions for it. Finally, defining democracy as we have emphasizes its variable character. Democracy is seen as a characteristic which can exist to a greater or lesser extent at any point in time, rather than as a rigid category into which a political system may fall. To study public opinion, then, is to engage in the formulation and evaluation of democratic theory.[3]

PUBLIC OPINION AS DEMOCRACY

Formulating a definition of democracy hardly settles the problem of the role of the public. Even if everyone agreed with the idea that democracy consists of the influence of public opinion on government, there would still be disagreement as to whether the United States (or any other country) is "democratic." In part, the controversy would continue because of a failure to agree upon just what constitutes "public opinion."

For our purposes, the term may be defined very simply: *public opinion is the distribution of individual preferences within a population*. In other words, *public* opinion is simply the sum or aggregation of *private* opinions on any particular issue or set of issues. There are, however, some other aspects of the meaning of public opinion that deserve particular comment.

[3] Concepts of "democracy" can also be divided into those emphasizing what classical philosophy called *posis* (the results produced by a political system) and *praxis* (the way in which those actions were made). The definition we are using is of the latter variety. See Donald J. Devine, *The Attentive Public: Polyarchical Democracy* (Chicago: Rand McNally, 1970), chap. 1 and 2 for a discussion of these approaches. Braybrooke suggests that the United States probably fulfills the criterion of representing "collective preference" in policy decisions better than other examples of a *posis* nature. See David Braybrooke, *Three Tests for Democracy: Personal Rights, Human Welfare, Collective Preference* (New York: Random House, 1968).

As suggested in the definition, we are interested in the distribution of opinions. This has two implications. First, we expect that the population under study will not all be of the same opinion. There will instead generally be at least two sides to the question and a number of individuals on each side. Students of public opinion are concerned not simply with which side is larger, but with the relative numbers of people holding each position. We would like to know not simply that public opinion generally favors prayer in public schools, but rather that 75 percent believe it should be allowed, and about 13 percent oppose it, with the rest not inclined to express feelings one way or another. Secondly, we are often not content with simply knowing *how many* people hold an opinion, but also with *who* they are and *how strongly* they hold their opinions. Analyses of public opinion usually consider whether members of various social groups hold different opinions and how an individual's opinion on one issue affects his opinion on another.

The definition of public opinion makes reference to a "population." This word refers to the group of people whose opinions are being described. For many purposes, the "population" in question is just that—the whole population (or at least the adult population) of the country. In other cases, one may be interested in describing a smaller population, such as members of a minority group or those people who have a sufficient degree of knowledge about a technical question to be able to formulate an opinion. If we are concerned with U.S. policy in Asia, the whole adult population would probably be sampled, whereas the relevant population for an evaluation of the current agricultural price-support program might be only those people whose families are engaged in farming. Any population may be validly dealt with as a "public," provided that one specifies precisely who is included in that population.

A problematic aspect of our definition is the extent to which an individual must *express* a preference before it is counted as an opinion. Must he volunteer his views in a public forum? Or will an unstated and even subconscious feeling suffice? The theoretical problem here is that there are different levels of cognition and evaluation which vary in their specificity and expression. Terms such as "values" or "beliefs" generally refer to the most basic, deep-seated, and even subconscious aspects of a person's view of the world. "Attitudes" implies a general sort of orientation toward one category of object in the world. At the most conscious and specific level are what we usually call "opinions," which are statements of preference about a particular question. The most manifest level is that of "overt behavior," including verbal expression of an opinion, casting of a vote, or choice of a particular medium of information. We can order these el-

Figure 1-1
Levels of Preference

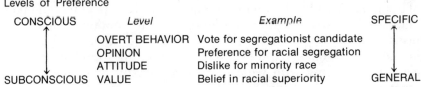

CONSCIOUS	*Level*	*Example*	SPECIFIC
	OVERT BEHAVIOR	Vote for segregationist candidate	
	OPINION	Preference for racial segregation	
	ATTITUDE	Dislike for minority race	
SUBCONSCIOUS	VALUE	Belief in racial superiority	GENERAL

ements on the basis of their specificity and nearness to the psychological surface, as is done in Figure 1-1.

The fact that one can differentiate these phenomena in theory does not mean that it is possible to do so in a practical sense. Of necessity, we can only measure actual behavior, such as the response a person gives to a question on a survey. Such answers may reflect specific opinions, but they also tap underlying attitudes and values. As will be made clear in Chapter 3, specific opinions are largely a reflection of these more deep-seated elements and are generally consistent with them. For these reasons, it can be misleading to press too far a distinction between opinions, attitudes, and values. In this book, we shall attempt to use such terms in a manner consistent with our theoretical understanding of their meaning, but the reader should remember that the distinctions are largely artificial.

The concept of public opinion that has been presented here is essentially one that most students of the subject and professionals in the field of opinion measurement would accept. However, this view of public opinion does not reflect the meaning implicitly held by some persons, particularly those with more extreme ideological positions. The basic source of disagreement is one arising out of an elitist-populist dichotomy. We have defined public opinion in basically *populist* terms (i.e., the opinions of every individual within a given population are theoretically weighted equally in our estimation of the opinion for that particular public). But there are others who have a fundamental disagreement with this populist assumption, and their views should be acknowledged.

Alternatives to the populist concept of public opinion generally involve some element of *elitism* (i.e., the idea that the opinions of certain people should necessarily count for more than those of other individuals). This position has been most clearly advanced at times in the past when out-and-out elitism was a more popular position. "Public opinion" was then thought to be the consensus held by the "best" people, those with the social status and ability required for participation in public affairs of the day. Such open expression of elitism grates upon the ears of an egalitarian age, yet the concept lingers on in other languages. For example, some spokesmen for the political Left seem implicitly to impose some additional criteria for inclusion into the public whose opinion they deem relevant. According to this view, only those opinions that are ideologically correct or intensely expressed should be heeded. The orator who calls for "all power to the people" probably does not mean this in the literal, populist sense; rather, he means "all power to people who hold my views." Advocates of all persuasions tend to argue that only the opinions of those who are as well educated and informed as they are ought to be included in an assessment of public sentiment.

Although these may be morally defensible positions, it is important that their implicit assumptions be made clear. Definitions are always arbitrary, but must be made clear as to their meaning, for definitions have implications. For example, an elitist concept of public opinion might well lead one to measure feeling on an issue by measuring the *overt expression* of intensely held opinions through such means as participation in demonstrations, letters written to public officials, and the like. A populist conception, on the other hand, suggests reliance on means that give equal opportunity for expression to all members of a population, such as public opinion polling. As we shall see in Chapter 2, there are apt to be very different estimates of public opinion produced by these two methods. Hence, it is important to make clear the nature and implications of the concept of public opinion which is being used.

Finally, it is important to distinguish the normative values inherent in our conceptualization from the empirical assumptions. In particular, one might infer from the preceding discussion that we are assuming that all individuals have the same influence upon the political process. Nothing could be farther from the truth. The elitist, whatever his political philosophy, is undoubtedly correct in his belief that the informed, articulate, and organized public often has more than its share of influence on government policy. Whether this situation is "right" or not is a subjective judgment. The point is that an assessment of the relative impact of public opinion on public policy in the populist "one man-one opinion" sense, versus that held by intense or organized groups within the population, is an *empirical* question to be answered by careful analysis of the workings of the political process. To begin by more narrowly defining the relevant public would be to create a self-fulfilling prophecy. It is only by starting with a definition of the public as including everyone's opinion that we can evaluate the possibility that there is a direct relationship between public opinion and public policy. Considerable attention will be given to that question in the concluding chapters of this book. It should be noted, also, that our populist conception of public opinion does not exclude the possibility of measuring the intensity and expression of opinions within subgroups of the population, though it does require that this measurement be done in a systematic and objective fashion.

As should now be clear, the concept of public opinion used in this book is inherently related to our concept of democracy as a characteristic of the political process. We are not assuming here that democracy is desirable, that it now necessarily exists, or that it is likely to exist in the future.[4] What we are saying is that the question of democracy in America is worth careful analysis and that the study of public opinion is necessary to make any general evaluation of either the desirability or the possibility of a truly democratic society.

THE REQUISITES OF PUBLIC OPINION IN DEMOCRATIC THEORY

Political thinkers have speculated on the role of the public in the political process for many centuries. Long before the term "public opinion" was ever coined, philosophers suggested that the citizens who made up a political system would have to meet certain criteria in order for any sort of democratic policy to exist. While the concerns of those philosophers were normative (i.e., what was the "best" society and how might it be achieved), their comments about the mass public essentially had to do with questions of fact (e.g., whether citizens were sufficiently rational to take part in the formation of public policy). The long legacy of political philosophy thus provides a number of testable hypotheses for the scientific study of public opinion. While the philosopher of the past could at best speculate about the nature of the public and draw upon his own personal experience, modern social science is now able to reach some more general conclusions. As Berelson says, "The tools of social research have made it possible, for the first time, to determine with reasonable precision and objectivity the extent to which the practice of politics by the citizens of a democratic state conforms to the requirements and the assumptio s of the theory of democractic politics. . . ." [5] What are some of those requirements and assumptions?

The Individual Citizen: Theory. Several assumptions are common in the literature of democratic theory about the quality of a citizen's

[4] For a thorough attempt to find a general justification for democracy, see Thomas Landon Thorson, *The Logic of Democracy* (New York: Holt, Rinehart, and Winston, 1962).
[5] Bernard Berelson, "Democratic Theory and Public Opinion," *Public Opinion Quarterly*, 16 (1952), 314.

involvement in politics.[6] First, the level of citizen interest, ideally, is expected to be high. It is assumed that political and public affairs are among the primary concerns of the average man, that he will follow the actions of government fairly closely even if the direct impact of those actions on his own personal life is minimal. Secondly, if the average citizen is to have an impact on public policy, he must have a general notion of what current problems and policies are, and what alternative courses of action seem feasible. Finally, in classical theory, the citizen must be ready to participate actively in the political process in order to communicate his preferences. At a minimum he must vote. Given the realities and complexities of modern politics, he should also avail himself of additional means of communication, such as writing letters to public officials and to the news media, and he should at least consider the utility of joining a political party and actively supporting candidates who share his views. Many writers would insist, further, that citizens share a widespread consensus as to the "rules of the game." Democracy, it is said, cannot survive unless its citizens wholeheartedly support the right of political minorities to express their views and to attempt to become majorities. Losers must accept the verdict of the electoral process, and winners must not try to eliminate their opponents from competition. The citizen is expected to be highly politicized, yet at the same time, be tolerant of those with whom he disagrees.

The most basic theoretical assumption about voters is that their choice of candidates and parties is based upon their opinions on the political issues of the day. Emotions, candidate personalities, and past voting habits are all assumed to be secondary to pressing public questions and the positions on these advanced by the candidates. Thus, the theory goes, voters directly express their preferences by their choice of candidates. Secondly, there is a presumption that most voters will be "public-regarding" in their political motivations (i.e., citizens will be motivated by a concern with what is good for the larger community rather than with what will benefit themselves personally). For example, the ideal citizen would choose among alternative candidates on the basis of who would be the most honest, efficient, and likely to solve social problems, rather than choosing

[6] Berelson, *ibid.*, collects quite a number of these assumptions. It should be noted that he writes from the viewpoint of a social researcher, rather than as a political philosopher, and that his description of the "classical theory" (like that presented here) is somewhat oversimplified. For a more complete analysis see Carole Pateman, *Participation and Democratic Theory* (Cambridge: Cambridge University Press, 1970), chap. 1. For an extended survey of the use and application of the concept of "democracy" in political thought, see Jens A. Christopherson, *The Meaning of Democracy* (Oslo: Universitatsforlaget, 1968).

the candidate who promises the voter a public job or a tax policy which will benefit him to the detriment of others. Finally, many theorists seem to assume that the average citizen is a bit of a political philosopher himself. He is assumed to hold a consistent set of political beliefs, preferences, and opinions (i.e., a political ideology). Candidates or political parties need only present a coherent liberal or conservative position across a broad range of issues and the ideologically attuned voter can decide which philosophy best represents his own. According to these theories, the voter is not merely interested in politics and well informed, he also has a well-developed set of preferences that he will use to structure his political participation and therefore influence the course of government policy.

This listing of theoretical requirements for a democratic citizenry is not exhaustive; many nuances of particular authors could be added. The case here may have been overdrawn. Certainly, many theorists do not suggest that these qualifications must be universal or absolute. However, the point remains: *classical democratic theory assumes that an "ideal" public is necessary for the existence of democracy.*

The Individual Citizen: Empirical Realities.   While such theoretical requirements as those outlined above are largely the product of a priori speculation, they constitute generalizations whose validity may be tested by observation of the real political world. Despite the fact that writers who should have known better have been content to uncritically repeat these assumptions, there is a large body of knowledge that leads to serious questioning of the ideal character of the mass public. Indeed, it hardly requires an academic knowledge of social research to doubt the truth of these assumptions. Even the least sophisticated political observer might suspect that a sizable number of voters are motivated by emotional appeals, candidate images, or the prospect of personal gain. Since much of this book is devoted to analyzing the nature of individual political psychology, much data will be presented later which bear upon this point. For the moment, a few examples will suffice:

—Over one-half of the voters in the 1958 congressional elections said that they had neither read nor heard anything about either candidate for Congress in their district; less than one-fifth professed to have some knowledge about both contenders.[7]

—Only 12 to 15 percent of the American electorate can be clas-

[7] Donald E. Stokes and Warren E. Miller, "Party Government and the Salience of Congress," *Public Opinion Quarterly*, 26 (1962), 531–46.

sified as ideological in their voting habits, while a fifth appear to lack even the most minimal issue content.[8]

—Sizable proportions of the population express reservations about the application of political freedoms to persons holding unpopular views.[9]

—Less than two-thirds of the potential electorate votes in presidential elections, and only about half turn out for off-year general elections, with even much lower rates for local elections.

—Only about 15 percent of the population reports ever having written a letter to a public official, and no more than 3 percent have ever written to a newspaper or magazine.[10]

Examples such as these—and they could be easily multiplied a hundred-fold—do not prove the point that the electorate is incompetent to govern. They do, however, cast the strongest of doubts upon the classical assumptions about the ideal democratic citizen. The weight of empirical evidence suggests therefore that we must carefully evaluate the assumptions about what is required of the public for a functioning democracy and what is required of the political process.

Some Challenges for Empirical Study. The preceding comparison of political theory and political reality suggests the potential contributions that an analysis of public opinion and its role at the individual, aggregate, and institutional levels can make to a better understanding of democratic theory. Following are several basic questions about the political process upon which an objective study of public opinion can shed much light.

—When people express their opinions and make their voting decisions, do these choices really reflect their preferences for public policy?

—Is public opinion susceptible to manipulation by those who control the mass media?

[8] Angus Campbell *et al.*, *The American Voter* (New York: John Wiley, 1960), chap. 10.

[9] Herbert McClosky, "Consensus and Ideology in American Politics," *American Political Science Review*, 58 (1964), 361–82. See also James W. Prothro and C. W. Griff, "Fundamental Principles of Democracy: Bases of Agreement and Disagreement," *Journal of Politics*, 22 (1960), 276–94.

[10] Philip E. Converse, Aage R. Clausen, and Warren E. Miller, "Electoral Myth and Reality: The 1964 Election," *American Political Science Review*, 59 (1965), 321–36. For other aspects of political involvement, see Lester W. Milbrath, *Political Participation: How and Why Do People Get Involved in Politics* (Chicago: Rand McNally, 1965), pp. 16–22.

—Does public opinion as a total quantity speak with such specific clarity and force that it can be heeded by those in power?

—Do election results convey any necessary policy implications to government?

—Do those who hold political power heed public opinion?

—If public opinion does not determine public policy, where does the fault lie?

Questions such as these are both broad and difficult. This book will not pretend to give authoritative answers to any of them. What will be attempted is to bring the full weight of existing theory and evidence to bear upon these issues, so that the reader can better make his own evaluations.

We live in a time of great evaluation and criticism of ourselves, of modern society, and of the political process. Many would argue that a meaningful degree of political democracy has not been achieved in this or other nations.[11] The notion of public opinion as a major influence upon politics, it is alleged, is but a falsehood promoted by those who alternately manipulate and ignore the desires of the mass public. At the root of much of this critical literature are some generalizations about public opinion that are at least partially amenable to scientific inquiry. The study of public opinion has always been an important one for those concerned about the basic character of the political process. It is of the greatest importance at the present.

---

[11] The reference here is to the line of argument exemplified by C. Wright Mills in *The Power Elite* (New York: Oxford University Press, 1956) and continued by a host of others in both academic and popular publications. Recent works continuing this argument include G. William Domhoff, *The Higher Circles: The Governing Class in America* (New York: Random House, 1970), and Kenneth Prewitt and Alan Stone, *The Ruling Elites: Elite Theory, Power, and American Democracy* (New York: Harper and Row, 1973).

The Measurement of Public Opinion

2

"MYTH AND REALITY" IN 1964: A CASE STUDY IN MISPERCEPTION OF OPINION [1]

To most political analysts, the outcome of the 1964 presidential election was quite predictable. The Republican candidate was the minority candidate of a minority party. He had apparently taken unpopular positions on many of the leading issues of the day, thereby causing massive defections from his own party as well as the loss of Democrats and independents who had supported Republicans in the past. With all of this, it was hardly surprising that the Republican share of the vote dropped to less than 40 percent and Barry Goldwater carried only six states, five of them in the deep South.

Some, however, were surprised by the magnitude, if not by the fact, of Goldwater's defeat—namely, those who had advocated and supported his candidacy and planned the Republican campaign. They had assumed that there was strong support for a "real conservative," if only the Republican party would offer "a choice, not an echo." Public opinion polls notwithstanding, these Goldwater supporters believed that a campaign based upon a strong conservative ideology would have wide popularity among voters of all political persuasions, and the whole Republican presidential campaign was structured around this belief.[2] Their assumption was wrong. After the election, many Goldwater supporters attributed the defeat to the unfortunate image of their candidate that was projected by the mass media, an interpretation which had little basis in fact.[3] There is

---

[1] This case study draws heavily on Philip E. Converse, Aage R. Clausen, and Warren E. Miller, "Electoral Myth and Reality: The 1964 Election," *American Political Science Review*, 59 (1965), 321–36.

[2] It appears that various conservative strategists (such as Raymond Moley) actually believed in the existence of a "silent vote" that was untapped by opinion polls and that was expected to vindicate the senator's positions on election day. See Karl A. Lamb and Paul A. Smith, *Campaign Decision-Making: The Presidential Election of 1964* (Belmont, Calif.: Wadsworth, 1968), chaps. 3 and 4.

[3] Surveys revealed that voters tended to perceive Goldwater's personal qualities less unfavorably than his policies; Converse *et al.*, "Electoral Myth," p. 331.

abundant evidence that American voters simply did not agree with the Goldwater philosophy.

The interesting question is, why had the Goldwater team (many of them experienced political professionals) so miscalculated the mood of the public? The analysts of the Survey Research Center (see Postscript to Part I) suggest that it may have been because they paid too much attention to that segment of the public which bothers to make its opinions known. In other words, they paid too much attention to the letters they received! Rejecting public opinion polls as misleading, they were swayed by what seemed to be a massive outpouring of grass-roots support for their position. And, consequently, they went down to defeat.

This explanation is borne out by analysis of the center's survey on the 1964 election. The respondents were divided into two categories: those who claimed to have written letters to public officials or to the press, and those who had not. The "letter writer" category was by far the smaller, comprising only 15 percent of the total, with about 3 percent of this total accounting for two-thirds of the actual letters. This group of letter writers was then compared to the whole sample in terms of opinions on various issues. Some of these comparisons are shown graphically in Figure 2-1. It is easy to see that there are great differences between those who were inclined to write and the mass public. The Goldwater organization was correct in its assessment of the more articulate part of the public, for the writers favored Goldwater, were ideologically committed, and agreed with the conservative campaign he was waging on several issues. Unfortunately for the Republican party, elections are conducted among the public as a whole—and they were distinctly not in favor of Goldwater, his ideology, or his issue positions. This distortion of opinion in the letter-writing group is increased by the fact that most letters are written by an even smaller number of people who send many.

There is a striking parallel between this aspect of the 1964 election and the experience of the McGovern campaign in 1972. A number of McGovern workers denied (at least publicly) the validity of polls that showed their candidate to be far behind. Their thinking may have been influenced by the previous experience of successfully waging a nominating campaign for a candidate who began his efforts when he was the choice of only a tiny percentage of the electorate. But the McGovern partisans may have failed to realize that the ability to win primaries (often contested by more than two candidates) within the electorate of one party and to gain delegate votes through systems of caucuses of party activists was a poor indicator of popularity with the mass public.

There are several practical lessons here. The first is that there is

Figure 2-1
The Distribution of Opinions Among Letter Writers and the Mass Public, 1964 *

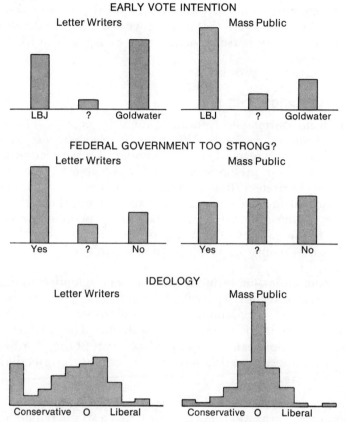

Source: Philip E. Converse, Aage R. Clausen, and Warren E. Miller, "Electoral Myth and Reality: The 1964 Election," *American Political Science Review,* 59 (1965), 334.

* The opinions of the letter writers are weighted by the relative number of letters written.

apt to be a difference between the opinions held by the articulate public and those held by the mass public. This means that our measures of public opinion must not rely upon those people who desire to make their preferences known. Secondly, the misperception that occurred in 1964 points up the implications of the populist definition of "public opinion" that we advanced in Chapter 1. According to an elitist definition, the method apparently used by the Goldwater forces would have been quite proper. Elections, however, include participation by large numbers of people with weak preferences. Finally, the results of the 1964 election suggest that some form of public opinion polling is likely to better measure public opinion than the timeworn methods of reading letters, cataloging newspaper editorials, and keeping in touch with local political activists The reader should likewise be aware that judging what the public thinks on the basis of what a few personal acquaintances say is also likely to be quite incorrect.

SURVEY RESEARCH: THE HARDWARE

Almost all measurement of public opinion is accomplished through the use of survey research. This type of research, also known as "polling," simply means that some sample of a population is questioned as to their preferences on various subjects. Through this method an accurate estimate of public opinion can be obtained. Since much of the material that appears in later chapters is based upon the results of surveys, and since many people express skepticism as to the validity of surveys, we shall devote considerable attention at this point to a justification and explanation of the survey method.

Two assumptions underlie the faith of social scientists in the validity of survey research: (1) a relatively small sample can accurately represent a large population, and (2) the answers that individuals give in response to interviews are meaningful. The first assumption is mathematical and can be described as a part of the "hardware" of this method; the second is behavioral and can be described as a part of the "software."

The Logic of Sampling. There is a natural tendency to doubt whether a small part can accurately describe a whole population. National surveys generally use a sample size of less than two thousand people to represent a population of over one hundred million adults. Common sense tells us that this simply cannot work—yet it does, as witness the close approximations of election results achieved by pollsters such as George Gallup.[4] While we may have commonsense doubts about the sampling, there is also present a commonsense sort of justification. Suppose that we needed to determine the chemical composition of a carload of ore. It would be quite impractical to attempt to analyze the entire amount—and quite unnecessary. We would simply select a number of small samples from throughout the total bulk and then analyze them. As the old saying goes, "You don't

---

[4] From 1936 to 1964, the final Gallup pre-election poll erred by an average of 2.9 percentage points from the actual vote in presidential and congressional elections. Since 1948, the average error has been only 1.9 percentage points. *Gallup Political Index*, no. 9 (February 1966), 40.

have to drink all of the soup to see if it's salty!" This is the basic idea used in industrial quality control—only a small fraction of the items that come off the production line are thoroughly tested. The method is not completely accurate, for the sample may be an unusual one, but the degree of error is small. What is more important, the degree of possible error is a known factor.

Although this is a commonsense justification for using samples, it rests upon a firm mathematical basis in the laws of probability. Suppose that a person was faced with the task of determining the relative number of red and black marbles in a bushel basket. If he drew only one marble, then this would tell him almost nothing about the composition of the basket. As he started to pick out more and more, a pattern would start to emerge. By the time a hundred marbles had been selected, the proportion of red to black would resemble that of the whole basketful. As his sample got larger and larger, the proportions would remain fairly constant and closely parallel the true values. A basic principle of statistics is that if sufficiently large random samples of a population are taken, they will tend to approximate that population. Furthermore, the distribution of these samples tends to take the form of a "normal" distribution (the "bell-shaped" curve), and this characteristic allows us to estimate the accuracy of a particular sample. Therefore, we can use the results of a sample of a population to represent the whole and do so with a known degree of accuracy.

Sample Size—How Large?   There is no single size that can be specified as "sufficiently large." The larger the sample the more accurate it will tend to be, but the exact size chosen for a particular survey will depend upon many factors. Table 2-1 shows the relationship between sample size and accuracy. The column headed "maximum

Table 2-1
Sample Size and Accuracy *

Sample Size	Maximum Error (95% Confidence)	Probable Error (50% Confidence)
10	±44%	±15%
25	±31	±11
50	±14	±5
100	±10	±3
500	±4	±2
1,000	±3	±1
5,000	±1	±½
10,000	±1	Less than ½

* These figures assume simple random sampling.

error" gives the range of results we can expect 95 percent of the time. Suppose that the sample size was 1,000. In 95 such samples out of 100, we could expect that our sample results would be within about 3 percent of the true value. In other words, if our sample yielded the prediction that the Democratic candidate would get 55 percent of the vote, we could be quite confident that he would actually get somewhere between 52 and 58 percent on election day. Only five times out of one hundred would we be off by more than 3 percent.

It is also instructive to look at the degree of error that we should expect to have. This is shown in the column labeled "probable error." This figure is the amount that our sample will deviate from the true population value 50 percent of the time. In other words, half the time we will be closer than this and half the time we will be more in error. In the case of a sample size of 1,000, we could expect that our results would be, on the average, about 1 percent off the true value for the population.

Obviously, the larger the sample size, the less the error. But it is not a simple relationship. The error is proportional to the square root of the sample size. Hence, if one increases his sample size by a factor of four, his error is only halved. This effect is shown in Figure 2-2. For this reason, no one today would ever use a sample size of

Figure 2-2
The Relationship Between Sample Size and Accuracy

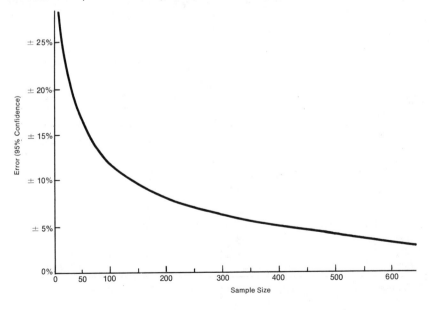

10,000 for most social research purposes. The increase in sample size (and therefore cost) would not be great enough to justify the small reduction in error that the increase would produce.

The decision as to how large a sample should be is a practical one. The first criterion is financial—the larger the sample, the more costly the survey. Secondly, the size depends upon the purpose of the research. If someone is concerned with testing the production of a pharmaceutical factory to make sure that no poisons are being accidentally introduced into medicines, then he would (hopefully) require a high degree of accuracy and a correspondingly large sample size. On the other hand, an attempt to survey the population generally to get a notion of attitudes toward government would not require such a degree of precision. Finally, it must be noted that there are many sources of error in survey research besides the probabilistic error introduced in sampling. These other sources—which are not easily measurable—include all of the sources of "human error" that we shall discuss in later sections of this chapter. There is no point in reducing sampling error to a mathematical minimum when other sources of imprecision are still present.

There are two other variables that affect the accuracy of samples. One is the relative frequency of a characteristic in the population. If the item being measured by a survey is found in only a small part of the population (say, 10 percent) or in almost all of the individuals (90 percent), then the degree of error will be less. Accuracy is lowest when the distribution of the characteristic is 50 percent. (The figures in Table 2-1 assume that this is the case.) Since voting intentions tend to divide fairly equally between the two parties, elections are somewhat hard to predict.

How large the sample size is in relation to the size of the total population also makes a difference. The larger the proportion of the total included in the sample, the greater the degree of accuracy. However, the mathematics of this are such that there is no significant increase in accuracy from this effect until at least a fifth of the total population is sampled. Thus, a sample of 1,000 cases from a population of 20,000 is more accurate than the same sample from a population of millions by only a tiny amount. This is why a good survey of a state or city will require almost as many interviews as a survey of the whole nation.

Types of Samples: Random and Other. Throughout the previous discussion, we have been assuming that samples were *random*. A purely random sample is one in which *each individual within the population has an equal chance of being selected.* There are many ways of selecting a random sample, ranging from drawing names out of a proverbial hat to using a computer to select individuals randomly. All of these methods, however, require the use of a list of all individuals within the population. Such lists are generally not available in survey research. While one might have a virtually complete listing of all students on a college campus or even of all voters in a city (though listings like these are often erroneous), there is no list of the adult population of the United States, or even of any single state. Therefore, other methods must be used in sampling most populations.

There is another reason for not attempting a simple random sample in many practical instances. This is the problem of geographic dispersion. Since Idaho contains only .0035 of the population of the United States, a random sample of 1,000 should produce only 3 or 4 respondents in that state. The same sample would call for about 20 persons throughout the 500-mile expanse of Tennessee. To send interviewers throughout the country or to hire local interviewers in such widely separated areas would raise the cost of survey research tremendously. Therefore, almost all survey research, even at the state and local level, utilizes a technique known as *cluster sampling*. This method involves the selection of a number of geographic units ("clusters") within which individuals are sampled. There are generally a number of stages in this process. A national sample might be drawn up along these lines:

1. The country is divided into four major regions.

2. Within each region, a number of counties are randomly selected.

3. From each selected county, a number of census tracts or other comparable units are randomly selected.

4. Within each selected tract (in urban areas), certain blocks are selected.

5. In each block, certain households are selected according to some established rule.

6. In each household, one person of voting age would be interviewed.[5]

The result of this procedure would be a national sample that would give every individual an equal chance of selection. For various statistical reasons, such a sample is less "efficient" than a pure, random sample (i.e., its level of accuracy for any given sample size is some-

[5] A standard work on the use of samples in survey research is Frederick F. Stephan and Philip J. McCarthy, *Sampling Opinions: An Analysis of Survey Procedures* (New York: John Wiley, 1958). A complete discussion of the technicalities involved in cluster sampling is found in Leslie Kish, *Survey Sampling* (New York: John Wiley, 1965).

what less). As a general rule of thumb, national cluster samples, which are usually samples of about 1,500, have roughly the same accuracy as a simple random sample of about 1,000. It is possible, therefore, to select a sample of the entire country that will be accurate within known limits.

While most professionally done survey research today uses the cluster method, thereby avoiding error, there are also cases of nonrandom sampling. These occur most commonly as "straw polls" conducted by journalists. One such method would be the "street corner sample," a procedure that can best be described as haphazard. The street corner interviewer is just that. He interviews whomever he can find, wherever he can find them—on street corners, in shopping centers, on the courthouse steps. Such a procedure is full of opportunities for error. For instance, it will make a considerable difference whether the "street corner" is in the central city, at the edge of a university campus, or in a suburban shopping center. And even if a number of locations are used, a number of segments of the population will not be reached, such as housewives with small children, people at work, and shut-ins. Such "pools" are sometimes relatively accurate in predicting election outcomes, but there is no guarantee of success. Furthermore, their possible sampling error cannot be calculated—for they have not really "sampled" any particular population. Efforts like these may make good newspaper copy, but they make bad research.

An even more inaccurate method of taking a straw poll is to request that people clip coupons from a newspaper and send them in with their preferences. The problem here is that only a tiny fragment of the population will bother to do this and that segment of the population is the same one that writes letters. As we saw earlier, this is hardly a representative sample of the mass public.

It was this method which produced the prediction by the *Literary Digest* in 1936 that Landon would win a stunning victory over Roosevelt. First of all, the *Digest* sent ballots to people selected only from lists of those who had cars or telephones. This produced a serious overrepresentation of the middle and upper classes during that Depression year. Secondly, since the person being polled had to go to the trouble of returning his ballot through the mail, the responses came from that small and articulate segment of the sample. It is hard to imagine a more error-ridden attempt at public opinion measurement.

Another method of sampling which has less serious faults is that of *quota sampling*. In this approach, interviewers are told that they must find a certain number of blue-collar workers, Catholics, blacks, farmers, men under thirty, etc. This is guaranteed to produce a sample that is representative of the population with respect to those demographic characteristics for which quotas are set, but it may well introduce biases on other kinds of variables. The key problem is that it is left up to the interviewer as to which male blue-collar worker, for example, is interviewed. Thus, the interviewer (usually a middle-class woman) might select the male blue-collar worker who seems the most meek or inoffensive. The farmers selected might be those who were in town on business, rather than those who were unable to leave their farm. Hence, severe questions can be raised about the validity of quota sampling. While it has been used by reputable national organizations, such as Gallup in the 1940s, almost all professionals have switched to preselected cluster samples of the type described earlier. Actually, there is no advantage to quota sampling, as a valid probability sample will yield a group of respondents representative of the population on demographic characteristics.

This has been a brief introduction to the do's and don'ts of selecting respondents—the simpler and less problematical aspect of survey research. Few efforts at public opinion measurement fall into error at this stage (save for the street corner samples). The serious problems come in what the respondent is asked, how he is interviewed, who does the interviewing, and how the results are interpreted.

SURVEY RESEARCH: THE SOFTWARE

The Questions.   What sorts of questions do public opinion surveys ask? Since the range of survey research is very broad, the nature of interview items can only be outlined. Let us first consider the form of questions. Basically, questionnaire items are either *closed-end* or *open-end*. Closed-end questions are those for which the alternatives are specified for the respondent. Most common is the dichotomous set of responses, in which the respondent must answer "yes" or "no," agree or disagree, etc. Actually, such questions always have at least three responses, for some respondents may have no opinion, be undecided, or decline to answer. Such questions are simple to ask and easy to analyze, but they fail to catch any hint of the intensity of feeling. Two people may both respond that they generally approve of the president's performance in office, but one may be an enthusiastic partisan while the other has never given the matter any thought before. In order to measure the intensity of opinions more precisely, several methods involving closed-end items may be used.

First, the question may simply pose a more complex set of responses, such as "disagree strongly," "agree," or "agree strongly." Secondly, the interviewer may provide the respondent with a visual scale of some sort and ask him to place himself on it with reference to the issue. This might simply be a horizontal line with some marking between two extremes. In their study of the 1968 election, the Survey Research Center presented subjects with a "feeling thermometer" and asked them to evaluate each of twelve major political figures on it, zero being the most negative reaction and one hundred degrees the most favorable, with fifty as the point of indifference.[6] Perhaps the most sophisticated use of closed-end questions to tap degrees of feeling is found in the technique of *scaling*. An example of this technique is Bogardus's "Social Distance Scale," which is reproduced in Table 2-2.[7] In this set of questions, the respondent is asked about what degrees of association he would permit with members of various racial or ethnic groups. The various items tend to form a single dimension of acceptance or rejection of each group. If the respondent would accept a group member as an in-law, it is assumed he would approve of all of the other "steps." If he would not want the person as a fellow citizen, it is assumed he would exclude him from all other forms of association. Thus, responses to a scale such as this would tend to form a pattern like the one shown in the

Table 2-2
The Bogardus Social Distance Scale

"Put a cross after each race in as many categories as your feelings dictate."

Category	English	Poles	Negroes	Chinese	etc.
1. To close kinship by marriage.					
2. To my club as personal chums.					
3. To my street as neighbors.					
4. To employment in my occupation.					
5. To citizenship in my country.					
6. As visitors only to my country.					

Respondent	Marriage (1)	Club (2)	Neighbors (3)	Employ (4)	Citizen (5)	Visitor (6)
Andrews	+	+	+	+	+	+
Brown		+	+	+	+	+
Charles			+	+	+	+
Daniels				+	+	+
Edwards					+	+
Franklin						+

Source: Scale version adapted from John P. Robinson, Jerrold G. Rusk, and Kendra B. Head, *Measures of Political Attitudes* (Ann Arbor: Survey Research Center, Institute for Social Research, University of Michigan, 1968), p. 244.

[6] Philip E. Converse *et al.*, "Continuity and Change in American Politics: Parties and Issues in the 1968 Election," *American Political Science Review*, 63 (1969), 1088–90.

[7] Emory S. Bogardus, *Social Distance* (Yellow Springs, Ohio: Antioch Press, 1959).

lower portion of Table 2-2. Each respondent could then be classified with a precise scale score. In the example shown, Andrews would receive a score of one, as the most accepting, while Franklin would receive a six as the least accepting. Not all sets of questions will prove to form a single dimension as this does. There are statistical tests to determine whether patterns of responses tend to form a single scale. Scales have been devised to measure all manner of attitudes, such as liberalism-conservatism, hostility, and faith in government. Thus, the simple, dichotomous, closed-end question can be used to determine precisely the extent of one's feelings on a complex issue.

Open-end questions are just that. The respondent is asked a question and no categories are supplied. Rather, his answer is recorded verbatim by the interviewer. The advantage to this method is that it avoids putting words into the respondent's mouth. If a person is asked what policy the president should adopt toward foreign economic competition, he may very well have no specific answer. If, however, he is given a choice of several alternative policies, he may well pick one simply to avoid appearing ignorant. In such a situation, the open-end item would yield more valid results. The open-end item also avoids restricting the scope of the question and imposing the biases of the designer of the survey on the public. For instance, a closed-end item which asked whether foreign affairs, economic problems, or racial tensions were the most pressing problems facing the nation would not allow for the respondent who perceived farm prices, crime, and a lack of religion as the key issues of the day. The practical drawback to open-end questions, aside from the fact that they take longer to administer, is that verbatim responses, as such, cannot be statistically analyzed. Some sort of standardized code must be imposed upon the answers, and this is done after the interviewing has been completed. For example, the Survey Research Center uses hundreds of different categories for answers to the question "What do you personally feel are the most important problems which the government in Washington should try to take care of?" Most coding schemes are not nearly so complex as this, but even a much simpler set of categories can allow for a detailed analysis of responses. Thus, through the use of both open-end and closed-end questionnaire items, surveys can tap precisely the almost infinite variety of individual attitudes and preferences.

Interviewing. This discussion of surveys has been presented in terms of personally conducted interviews, for this is the most commonly used method in large-scale opinion research. Interviews are conducted with the individuals sampled, generally in their own homes. A few other possible methods should be mentioned. One approach that sometimes occurs to persons who need to do a survey, but have limited financial resources, is to mail out their questionnaires and wait for the returns. The problem with this approach is one we have already come across—only a small percentage of the population will return the questionnaires, and they will be a very unrepresentative sample. Hence, the mail approach has almost no usefulness in surveying the general population. Mail questionnaires have been used, however, for specialized populations, such as members of a particular profession or persons holding some level of political office. In such instances, a well-done project can yield a high rate of return.[8] Another possibility is interviews conducted over the telephone. Obviously some households without telephone service are excluded, but this presently includes no more than 10 percent of all households. And since telephone numbers can be randomly selected (by computer) from the block of all possible numbers in a telephone exchange, there is no bias against persons with unlisted numbers. There are several advantages to telephone interviewing: the cost is somewhat lower; the time required to initiate and complete the project is significantly less; and it is much more efficient to make call-backs to persons not at home than it would be in personal interviewing. The greatest disadvantage is that the survey must be quite short (five to ten items) and therefore the more sophisticated measurement techniques cannot be used. Thus, the main use of telephone interviewing would be for a situation in which a quick reading of public opinion on a single subject is desired; political campaigns offer a prime instance.

Most of the professional interviewing done by commercial firms in the United States is done by "housewife" types—middle-aged women of reasonably high education who work part-time. In most instances who the interviewer is poses no problem, but in some cases it can adversely affect the quality of the interview. The most obvious problem comes when the interviewer is significantly different from the respondent either in race or social class. Whether the attitude of the respondent is deference or hostility, the response to the questionnaire may be, in part, a reaction to the interviewer. In cases where a major goal of the survey is to measure attitudes among minority groups, interviewers are often hired from the racial or ethnic community where the interviewing is to be done. The decision as to whether to use amateurs or professionals is another interviewer problem that may affect some projects. (This is a question that most often faces polls conducted by political organizations.) The evidence

---

[8] See William J. Crotty, "The Utilization of Mail Questionnaires and the Problem of a Representative Return Rate," *Western Political Quarterly,* 19 (1966), 44–53, for a discussion of how surveys by mail can be done validly.

seems to favor the use of paid workers, rather than volunteers, not only because of a need for expertise, but because volunteers are more likely to project their own feelings into the interviewing process. Therefore most political campaigns (if they have the resources) rely entirely on polls done by commercial organizations entirely separate from party workers and campaign volunteers.

Interviewing techniques are not complex, though they require experience to be performed well. For the most part they simply consist of the application of common sense. The interviewer should be polite, understanding, and, above all, objective. At all costs, the introduction of any bias on the part of the interviewer, whether intentional or not, must be avoided. The interviewer should be able to develop a knack for drawing out the respondent; at the same time she must know when to move away from a subject that seems to be introducing hostility or fear in the respondent. Survey interviewing in the United States is usually a relatively easy task, for Americans are much more willing to answer questions from strangers than are people in many other cultures. Given a skilled interviewer and a willing respondent, an interview can elicit an astonishing amount of information on even the most personal subject.

Problems in Survey Interpretation.   Thus far, we have been discussing the correct way to do a survey: how a proper sample can be taken, how interviewing ought to be conducted. What are some of the pitfalls that can cause a survey to produce invalid or misleading results?

The most obvious blunder that might be made in a survey is to use questions that are biased, leading, or loaded in some way. A question of the "Have you stopped beating your wife?" variety is not likely, but some almost as bad have been known to appear. An interview that asks whether one "is opposed to throwing more tax dollars down the ratholes of ungrateful foreign countries," will be as predictable in its results as one that asks whether or not "we should live up to our promises in assisting our valiant allies in their struggles against communism." Both are equally bad as indicators of attitude toward foreign aid. Such clear cases of biased wording are rare, for they render the question useless as a research tool. There are cases, however, where someone might use such an unfortunate item in order to achieve results that would justify his own position. An occasional congressman has been known to slip this sort of item in on a postcard ballot sent to his constituents.

A greater difficulty comes with interpretation of the meaning of responses to objectively worded questions. The problem is such that two nationally published polls can deal with the same topic at about the same time, using slightly different questions, and receive seemingly conflicting results about what the American people think. Let us take one case in point. In December of 1970 George Gallup headlined his poll column "Voters Shun Extremist Labels." [9] By this he meant that relatively few Americans were willing to classify themselves as "very conservative" or "very liberal," most sticking to "fairly" conservative or liberal, or "middle of the road." One month later, pollster Louis Harris devoted his newspaper column to the same subject.[10] This time the headline read, "U.S. Political Center Shrinks." Harris, using the same self-classification question as Gallup, found that only 28 percent of the population were in the "Center," as opposed to being "Right of Center" or "Left of Center." From this sequence of polls, a reader might assume that there had been a great upheaval in public sentiment over the holidays. Or a more reasonable suspicion would be that one of the pollsters had reached a biased sample. Neither of these, however, appears to be the case. What had happened was that Harris had put all liberals and conservatives together with those on the Left and Right wings, while Gallup considered "fairly" conservative and "fairly" liberal Americans to be part of the center. The problem, therefore, was not one of substance, but of *interpretation.*

The lesson to be gained from occurrences like these is a double one. The public opinion researcher must not only be careful at all times to use the most precise measures available, but must also look very carefully at his results to avoid unwarranted conclusions. The student of public opinion must be willing to go behind the headlines and the generalizations to evaluate the actual data the researcher has collected and draw his own conclusions.

NONSURVEY METHODS OF OPINION MEASUREMENT

While most of our information about public opinion comes from survey research, other techniques are sometimes used to estimate popular preferences or to analyze related phenomena. It is useful to introduce some of these techniques, as we shall have occasion to draw upon them later. Moreover, they may offer an alternative tool to the costly use of large-scale surveys.

One technique which is a sort of survey research is that of *intensive interviewing* of a limited sample. In this approach, the researcher selects only a handful of subjects, but employs a variety of interviewing techniques, possibly including psychoanalytic meth-

[9] *Chicago Sun-Times,* December 6, 1970.
[10] *Chicago Tribune,* January 11, 1971.

ods, over an extended period of time, from a few hours to several weeks. By utilizing such an approach, the researcher may be able not only to explore the opinions a respondent holds, but also to determine the structure of his belief system and the fundamental reasons why certain beliefs are present. Because the research has been confined to a very small and often unrepresentative sample, it would not be valid to generalize the findings to a larger population. However, intensive interviewing can give insights into human behavior and can generate hypotheses which might be tested by more conventional means on larger samples. Among the leading examples of such an approach are Lane's study of the political beliefs of working-class men [11] and Keniston's studies of alienation and political involvement among college students.[12] Many of the most important concepts for understanding the nature of public opinion have sprung from this intensive form of interviewing (such as the theory of psychological functionalism, discussed in Chapter 3).

There are many occasions when it is impossible to do any sort of survey work. If we are concerned with the past, for instance, we are unable to administer interviews, and if the time period is prior to about 1935, there are no existing survey data to be consulted. Can no statements about public opinion be made under such circumstances? Fortunately it is often possible to make some judgment in the absence of survey research through the use of *aggregate analysis,* which employs data that is available on groups of people, usually in some geographic units, instead of on individuals. Most frequently, these data consist of election returns, supplemented by a great amount of census data on a large number of variables. The characteristic pattern of analysis here is to investigate the relationship between the presence of some social characteristic in geographic units and a tendency to vote for a particular candidate or party. Thus, we might be able to ascertain the relationship between the economic distress of farmers and support for Populist candidates in the 1890s or look for religious influences on voting in the 1928 presidential election. We shall see a number of examples of the usefulness of aggregate analysis in Chapter 6 as we explore the role of historical and cultural factors in influencing public opinion.

There are some serious problems that can arise when we attempt to use aggregate methods to tell us something about what individuals

[11] Robert E. Lane, *Political Ideology: Why the American Common Man Believes What He Does* (New York: Free Press, 1963). Lane's *Political Thinking and Consciousness: The Private Life of the Political Mind* (Chicago: Markham Publishing Co., 1969) uses the same approach.
[12] Kenneth Keniston, *The Uncommitted: Alienated Youth in American Society* (New York: Harcourt, Brace and World, 1965) and *Young Radicals: Notes on Committed Youth* (New York: Harcourt, Brace and World, 1968).

are thinking. One problem is that of interpreting the evidence correctly. We must be careful not to read too much into the act of voting, for instance. To assume that the tendency of a group to vote for Nixon in 1968 was necessarily an indicator of a certain feeling on Vietnam, civil disorders, or the economy would probably not be valid, for the tendency undoubtedly resulted from a combination of these factors and many others. We may find shifts in the voting patterns of persons of German descent during the 1920s, but was this a response to World War I, to prohibition, or to something entirely different? Some inferences can be made, but there is always a possibility of misinterpretation.

Another problem in the use of aggregate data stems from the fact that we are trying to use information about groups to make statements about individuals. This can lead to what has been called the "ecological fallacy." Briefly, the difficulty is that the population groupings we analyze are not homogeneous—and the part of the group that is displaying the behavior in question may not be the one it appears to be. Consider this example: if we compare the vote for George Wallace in 1968 in southern congressional districts with a number of demographic characteristics of those counties, we find a strong positive relationship between support for Wallace and the percentage of the population that is black.[13] Since we doubt that black voters were inclined to vote the American Independent ticket, we can construct the explanation that white southerners in heavily black areas are more concerned with the racial issue than those where there are few blacks. Hence, we would not accept the apparent conclusion that Wallace received black support. But if the analysis dealt with religious voting in the 1880s, the fallacy might not be so apparent. One way to reduce the possibility of falling into such an error is to use smaller, and therefore more homogeneous, units of analysis. In the 1968 example, the positive relationship between percent black and Wallace voting would probably disappear if we could compare precincts, rather than counties.

A basic problem in utilizing survey data for many purposes is that we frequently do not have sufficient numbers of cases from subgroups within the population to analyze them independently. This is particularly a problem when we desire to estimate the distribution of opinions within states or lesser geographic areas. There are a number of national polls before every presidential election, but the three or four cases from Idaho, or the twenty from Tennessee, do not allow a precise prediction as to how the election will turn out in

[13] Robert A. Schoenberger and David R. Segal, "The Ecology of Dissent: The Southern Wallace Vote in 1968," *Midwest Journal of Political Science*, 15 (1971), 583–86.

those states. However, it is possible, through the process of *simulation*, to combine national survey data with census data for smaller areas, in order to produce estimates of opinion distribution within those smaller areas. This technique was developed for use by the Kennedy campaign in 1960,[14] and it has since been used for estimating public opinion on common issues in different states, for the purpose of comparative analysis.[15] Techniques of simulation offer great promise for more precise measurement of public opinion and understanding of how it operates.

A final technique, used more for studying related subjects than for measuring public opinion itself, is *content analysis* of communications. Content analysis has been defined as "any technique for making inferences by objectively and systematically identifying specified characteristics of messages." [16] A content analysis breaks a communication down into parts (words, sentences, etc.) and then sorts them into some established categories. This technique has been used for all manner of purposes, including establishing the authorship of historical writings and measuring the buildup of hostility between nations as reflected in diplomatic communications. In the field of public opinion research it has been most used for evaluating mass media messages for evidence of bias. During World War II, social scientists developed content analysis techniques for determining what material might be prosecuted as enemy propaganda.[17] The content of the news media has been frequently analyzed for evidence of favoritism. Such analysis can be quite simple, for example, counting the column inches devoted to stories about different candidates or ascertaining the relative number of papers with Republican or Democratic editorial leanings. It can also be quite complex and detailed, as in the case of a current and controversial study of bias in network news coverage of the 1968 election.[18] Content analysis thus offers a means of precisely evaluating sources of public information and attempts to influence public opinion.

[14] The "Simulmatics" project is explained by Ithiel de Sola Pool, Robert P. Ableson, and Samuel Popkin, *Candidates, Issues and Strategies: A Computer Simulation of the 1960 and 1964 Presidential Elections* (Cambridge: M.I.T. Press, 1964). A fictional work that explores the use of this technique to gain political power is Eugene Burdick, *The 480* (New York: McGraw-Hill, 1964).

[15] Ronald E. Weber, *Public Policy Preferences in the States: A Simulation Approach* (Bloomington, Ind.: Institute of Public Administration, Indiana University, 1971). See also Ronald E. Weber and William R. Schaffer, "Public Opinion and American State Policy-making," *Midwest Journal of Political Science*, 16 (1972), 683–99.

[16] Ole R. Holsti, *Content Analysis for Social Science and Humanities* (Reading, Mass.: Addison-Wesley, 1969), p. 14.

[17] Harold D. Lasswell *et al.*, *The Language of Politics: Studies in Quantitative Semantics* (Cambridge: M.I.T. Press, 1965), chap. 9.

[18] Edith Efron, *The News Twisters* (Los Angeles: Nash Publishers, 1971).

EVALUATING PUBLIC
OPINION RESEARCH

Our survey of public opinion research techniques has necessarily been cursory. Anyone who contemplates initiating a serious research project would be well advised to consult more detailed sources.[19] But most of us are likely to remain simply consumers of other people's efforts. Knowing something about both the "hardware" and "software" involved in survey research can enable us to make our own judgments about the validity and the meaning of the findings we encounter.

A rough knowledge of the relationship between sample size and accuracy can be helpful. Most published polls use an adequately large sample to achieve a substantial minimization of error. But this degree of accuracy does not extend to *parts* of the total sample. A national survey would probably be within plus or minus three percentage points almost all of the time in its estimate of the proportion of the population holding a particular view. But the pollster may offer a breakdown along racial lines, in which the nonwhite portion of the sample would only be two hundred cases or less. The sample size for nonwhites is then only two hundred, and the "maximum error" range would be about seven percentage points either way. Knowledge of sampling error is also useful in interpreting differences between polls. Late in a presidential campaign, a poll may report that a candidate has gained 1 percent on his rival. The student of these matters will recall that this change is well within the range of sampling error and does not necessarily signify any trend in voter preference.

Evaluating the "software" problems of surveys is a more difficult task. Interview questions can be evaluated on two criteria: *reliability* and *validity*. A reliable item is one that produces the same response every time from the same person under the same conditions. This is a measurable criterion, and carefully done projects often include data on the degree of reliability. "Validity" refers to the idea that the item measures what it is intended to measure, and this is a difficult thing to ascertain. One way is to cross-check a measure against other indicators of the same thing. If a measure of social class that is based upon the interviewer's rating of the appearance of the household proves to have little relationship to respondents' income, occupation, or education, then we would suspect that it is of doubtful validity.

[19] There are two particularly useful texts on the subject of survey research, which deal with both theoretical and practical problems: Charles H. Backstrom and Gerald D. Hursh, *Survey Research* (Evanston, Ill.: Northwestern University Press, 1963), and Earl R. Babbie, *Survey Research Methods* (Belmont, Calif.: Wadsworth, 1973).

Many times the evaluation simply comes down to "face validity"—does the question *appear* to measure what it is alleged to. If one sees a research project in which preference for a certain candidate is taken as an indicator of opinion on foreign policy, then he ought to seriously question the validity of the item. Again, however, the problems of survey research are seldom in the method, but in the interpretation of the findings.

It should now be clear to the reader that survey research and other methods of opinion measurement are neither the gimmicks of charlatans to mislead the gullible nor magic wands to reveal the public mind. They are simply useful tools with which to investigate the distribution of popular preference. Like all tools, these techniques can be of great value if they are used correctly and if their products are viewed with an informed and critical eye.

Postscript to Part I

THE USES OF OPINION MEASUREMENT

Who uses survey research to measure public opinion, why do they do it, and are there any benefits or dangers to society involved? To answer the first two questions: there are several different types of organizations engaged in large-scale survey research, and they are engaged in it for different purposes.

The most well known of these are the polls conducted for *journalistic* purposes (i.e., for public consumption). The leading practitioners of this trade are the Gallup poll (corporately known as the American Institute of Public Opinion) and its affiliates in a number of other countries, and the Harris poll (Louis Harris and Associates, Inc.). These organizations conduct regular surveys and sell the results to newspapers, which provide their main source of income. Methodologically, these surveys are done quite well and their results prove to be reliable. Their limitations come from the fact that they are designed for consumption by the average reader. Their survey instruments therefore usually consist of simple closed-end questions, and the only analysis presented is in the form of simple percentage tables. Also, because their surveys are designed for popular consumption, these organizations sometimes devote their resources to topics of passing topical interest, such as "most admired historical figures," interest in sports, and reactions to new fashion trends. Still, they provide the largest available body of data on American public opinion, and the fact that they have made this complete data available to survey "data banks" allows scholars to perform more sophisticated analyses. It is important to distinguish these professional polls from those sometimes conducted by journalists themselves during elections; the latter are frequently of the "street corner" or "straw poll" variety, with all of the attendant problems discussed earlier.

Less well known to the public are the surveys conducted by the "private polls" (i.e., commercial firms that conduct surveys on a contract basis for specific clients). The results of these polls are usually not available to the public and, in fact, steps are often taken to preserve their complete secrecy. The largest volume of this type of research is done for businesses, to test marketing techniques and public reaction to products. Clients also include political candidates and parties, which are increasingly using survey research in order to make election campaign decisions. The quality of this research undoubtedly varies, depending on the firm and on the resources and knowledge of the political client. In some cases, the most sophisticated techniques of measurement and analysis are employed.

The last category is survey research conducted by academic researchers for *scientific* purposes (i.e., to test hypotheses about the beliefs and behavior of the mass public). There are a number of permanently established organizations engaged in this, most notably the Survey Research Center (now the Center for Political Studies) at the University of Michigan and the National Opinion Research Center at the University of Chicago. Most of the results of studies conducted by centers such as these are also made available to other interested academics for further analysis. Research done by this type of organization is probably the best in methodology and uses the most complex means of measurement and analysis. Scholars also conduct surveys on their own for particular projects, though they rarely have the resources available for national samples.

While there are some obvious advantages to be gained from the intelligent use of survey research, there are critics who see dangers in its proliferation. Perhaps the most prevalent of these criticisms is that the publication of survey results will affect public opinion in the future. We shall attempt to demonstrate the lack of empirical support for this proposition in Chapter 7. Another fear is that politicians may make policy decisions purely on the basis of what the polls say. Whether this is desirable or undesirable is a normative question. Consider this aspect, however: if political leaders are inclined to follow what they suppose public opinion to be, the use of survey research will at least allow them to work on the basis of correct information. Finally, given that survey research is useful to a political candidate, it has been pointed out that many candidates cannot afford the considerable expense involved, giving an unfair advantage to those who can. This is an important consideration, but its remedy would seem to lie in some solution to the whole problem of financing political campaigns, not in curtailing the use of survey research.

The use of scientific techniques to measure public opinion has advantages for the particular client who uses it, whether business corporation or candidate for office. The academic researcher would also point out its merits for the purpose of pure science—finding out more about the world. We can also suggest some general benefits for the political system. Survey research, properly done, ought to make government more responsive to public opinion. Whether or not political decision makers should or will follow popular majorities, it is useful to know what those majorities are thinking. The politician who knows from poll results that the public is evenly divided on the question of legalizing abortion and is definitely in favor of gun control legislation may not so easily be intimidated by the more articulate voices of organized minorities. And, to the interested citizen, a knowledge of the preferences of the mass public allows a more meaningful evaluation of the responsiveness of government. If we accept the definition of democracy as the relationship between public opinion and public policy, we can hardly oppose the use of the most valid means of measuring public opinion.

PART II

OPINION FORMATION: MICRO-POLITICS

The Psychology of Opinions

3

As we noted in Chapter 1, most classical theorists who have discussed democracy assume that citizens in a democratic political system must possess a number of ideal attributes. At the root of most of these assumptions is the notion that men develop their opinions on public matters rationally.[1] Not all political observers would accept such a notion as empirically valid. Cynical observers of human nature argue that political opinions are often quite irrational, that they are either random preferences or simply the product of external social pressures. An orthodox Marxist would hold that political opinions, like all other forms of behavior, simply reflect one's place in the existing hierarchy of economic organization. This list of ideas on the nature of individual opinion formation might be continued at length if we were to go into varieties of sociological and psychological thought. The point is that there are a number of competing theories as to how people develop their political opinions and that it will take some effort to sort out and evaluate these different modes of explanation.

Just as there are different theories of opinion formation, so there are different approaches that have been used to study that phenomenon, each suggesting the importance of certain kinds of influences on the opinions held by individuals. A brief summary of these approaches is illustrative both of their substantive contributions and of the theoretical issues they raise.[2]

One of the early landmarks of scientific investigation into the political behavior of the mass public was the research carried out by a

[1] A uniform definition of "rationality" has never been accepted in social theory; the term usually implies the sort of assumption made in economics, for example, "the individual when confronted with a real choice will choose more, rather than less . . . man is a utility maximizer." James M. Buchanan and Gordon Tullock, *The Calculus of Consent* (Ann Arbor: University of Michigan Press, 1962), p. 18.

[2] For a methodological and substantive history of these research traditions, see Peter Rossi, "Four Landmarks in Voting Behavior Research," in *American Voting Behavior*, ed. E. Burdick and A. Brodbeck (Glencoe: Free Press, 1959), chap. 4.

team of researchers from Columbia University on the 1940 and 1948 presidential elections.[3] Their concern was with voter preference as a type of consumer preference, and their method emphasized the importance of social groupings. The success they achieved in relating characteristics such as economic status, religion, and urban versus rural residence to the partisan voting choice of their respondents led them to argue that it was these demographic variables that determined political opinions and behavior. At one point the conclusion was drawn that "A person thinks, politically, as he is, socially. Social characteristics determine political preference." [4] Hence, the significance of these early studies is that they emphasize the more constant and nonrational influences upon an individual's opinions. This is brought out by their reliance upon the S-O-R (stimulus-organism-response) model of human decision making.[5] In this model, the decision-making process is viewed much as a biological experiment would be: external stimuli are received by the subject, who implements a pattern of responses. In this case, communications about politics represent the stimuli; social characteristics of the voter predispose him to react in certain ways; and the voter's opinions and political behavior constitute the response. While the authors of these studies made some allowance for the selectivity exercised by the individual in accepting stimuli and in constructing his responses in accordance with his previously determined dispositions, the main thrust of their argument was that opinions are largely determined by the external forces with which an individual comes in contact. Thus, any attempt to explain the sources of individual opinions must necessarily take into account the individual's position in society—as we will do in Chapter 5.

Following upon these early voting studies was the work of the Survey Research Center. While building upon the earlier work, this line of research, which culminated with the publication of *The American Voter*, emphasizes the *cognitive aspects* of political behavior.[6] Though social characteristics are seen to play an important background role, beliefs and attitudes are thought to be the factors that really are responsible for electoral choice. Chief among these is the

[3] Paul Lazarsfeld, Bernard Berelson, and Hazel Gaudet, *The People's Choice* (New York: Duell, Sloan and Pearce, 1944), and Bernard Berelson, Paul F. Lazersfeld, and William N. McPhee, *Voting: A Study of Opinion Formation in a Presidential Campaign* (Chicago: University of Chicago Press, 1954).

[4] Lazarsfeld *et al.*, *ibid.*, p. 27.

[5] Berelson *et al.*, *Voting*, pp. 277–80.

[6] Angus Campbell *et al.*, *The American Voter* (New York: John Wiley, 1960). Earlier works based on some of the same survey data were Angus Campbell and Robert L. Kahn, *The People Elect a President* (Ann Arbor: University of Michigan, Institute for Social Research, Survey Research Center, 1952), and Angus Campbell, Gerald Gurin, and Warren Miller, *The Voter Decides* (Evanston: Row, Peterson, 1954).

concept of party identification, which appears to be central in the complex of social and psychological determinants of political behavior. Thus, this line of research suggests that while political behavior is responsive to external forces, opinions and voting are internally determined by the individual.

A third line of research into the political behavior of the mass public deals with the way in which people learn about politics (i.e., acquiring both factual knowledge and subjective preferences), particularly as this process occurs in the formative years. While political observers throughout history have been concerned with this process, it was only in the late 1950s that the idea of *political socialization* began to be intensively studied.[7] These studies showed that many basic political orientations are established by the time a child finishes elementary school and that some of these—particularly party identification—tend to persist through adulthood. Thus, political socialization research suggests that in order to understand a person's opinions, we must consider what he has learned in the past, particularly from parents and teachers. The topic is investigated at length in Chapter 4.

A final line of research—in this case, one that has been pursued from the 1940s on throughout the entire period of scientific study of political behavior—deals with the political activity of the mass public at an aggregate level.[8] Research in this area is largely concerned with the patterns of stability and change within different geographic areas. For instance, an examination both of the distribution of opinions on certain topics and of electoral support for political parties reveals differences between regions that cannot be explained by reference to the distribution of demographic characteristics within those regions. Many such patterns can be explained only by reference to historical circumstances that have become institutionalized into regional cultural patterns. Much the same sort of phenomenon can be observed for nongeographic patterns of opinion, such as those within religious or ethnic groups. Any attempt to discover the sources of individual opinions therefore must include an examination of the particular culture or subculture into which the individual

[7] The book that acted as the catalyst for much of the later socialization research was Herbert Hyman, *Political Socialization* (New York: Free Press, 1959). Among the many empirical studies which have emerged since that time, the most important have been Fred I. Greenstein, *Children and Politics* (New Haven: Yale University Press, 1965); Robert D. Hess and Judith V. Torney, *The Development of Political Attitudes in Children* (Chicago: Aldine, 1967); and Kenneth P. Langton, *Political Socialization* (New York: Oxford University Press, 1969).

[8] This concern with the aggregate has increased, as typified by the change in perspective from *The American Voter* to Angus Campbell *et al.*, *Elections and the Political Order* (New York: John Wiley, 1966).

has been socialized. We will attempt to unravel the twisted strands of history, geography, and culture in Chapter 6.

As should be clear from the preceding summary, social research on the political behavior of the mass public over the last several decades has suggested a number of different types of sources of individual opinions. Yet even the most thorough catalog of such sources neglects the most crucial element of the opinion-formation process: *the way in which individuals combine these inputs to produce opinions.* To ignore the "organism" of the S-O-R model or the thinking processes of the "rational man" is to fail to understand public opinion. The remainder of this chapter will be devoted to an explication of some psychological approaches that may prove useful in understanding how people form their opinions on public affairs.

PERSONALITY: POTENTIAL AND PROBLEMS

If one proposes to understand the root causes of any kind of human behavior, then an obvious starting point is *personality.* To offer a single general definition of "personality" is difficult, for psychologists themselves cannot agree.[9] At the heart of most concepts of personality is the commonsense notion of an individual's "personality" as his *characteristic pattern of behavior.* A definition along these lines, while logically acceptable, has the defect of being too broad to put into practical use. Almost all psychologists would agree, however, that personality is an "inferred entity" (i.e., an abstract notion used to account for regularities in human behavior).[10] In other words, personalities are not real objects; they are only elements of theories that may be useful in understanding the human mind. As such, their characteristics are dependent upon the psychological theories of which they are a part.

While the concept of personality has been widely used in explaining human behavior, the practical constraints of data collection have largely limited its application in the study of political behavior to three types of inquiry.[11] First, there have been a number of psychoanalytic case studies of single political actors, typically persons who have achieved a major place in history.[12] Secondly, there have been

[9] To discuss even briefly the different types of personality definitions would require an entire chapter. For a general discussion of the nature of personality and the problems involved, see Calvin S. Hall and Gardner Lindzey, *Theories of Personality,* 2nd ed. (New York: John Wiley, 1970), chap. 1.

[10] Fred I. Greenstein, *Personality and Politics* (Chicago: Markham Publishing Co., 1969), p. 3.

[11] *Ibid.,* pp. 14–17.

[12] E.g., Erik Erikson, *Young Man Luther* (New York: Norton, 1958); Alexander George and Juliette L. George, *Woodrow Wilson and Colonel House* (New York: John Day, 1956); and Arnold Rogow, *James Forrestal* (New York: Macmillan, 1963), to cite only a few of the most notable examples.

a number of attempts to characterize the model personality types of entire nations, a phenomenon once known as "national character." Both of these approaches can necessarily do little to aid the study of public opinion, as the first deals with too few and unusual individuals, and the second deals with whole political systems rather than the individuals within them. The remaining type of personality inquiry to be considered here—and the most relevant for our own investigation—consists of *typological* studies, which attempt to identify and measure the presence of certain personality "traits" within a population, as well as to discover the behavior patterns typical of people who possess these traits. It is this type of inquiry that is most similar to studies of public opinion per se, and it is the one upon which we shall concentrate.

Personality Traits and Political Behavior. The typological approach to personality begins by identifying certain relevant personality traits, and then attempts to measure their distribution within a population by means of some sort of test or scale that can be used in survey research. The relationship of these traits to other characteristics is then investigated. Among the sorts of personality traits that have been suggested as being relevant to political opinions and behavior are such traits as "sociability," "alienation," "efficacy," "dominance," and "intellectuality." [13] The basic rationale behind most uses of these concepts in political science is the argument that an individual's personality traits in purely private life will carry over into his political behavior and his opinions on public affairs. Thus, persons who are cynical and alienated in their personal life would tend to be withdrawn from political participation and to express little confidence in political leadership. Those who develop hostility in their personal affairs are hypothesized to transfer this hostility to the political arena. While some would argue that, considered in this manner, personality traits can explain many variations in individual opinion, this approach has generally not proved useful in the analysis of the mass public, aside from the area of political participation. Persons who exhibit personality traits such as alienation, anomie, and dominance tend to be less active in politics; beyond this, there is little prediction possible about the nature of their opinions. On the other hand, there have been a few notable attempts to discover the interrelationship between political belief systems and personality traits, and it is to these we shall now turn.

Personality, Authoritarianism, and Ideology. One of the most famous books in the history of social science is *The Authoritarian*

[13] Literature dealing with the effects of personality traits such as these on political behavior is discussed in Lester W. Milbrath, *Political Participation* (Chicago: Rand McNally, 1965), pp. 72–89.

Personality, published in 1950. The basic concern of this study was the "potentially fascist" individual (i.e., the authoritarian anti-Semite). The basic assumptions of the researchers were "[that] the political, economic, and social convictions of an individual often form a broad and coherent pattern, as if bound together by a 'mentality' or 'spirit' and that this pattern is an expression of deep-lying trends in his personality." [14] Their hypothesis was that there is a certain type of individual who, as a result of certain internal hostilities, manifests an "authoritarian personality" that results in fascist beliefs. The basic method of testing this idea was to develop three attitudinal scales: F (authoritarianism), E (ethnocentrism), and PEC (political-economic conservatism). Various versions of these scales were administered to a number of groups, and the results were supplemented by a number of intensive interviews with a number of individuals selected because of their high or low scores.

To summarize a work of this magnitude briefly is difficult. However, the main substantive finding seems to be that the three scales are highly interrelated: the authoritarian is also prejudiced and conservative. Certain demographic variables were also found to be related: the higher the level of education, social status, and intelligence, the less the authoritarianism, prejudice, and conservatism. However, little relationship was found between political party identification and the three scales. Thus, *The Authoritarian Personality* suggests that there is a direct linkage between personality and several dimensions of attitudes and opinions.

While the book was widely accepted, there are a number of serious weaknesses in its approach that raise critical questions as to the validity of its findings.[15] Many of these deal with practical aspects of the research. First, the original study made no attempt to use a random sample. Interviews were received from a hodgepodge of groups, most of whose members were of middle or upper levels of education or status, and no members of racial or religious minorities were included. There was also a serious problem with scale construction, for the PEC scale (conservatism) was purposely constructed only from those items that had previously proved to be related to the F scale. Hence, the positive correlations between the three scales prove nothing about the real relationship between political beliefs. Finally, all of the items on the original scales were in the form of statements

[14] T. W. Adorno *et al., The Authoritarian Personality* (New York: Harper and Row, 1950), p. 1. We shall give considerable attention to this work and to that of Herbert McClosky, primarily on the grounds of the wide attention they have commanded in political science and sociology.

[15] Many of these criticisms are contained in Richard Christie and Marie Johoda, eds., *Studies in the Scope and Method of "The Authoritarian Personality"* (Glencoe: Free Press, 1954).

with which the respondent was asked to agree or disagree. Since virtually all of these statements were supposed to reflect the more authoritarian or conservative point of view, it followed that anyone who uncritically accepted most of the statements was therefore a "potential fascist." And since less educated persons are more likely to agree with impressive-sounding statements, it was almost inevitable that they tended to have higher F, PEC, and E scores.

While many of these defects were corrected in later applications of the scales, some inherent theoretical problems remain with regard to this study. The most serious of these is the confusion between personality traits and the norms and values that an individual has learned. The authors of *The Authoritarian Personality* assumed that prejudice toward a minority group was necessarily a pathological outgrowth of personality difficulties. Thus, according to their reasoning—and their research methodology—a large proportion of white southerners in past decades would have had the same extreme personality type, a conclusion that makes the whole concept of individual personality almost meaningless. What was overlooked was the fact that individuals, regardless of their personalities, acquire many values from their parents and peers, their experience, and the particular culture in which they live. This phenomenon of socialization could account for most of the findings cited previously, not only on prejudice (the E scale), but on authoritarianism and conservatism also (the F and PEC scales), as the items included many statements that resembled (or actually were) common proverbs and homilies. Thus, agreement with the adage "Familiarity breeds contempt" would raise the respondent's authoritarianism measure. Certainly, an individual's personality might affect the way in which he internalized these values and translated them into specific opinions, but it would seem much more reasonable to use those learned values as the explanatory device than personality.

Do these problems with the Adorno study mean that there is no such thing as an "authoritarian personality"? Not necessarily, for it is possible to extract some of the ideas and findings and present a more valid reformulation.[16] The central point of such a revision would be that the "authoritarian" has intense, yet ambivalent, feelings toward authority. He is outwardly subservient to higher authority, but also resents it. He has a "love-hate" orientation toward authority, and the "hate" part is repressed. Since repression always involves some psychological costs, this repressed hostility is likely to surface somewhere and be directed at those targets that the individual's value system defines as legitimate. These might include racial or ethnic

[16] Much of the following reformulation is drawn from Greenstein, *Personality and Politics*, pp. 106–10.

minorities or those who do not conform to traditional norms. This line of argument would explain and justify some of the findings of *The Authoritarian Personality*. Note, however, that the "authoritarian's" hostility might be directed at other targets provided by his value system, for example, big business, government, organized religion, people more successful in life than he, etc. We cannot predict just how authoritarianism or any other personality attribute might affect a person's opinions and behavior unless we are aware of his internalized values and their sources. Thus, even with a revision of the authoritarian theory, it still is clear that there is no simple correlation between personality and opinions.

Another attempt to investigate the effects of personality on political beliefs can be seen in McClosky's article "Conservatism and Personality." [17] The procedure employed in this research was, first, to examine a number of "conservative" writings, in order to extract common threads of belief. These were then combined into a scale designed to measure conservatism that was administered to a random sample of Minnesota residents, along with a number of other psychological scales. The items comprising McClosky's conservatism scale are reproduced in Table 3-1. The relationships between these various measures revealed some interesting results: conservatives were found to be low in education, awareness, and intellectuality. They tended to score at the "undesirable" end of a number of personality scales, tending to be submissive, anomic, pessimistic, bewildered, and alienated. And on clinical measures, conservatives tended to show higher degrees of hostility, rigidity, and paranoid tendencies, to mention only a few of the findings. Hence, it would be easy to infer a direct relationship between personality and basic political beliefs. However, some additional findings raise substantial doubts about this conclusion. McClosky notes that there are "fairly low" correlations between his conservatism measure and "party identification, attitudes on economic issues, and liberal-conservative self-identification." [18] Thus, one must have severe doubts as to whether those "conservatives" identified by McClosky are the same people who hold what are usually identified as "conservative" views in the political world.

If political conservatism is not what McClosky measured, what variable did he identify? An inspection of his complete scale reveals that almost all of the measures deal with what might be called "personal conservatism," that is, belief in the past and fear of change. [19]

[17] Herbert McClosky, "Conservatism and Personality," *American Political Science Review*, 52 (1959), 27–45.
[18] *Ibid.*, p. 44.
[19] A revised version of McClosky's complete scale is presented in John P. Robinson,

Table 3-1
Conservatism Scale Items from McClosky, "Conservatism and Personality"

(Agreement with each item indicates conservatism)

---

1. I prefer the practical man anytime to the man of ideas.
2. If you start trying to change things very much, you usually make them worse.
3. If something grows up after a long time, there will always be much wisdom to it.
4. It's better to stick by what you have than to be trying new things you don't really know about.
5. We must respect the work of our forefathers and not think that we know better than they did.
6. A man really doesn't have much wisdom until he is well along in years.
7. No matter how much we like to talk about it, political authority really comes not from us, but from some higher power.
8. I'd want to know that something would really work before I'd be willing to take a chance on it.
9. All groups can live in harmony in this country without changing the system in any way.

Source: John P. Robinson, Jerrold G. Rusk, and Kendra B. Head, *Measures of Political Attitudes* (Ann Arbor: Survey Research Center, Institute for Social Research, University of Michigan, 1968), p. 96.

The whole notion is summed up by this item: "It's better to stick to what you have than to be trying new things you don't really know about." That items of this sort were determined to be the essence of "conservatism" is understandable; this notion of the wisdom of the past is perhaps the single idea that is common to a whole host of conservative writers over several centuries. This fact, however, does not mean that an adequate measure of contemporary ideology has been discovered. Rather, one might speculate that what McClosky's conservatism scale has measured is simply the extent to which an individual is "traditionalistic," [20] finding that he cannot cope with contemporary society as well as he could with his image of the past. Such an hypothesis would explain the social correlates that were found—lesser education and intellectuality, plus personality attributes that indicate a feeling of failure to operate successfully in a modern environment. Hence, this attempt to relate personality to political attitudes largely demonstrates the interrelated character of personality itself.

While not all attempts to use personality to explain the political beliefs of the mass public contain the methodological and theoretical

---

Jerrold G. Rusk, and Kendra B. Head, *Measures of Political Attitudes* (Ann Arbor: Survey Research Center, Institute for Social Research, University of Michigan, 1968), pp. 94–97.

[20] At one point the author says that "traditionalism" and "conservatism" are "virtually synonymous." McClosky, "Conservatism and Personality," p. 32.

problems of the two examples cited above,[21] the typological approach has never lived up to its initial promise. Measures of personality traits sometimes will prove to be related to some dimensions of opinion on a particular subject, but even then the degree of explanation is generally not impressive. There are some basic reasons for this. First, most personality theory is inherently clinical in its origins and outlooks, largely as a result of its Freudian beginnings. Hence, it tends to concentrate upon pathological phenomena, which limits its applicability to populations that are presumably made up of psychologically healthy individuals. Secondly, total personalities are impossible to measure without extremely intensive observation. A typological approach therefore inevitably must deal with those particular personality traits that can be dealt with by survey techniques—and trait psychology is necessarily oversimplified. Finally, a complete reliance on personality neglects (or assumes) the nature of an individual's experience, learned values, perceptions, and received stimuli—all of which are an integral part of his process of opinion formation. In short, while personality theory has a great potential for explaining why an individual holds the opinions that he does, the practical problems associated with its application generally negate its promise.

Does this failure of personality theory to explain public opinion mean that the human mind must remain a "black box" in our inquiry? This, fortunately, is not the case, for psychological functionalism—itself an outgrowth of personality exploration—is able to demonstrate some important principles of opinion-holding.

PSYCHOLOGICAL FUNCTIONALISM:
THE USES OF AN OPINION

"Of what use to a man are his opinions?" It is with this question that Smith, Bruner, and White begin their classic study of the interrelatedness of personality needs and opinions, an analysis conducted along the lines of psychological functionalism.[22] The concept of functionalism, in this sense, begins with the observation that all individuals have certain psychological needs which must be met and that the personality must function so as to fulfill these needs. Opinions

[21] A number of studies have found personality traits to be related to opinions on various types of issues, particularly those in the area of foreign policy, e.g., Herbert McClosky, "Personality and Attitude Correlates of Foreign Policy," in *Domestic Sources of Foreign Policy,* ed. James N. Rosenau (New York: Free Press, 1967), pp. 51–109.

[22] M. Brewster Smith, Jerome S. Bruner, and Robert W. White, *Opinions and Personality* (New York: John Wiley, 1956).

are one way of performing the necessary functions; hence, they are a direct outgrowth of personality. The functional approach, then, is an attempt to understand why people hold their opinions by understanding the kinds of needs the opinion meets (i.e., how the individual is making use of his opinion). In order to accomplish this, it is necessary to suggest the kinds of functions an opinion might perform and how that might be accomplished. We will rely at this point on the classification advanced by Katz,[23] though there are variations advanced by other authors.

The Instrumental Function.   This function, also called the *utilitarian* or *adjustment* function, is a psychological version of the economic assumption that people will always try to maximize pleasure and minimize pain. Attitudes are one method the individual possesses of achieving those psychological states he desires and avoiding those he fears. If a person finds that certain attitudes seem to be rewarded and others punished, the former will be reinforced and the latter extinguished. While this may operate on an overt level—as when an employer or teacher attempts to condition a pattern of behavior—it may also occur in much more subtle and unintended ways. A white who has internalized egalitarian values may find that holding negative opinions about particular blacks whom he meets tends to result in uncomfortable guilt feelings, for instance. The social situation one finds himself in may also structure the instrumental response. For example, the person operating in a typical academic environment will find that different opinions are likely to bring agreement and approval from his peers than would be the case in a business or working-class setting. Thus, attitudes may in part be a response to a rationalistic drive for maximizing one's utility, though hardly in the sense envisioned by economic theory.

The Ego-Defense Function.   All individuals have a need to protect themselves—and the image they hold of themselves—from threats, both internal and external. This concept of a self that must be protected, the "ego," is perhaps the most fundamental in psychology. Inner challenges to the ego may arise from many sources: feelings of inferiority, past guilt, inability to cope with external demands, or perceived conflicts between responsibilities, to name only a few. These challenges must be dealt with, and a variety of tactics are employed for this purpose. The tactics may be primitive in nature, such as denying that the conflict exists or otherwise avoiding the problem. They may be more complex, such as a projection of one's own inadequacies onto others or a transfer of hostility from the original

[23] Daniel Katz, "The Functional Approach to the Study of Attitudes," *Public Opinion Quarterly*, 24 (1960), 163–204.

target to one that is socially acceptable.[24] In a sense, such devices are utilitarian, for they are designed to reduce psychological pain; but they differ from devices of the instrumental function in that the object of the opinion is not always the original one, but rather may be one selected as a substitute. And while one may very well be conscious that he is developing an opinion for instrumental reasons, ego-defense mechanisms are necessarily concealed from one's consciousness. If one is aware that he is rationalizing, then the rationalization cannot serve its intended function. Thus, many attitudes toward public affairs are structured in response to private, and even subconscious, needs.

The Value-Expressive Function.   Just as there are sides to our personalities that we would like to suppress, there are other sides that demand amplification. The value-expressive function is this need to express attitudes or opinions that are consistent with and promote the way we would like ourselves to be. For instance, the man who prides himself on being a liberal may take every available opportunity to develop "liberal" opinions on a wide variety of topics. At one level, this may operate in an instrumental manner ("People expect me to be a liberal, so I mustn't disappoint them"), but it can also come in response to purely psychological expectations. In other words, certain values and expectations have become *internalized.* What is the source of this internalized self-image? To a great extent, individuals internalize those values that they see around them. They are *socialized* into roles—and certain belief systems accompany those roles. An understanding of the socialization process from childhood to adulthood is necessary therefore to explain why an individual expresses the opinions that he does.

The Knowledge Function.   A basic human need is for knowledge about the external world. Such a need, however, should not be interpreted as a quest for more information. Rather, what the individual needs is some method for interpreting and sorting the multitude of data he receives every day. The world is a complex source of stimuli, and no one could cope with even a small part of it unless he were able to sift or screen out a large part. Opinions play a definite role in this process. The structure of a person's beliefs comprises what is for him a coherent picture of the world. This view of the world serves as a model for evaluating new data: if the new piece of information does not fit into the existing picture, it may very well be discarded. Thus, information that does not complement existing beliefs and perceptions may simply be categorized as untrue and therefore

---

[24] An example of this phenomenon is to be found in the reformulated argument for the "authoritarian" discussed previously in this chapter.

discarded. Or the process may operate at a more sophisticated level; for example, the meaning of the information is distorted so that it is consistent with other beliefs. A man need not feel that he understands international economics in order to evaluate the government's new trade policy; he may be able to generalize from his attitude toward the president to the administration's latest venture in the area. Thus, the knowledge function—which is psychologically necessary—can lead to a less "rational" consideration of public affairs.

The Need for Consistency.   Perhaps the most basic of all needs and one that ties together those previously discussed is the need for psychological consistency.[25] Not only must the other functions be performed, but they must structure beliefs and perceptions so as to avoid any apparent contradiction. This is the case because such a contradiction would be psychologically painful and would set up a condition of *cognitive dissonance.* As Festinger argues,

The existence of dissonance, being psychologically uncomfortable, will motivate the person to try to reduce the dissonance and achieve consonance. . . . When dissonance is present, in addition to trying to avoid it, the person will actively avoid situations which would likely increase the dissonance.[26]

In performing the knowledge function, then, stimuli that would clash with existing attitudes are either screened out or reinterpreted so that the belief system is not threatened. In order for the ego-defensive and value-expressive functions to be properly maintained, a clear and consistent self-image must be retained. The various functions must not only be performed, they must also be performed so that they reinforce each other. Hence, as individual's attitudes are neither isolated conclusions nor random preferences. They are a complex of carefully (though often subconsciously) built-up patterns of orientation and perception that unite an individual's past experience, current values, and future expectations into a self-reinforcing and consistent set of responses to stimuli. An individual's beliefs will be—to him—logically related, and to attack one of them is to threaten his basic self-image.

BEHAVIORAL MANIFESTATIONS OF PSYCHOLOGICAL FUNCTIONALISM

All of the above generalizations are only theory, albeit well-established theory. Because they deal with purely mental and often

[25] There are some theoretical differences between "consistency" theory and "dissonance" theory; we shall not go into them in this discussion.
[26] Leon Festinger, *A Theory of Cognitive Dissonance* (Stanford: Stanford University Press, 1957), p. 3.

subconscious phenomena, it is probably impossible to offer empirical proof for them. To analyze an individual in these terms necessitates a great deal of information about him, such as that found in the intensive, almost psychoanalytic studies of Smith, Bruner, and White. This framework cannot therefore be applied to the public as a whole through the techniques of survey research. However, the functional and dissonance theory approach can be seen to operate in visible political phenomena and can thereby offer an explanation for behavior that would otherwise be incomprehensible.

Political Perception.   A number of examples demonstrating the behavioral consequences of psychological functionalism can be drawn from the voting literature. One of the clearest ones comes from data on the perception of the position taken by the two presidential candidates in 1948 on the Taft-Hartley Act.[27] Most voters, regardless of party affiliation, perceived the candidates' stands correctly, recognizing that Dewey supported the act and Truman opposed it.[28] However, some voters were in a situation that threatened to produce a psychological conflict. A Republican who opposed Taft-Hartley faced this conflict; his party loyalty called for favorable attitudes toward and a vote for Dewey, but to provide these would be to contradict his own position on a critical issue of the day. A Democrat who favored the measure was in a similar dilemma. It appears that many voters "solved" the problem by a complete distortion of the actual positions favored by the candidates. While 96 percent of those Republicans who favored the act saw Dewey as also favoring it, only 54 percent of those who opposed the act saw Dewey as being in favor of it. Thus, many Republicans handled the situation by incorrectly attributing their own point of view to the leader of their party. The same was true for the Democratic identifiers. Whereas only 10 percent of those Democrats who were against the Taft-Hartley Act believed that Truman favored it, 40 percent of those who favored the act thought that Truman agreed with them. A similar sort of distortion prevailed with respect to opposition candidates: Republicans tended to see Truman as taking the opposite position from themselves, while Democrats did the same for Dewey.

Such distortion on so visible an issue does not make much sense, except as we recognize that individuals, in order to protect their existing beliefs from challenge and possible disconfirmation, may adjust their perception of the external world. In the case just described,

---

[27] This particular election and issue offer a situation in which there had been long and heated debate, and each of the candidates had firmly committed himself to a position. There should have been little problem for the voter in ascertaining how the candidate stood on the Taft-Hartley question.

[28] This discussion is drawn from Berelson *et al.*, *Voting*, pp. 215–33.

other methods of dissonance avoidance are also in evidence. More of the voters who would have disagreed with their candidate's stand claimed a lack of knowledge as to his position or believed that he had none on that issue. And the more strongly the voter felt about his party's candidate, the more prone he was to distort his perception. This is just one example, but it illustrates the general principle. The same phenomena were observed with other issues in the 1948 election, and the tendency of the electorate to attribute their own preferences to the candidates they favor is a general one.

Other manifestations of attitudinal functionalism in political behavior might be cited, such as the tendency of persons subjected to "cross-pressures" (i.e., circumstances that predispose a person in opposing directions, whether attitudinal or social) to attempt to avoid the situation altogether in such ways as delaying an electoral decision or neglecting to vote entirely.[29] Moreover, people often exercise a screening process with regard to political communications; material favorable to the opposition is simply ignored. Many of these phenomena will be discussed in succeeding chapters. The point is that while the specific functions of attitudes may be hidden within the subconscious, the consequences of their functioning have a clear and important impact on the opinions that individuals express.

Techniques of Coping with Hostile Information. The examples cited suggest that the individual has a range of methods of dealing with situations that pose some threat to the functioning of his attitude structure. Indeed, the typical man has a wide repertoire of techniques for coping with new information that is disjunctive with his expectations. This is clear from the findings of *Opinions and Personality,* in which the subjects were confronted with "facts" and asked to interpret them. The following reactions emerged as characteristic responses to unpalatable items.

1. *Denial:* categorization of the item as false or unproven.
2. *Skepticism about source:* the veracity of the source is doubted and the item held at a distance.
3. *Ascription of motive:* the *ad hominem* argument that avoids direct evaluation of the alleged fact by questioning the motives for its having been advanced.
4. *Isolation:* neutralization of an item that is accepted by keeping it apart from the context of one's attitude.
5. *Minimization:* placing an accepted fact in context so that it appears unimportant or atypical.
6. *Interpretation:* placing an accepted fact in context so that it takes on a meaning other than the unwelcome one that it immediately presents.

[29] *Ibid.,* pp. 24–33; Lazarsfeld *et al., The People's Choice,* pp. 52–69; and Campbell *et al., The American Voter,* pp. 81–88.

7. *Misunderstanding:* distorted perception of the presented fact; a special case is motivated failure to perceive any meaning in the item.
8. *Thinking away:* moving from a correct original perception of the item to quite other conclusions, via a loose chain of thought.[30]

This, of course, is not an exclusive list of methods of dealing with new and threatening information. McGuire notes a number of other modes of reducing inconsistencies that are somewhat more subtle and complex.[31] Typically, more than one method is invoked in response to a given situation. Smith, Bruner, and White's analogy to the legendary old farmer is quite appropriate here: when accused of having broken a borrowed tool, the farmer replied that "he had returned it intact, it was broken when he had gotten it, and he had never borrowed it in the first place." [32] When faced with a circumstance that conflicts with one's expectations, particularly if some threat to one's self-image is implied, the human mind can go to great lengths to preserve psychological balance.

Almost any of these reactions, in an appropriate context, might be intellectually defensible. It would hardly be "rational" to believe everything one is told, and psychological balance could not be maintained if one adopted a new set of opinions with each issue of the daily paper. In practice, though, techniques such as these are used only to support one's existing attitudes, and the defense of the cognitive status quo takes precedence over an objective and balanced evaluation of information. Balance is maintained and psychological needs are met, but at the cost of a distorted view of the real world.

Opinion Change.   Perhaps the foregoing material has overstated a valid point. While there are strong strains toward psychological consistency, which tend to reinforce existing beliefs, *opinions do change,* sometimes to the point of reversal. Under what conditions is change most likely to occur?

A key variable affecting the susceptibility of an opinion to change is the *salience* of the subject matter to the individual. The more important a person considers an issue to be, the more he feels that some resolution of the issue would affect him personally; and the more extreme his opinions on the question, the less the probability of change will be. On the other hand, if an individual holds an opinion on a subject that seems far removed from him and is only of passing interest, then his opinion may easily change as a result of new information. In general, the issues involved in politics and public affairs are

[30] Smith *et al., Opinions and Personality,* p. 251.
[31] William J. McGuire, "The Current Status of Cognitive Consistency Theories," in *Cognitive Consistency,* ed. Shel Feldman (New York: Academic Press, 1966), pp. 10–14.
[32] Smith *et al., Opinions and Personality,* p. 251.

not of great salience to most Americans most of the time. This is particularly true of most questions of international policy and technical questions of science. Such issue areas may be of the greatest objective relevance for the future of man, but they are of lower salience to most people than mundane topics of taxation, local public expenditures, and labor relations. It must be noted that the importance of an issue is determined by the individual himself; while one union member is concerned with labor-management relations, another may ignore these and concentrate his political attentions on American policy toward another nation from which he has recently emigrated. The degree to which questions of economic and foreign policy are salient to these men would be different, and therefore the availability of their opinions to change would vary.

A second point to consider is the extent to which cognitive consistency has already been achieved. To the extent that there exists a measure of inconsistency among opinions or some ambiguity in orientations, the pressure will be for, rather than against, some change in attitudes. This is particularly true if the inconsistency has its roots in a deeper conflict in the individual's self-image. If the functioning of attitudes was always so successful as to completely meet all psychological needs, then attitude structures might become virtually impregnable to external stimuli. This, however, is not likely to occur, if only because of the changing nature of environment and the external pressures to which the self must adjust.

Finally, the susceptibility of opinions to change depends to a great extent on the particular type of function to which an opinion is linked. While an opinion is involved in the performance of several functions simultaneously, it may tend to be more related to one than the others, and the prime function will affect its responsiveness to differing stimuli. While generalizations are difficult, it would appear that the functions previously discussed might be ranked as follows from most to least susceptible to change: (a) *instrumental,* (b) *knowledge,* (c) *value-expressive,* and (d) *ego-defensive.* On one hand, if an opinion is held for purely utilitarian reasons, then a shift in the perceived rewards-and-punishments system of the external world should result in its reversal. On the other hand, an attitude that is directly engaged in defending the ego will be likely to change only as a basic adjustment of the self-image occurs, and hence the attitude would be relatively immune from external stimuli. Many of these principles will be discussed later in the context of the power of the mass media and its potential for persuasion. The point here is that the availability of an attitude for change and the nature of the stimuli that might bring it about are largely determined by factors that are internal to the individual.

CONCLUSION: INTERNAL CONDITIONS
AND EXTERNAL FORCES

If the reader expected this chapter to give him a simple method of predicting who will hold what preference on an issue, then he must be greatly disappointed. As we have seen, there is no simple correlation between personality attributes and opinions, even if the nature of personality can be adequately measured. What we have seen is that there is a complex interaction between the external environment and psychological predispositions, one result of which are opinions, attitudes, and beliefs. In order to understand and perhaps predict an individual's opinions, we must know the relevant characteristics of his position in the external world and the pressures upon him that this environment produces. As our brief survey of the literature suggested, there are a number of ways of conceptualizing this external situation and we shall devote several chapters to their analysis; for we must concur with Smith, Bruner, and White that "the opinions which develop in a man are multiple in their determinants." [33] But even the most sophisticated analysis of these multiple sources of an opinion will have little value if we are not at least aware of "the embeddedness of opinions in the functioning of personality." [34] *Personality*—however defined or measured—is not a *source* of opinions, but is rather a mechanism for translating a host of external inputs into a set of preferences and orientations that are consistent with individual needs.

[33] *Ibid.*, p. 278.
[34] *Ibid.*, p. 279.

Political Socialization: The Learning of Opinions

4

What are the sources of an opinion? How do people acquire their beliefs and perceptions about public affairs? One answer to this fundamental question is that opinions are *learned*—they are patterns of behavior acquired over a period of time. If this is so, then how early does the process start and how long do its effects remain? The evidence suggests that the acquisition of political knowledge begins during childhood and extends throughout the individual's lifetime.

This principle is clearly demonstrated in the case of one of the most important political attitudes a person holds: his identification with a political party. Early national surveys demonstrated that there is a strong similarity between the partisanship of a voter and that held by his parents. As Table 4–1 shows, most voters in 1952 identified with the same party they recalled their parents supporting. Among those who came from homes of unified party loyalty, about three-fourths favored that party, while only a fifth advocated the opposite. In cases where this family homogeneity was lacking, respondents were spread much more broadly over the partisan spectrum. This same finding of apparent "inheritance" of political preference has been substantiated in later studies, and the strength of the relationship seems to increase with the degree of political activity in the home.[1]

On first discovering this pattern of adoption of political partisanship from one's parents, some observers are likely to point out that this represents the pattern of growth in previous generations. Young people today, it is asserted, do not readily adopt the partisan loyalties of their parents. Instead, they are likely to disregard these loyalties or to actively rebel against them. It is alleged that early socialization is much less important for those now entering the political system than it was for their predecessors.

Is this assumption justified? Probably not, for many who would

[1] Angus Campbell *et al., The American Voter* (New York: John Wiley, 1960), pp. 146–48.

Table 4-1
Relation of Parents' Party Identification to That of Offspring, 1952

Party Identification of Respondent	Party Identification of Parents				
	Both Demo.	Both Repub.	One R., One D.	One R. or D., Other Unknown	Other Combinations
Strong Democrat	36%	7%	12%	14%	14%
Weak Democrat	36	9	32	23	22
Independent Democrat	10	6	10	13	14
Independent	3	4	—	10	10
Independent Republican	3	10	—	10	10
Weak Republican	6	30	22	12	11
Strong Republican	6	33	22	15	5
None, minor party, Not ascertained	—	1	2	3	14
Totals	100%	100%	100%	100%	100%
N	657	387	41	102	302

Source: Angus Campbell, *et al., The Voter Decides* (Evanston, Ill.: Row, Peterson, 1954), p. 99. "Other Combinations" category collapsed from the original table.

make it forget that while the group of recently enfranchised voters from eighteen through their early twenties lean much more heavily toward the Democratic and independent categories than toward the Republican, this is also true of their elders.[2] While there are some differences in the degree of partisan inheritance among younger voters today from those of earlier years, there is also considerable similarity. Table 4-2 shows data on the sources of party identification among students at one large midwestern university. It is clear that very few of the students in this survey adopted a party identification opposite to that of their parents, while almost three-fourths of those from politically homogeneous households gave at least nominal support to the parental party. There are some differences between this pattern and that of the whole electorate two decades before. The most important is that college students today are much more likely to identify themselves as some variety of political "independent," though most can still voice some party leaning. Another obvious conclusion is that there is an overall tendency to shift away from the Republican party and toward the Democratic party. Yet, on balance, the overall conclusion that much partisanship is a direct outgrowth of

[2] The political preferences of younger voters have been examined by a number of national surveys; Gallup's is reported in *Newsweek*, October 25, 1971, pp. 38–49.

Table 4-2

Relation of Parents' Party Identification to That of Offspring, College Students, 1974

Party Identification of Respondent	Party Identification of Parents				
	Both Demo.	Both Repub.	One R., One D.	One R. or D., Other Unknown	All Others
Strong Democrat	16%	2%	9%	4%	3%
Weak Democrat	28	4	20	12	6
Independent Democrat	36	10	29	29	24
Independent	11	11	16	23	32
Independent Republican	4	24	16	14	15
Weak Republican	2	32	8	10	7
Strong Republican	0	12	1	3	4
None, other, no response, etc.	3	4	1	4	8
Totals	100%	100%*	100%	100%*	100%*
* Totals in these columns fall short of 100% due to rounding.					
N	281	337	76	146	231

Source: Surveys conducted at Illinois State University by the author.

parental loyalties seems to hold for new voters today, just as it did for the previous generation.[3]

The purpose of introducing these findings is to suggest the importance of the political socialization process as a source for political beliefs. This evidence does not conclusively prove the point, for there are other possible reasons for the observed relationship. For example, some of the similarity between parent and child might simply be due to the fact that both hold the same position on a number of relevant demographic variables, such as race, religion, economic status, etc. However, the relationship is sufficiently striking to lead us to give considerable attention to the subject of socialization.

THE CONCEPT OF POLITICAL SOCIALIZATION

There are numerous theories and definitions of political socialization.[4] Perhaps the most useful is that it is the process "by which an

[3] The same conclusion can be drawn from data comparing the party identification of high school seniors with those of their parents as reported by M. Kent Jennings and Richard G. Niemi, "The Transmission of Political Values from Parent to Child," *American Political Science Review*, 62 (1968), 169–84.

[4] For a discussion of the concept and a summary of findings by a number of studies, see Richard E. Dawson, "Political Socialization," in *Political Science Annual: An In-*

individual learns politically relevant attitudinal dispositions and behavior patterns." [5] This is a very broad definition that potentially encompasses all phases of individual opinion formation. We shall concentrate at this point upon that political learning which occurs through interpersonal contact and which results in the acquisition of basic political attitudes.

The notion of political socialization rests upon that of socialization as a general phenomenon. When an individual lives within a social environment, there is an inevitable process of learning about that environment. This learning includes not only the objective "facts" of the situation, but also the evaluative judgments typically made by others and the distinctions as to which patterns of behavior are acceptable and which are not. This is not to say that the individual always accepts these judgments and behaves only in acceptable ways, though generally he does. The idea of political socialization refers particularly to those beliefs, values, and behavior patterns that are directed at political objects—governmental institutions, political leaders, ideological positions, and the like. The questions to be investigated here include these: when does the process of political learning start, from what sources does the knowledge come, and how does the process vary over the lifetime of an individual?

CHILDHOOD SOCIALIZATION

When Wordsworth said that "the child is father of the man," he was expressing an idea well confirmed by modern social science: the experiences and impressions of the earliest years can have an effect all through one's life. This notion has long been applied to the realm of politics. One of Plato's main concerns was the kind of upbringing the future rulers of his ideal state should receive. Systematic investigation of the nature of early political learning began with studies by Merriam and others that concentrated upon the role of formal instruction through public education in "civic training." [6] A number of important studies in the last decade have used survey techniques to measure the content of the child's view of the political world, and their findings are quite revealing.

The Political World of the Child. [7]   Children acquire basic political orientations in the first years of elementary school—though they may

ternational Review 1966, ed. James A. Robinson (Indianapolis: Bobbs-Merrill, 1966), pp. 1–84.

[5] Kenneth P. Langton, *Political Socialization* (New York: Oxford University Press, 1969), p. 5.

[6] Charles E. Merriam, *Civic Education in the United States* (New York: Charles Scribner's Sons, 1934).

[7] This section draws upon findings from a number of studies, including Fred I. Greenstein, "The Benevolent Leader: Children's Images of Political Authority,"

not even be aware of the idea of "politics." The first object of awareness is what can be called the "political community." This includes
the nation and associated symbols, such as the flag. At this stage
knowledge and attitude are quite diffuse; children recognize that
they are "Americans," that the American flag is the prettiest, that
their country has "freedom," etc. As knowledge increases, the first
specific concepts of institutions are added. However, children perceive formal governmental institutions almost entirely in *personalis-
tic* terms. The national government is seen as consisting of the president. Other structural roles, such as the vice-presidency or the
Senate, are pictured as his "helpers." At the local level, children
would at best probably be familiar with only the mayor (depending
upon their community) or with the policeman as an authority figure.
For children, then, government is a series of images of *individuals,*
almost always those in executive, rather than legislative or judicial
positions. More differentiated notions of governmental structures
and functions generally are not found until the last years of elementary school.

In this early period of socialization, when the images of the political system are diffuse and personalized, the affective orientation is
highly idealized. Children see their country as superior to others in
all ways and this uncritical appraisal holds true for their perceptions
of leaders. The view is typically expressed that the president is "the
best person in the world," and similar idealized appraisals are made
of other figures of political authority such as policemen. The same
sorts of favorable judgments are made toward nonpolitical figures
such as physicians, though to a less extreme degree. During the first
ten years of one's life the image of the political world is a series of
rather general perceptions of the political system as a collection of
idealized individuals exercising authority for good purposes.

Patterns of Socialization.   The sorts of findings reported above lead
us to some general conclusions about the process of socialization.
First, it seems that the child initially acquires an awareness and loyalty toward the political system as a whole (though in a decidedly
nonpolitical context). Secondly, it is clear that *evaluations* of the political structure precede specific *knowledge* about it. Finally, it may
be said that this first phase in the political socialization process is
generally completed by the start of adolescence.

We have described this pattern of acquiring political knowledge as
a learning process. How does this learning occur? Hess and Torney
suggest that there are at least four different ways in which the child

American Political Science Review, 54 (1960), 934–43; David Easton and Robert D.
Hess, "The Child's Political World," *Midwest Journal of Political Science*, 6 (1962),
229–46; and Robert D. Hess and Judith V. Torney, *The Development of Political Attitudes in Children* (Chicago: Aldine Publishing Co., 1967).

acquires various kinds of political orientations.[8] The simplest is *accumulation:* the child acquires various facts and ideas with no particular logical or emotional interrelationship among them. This mode of learning is brought about, for example, by the teacher who insists upon memorization of specifics about formal governmental structure by the student. Secondly, political learning may occur through *interpersonal transfer*. In this process, the child transfers his attitudes toward nonpolitical objects to the political system. For example, attitudes toward the father may be transferred to the president or other political authority figures, and feelings about social rules can affect orientations toward the legal system. Another mode of socialization is *identification* or *imitation*. The child observes that certain individuals whom he respects hold certain beliefs; therefore, he adopts those beliefs. In this way, a child can develop attitudes and opinions about political objects—such as political parties—about which he has virtually no knowledge. For most children, parents and teachers are the only adults with whom they have direct contact; hence, it is from them that orientations are adopted. (The relative contribution of each is discussed below.) Finally, political learning can involve *cognitive development*. This is the most advanced form of learning, for it requires both maturation and prior knowledge so that interrelated concepts and ideas can be internalized and put into perspective. Cognitive development could begin to some extent at an early age, though it typically occurs later than the other types.

Each of these types of learning can be used to explain the acquisition of different elements of political learning. Interpersonal transfer may account for the early formation of loyalties toward the political system as a whole. Accumulation seems to be the way children typically gain most of their factual knowledge of political structure. Identification with the attitudes of others is the way in which specific evaluations and loyalties, such as political partisanship, are established. For real understanding of the complex operation of the political system, cognitive development must occur. The process of political socialization in childhood is not a simple one in which the individual is automatically endowed with a standard set of political orientations. It is the beginning of an elaborate process of acquiring from different sources the political cognitions that eventually produce opinions and political behavior.

Sources of Socialization: The School and the Family.   Most students of childhood socialization would agree that the major sources of the political information learned by the child are parents and teachers, though there is some disagreement as to the relative impor-

[8] Hess and Torney, *Development of Political Attitudes in Children*, pp. 22–26.

tance of their respective contributions. (It might be noted that the impact of television viewing by children upon their political orientations has probably not received sufficient attention.) It is clear, however, that school and family introduce different, though interrelated, kinds of orientations.

It would appear that the greater part of socialization comes via the school. Hess and Torney conclude that "the public school appears to be the most important and effective instrument of political socialization in the United States." [9] It is here that the child acquires both information about the political world and the loyalties toward it that are expected of him. In school, it is the teacher who seems to be responsible for the opinions that the pupils acquire. Hess and Torney report a high degree of similarity in attitude between teachers and students on items dealing with the roles, powers, and performances of occupants of governmental positions.[10] Dissimilarities were most marked on items concerning trust versus cynicism in government, interest in politics, and the merits of strong partisanship. It would seem that it is in areas such as these that the family plays a greater role.

The data presented at the opening of this chapter obviously suggest that the family has a strong and lasting effect upon a person's identification with a political party. This is borne out by a number of investigations into childhood socialization. Greenstein finds that by the fourth grade, 60 percent of children expressed a party loyalty—a proportion identical to that of voters in their early twenties in the same city.[11] This loyalty does not, of course, grow out of perceptions and evaluations of parties, issues, and candidates, for the children displayed little or no knowledge of these. Rather, the child simply assumes the partisan identification expressed by his parents. "We're Republicans" is as natural and unconscious an assumption to the child as "We're Presbyterians!" Almost none of the children interviewed by Greenstein expressed a party loyalty contrary to that of their parents.

A similar, if less obvious, effect of family is revealed in the degree to which there is interest and involvement in politics. Children of politically active parents are themselves much more likely to be interested and involved in public affairs when they reach maturity. Less clear are transfers of ideologies and opinions on specific issues. Certainly, such direct transfers occur, but the specific strengths and limitations of the passing on of ideas have not been fully investi-

[9] *Ibid.*, p. 120.
[10] *Ibid.*, pp. 128–32.
[11] Fred I. Greenstein, *Children and Politics* (New Haven: Yale University Press, 1968), pp. 71–75.

gated.[12] One limiting factor on the ability of these learned opinions to persist over time is that while political party labels continue, issues depart from the political scene. To the extent that particular beliefs are carried over from the family, they presumably tend to reinforce the effects of party identification.

The family is important also as an agent of mediation between the child and other sources of socialization. There are important differences in the socialization patterns of children from different socioeconomic groups. Middle-class children tend to display greater feelings of political efficacy, greater awareness of partisan differences, and greater inclination to participate in politics than lower-class children of the same grade level. In short, the children from lower-class households have a somewhat different pattern of socialization into the political system. The explanation seems to be that while the values learned in school are reinforced by middle-class parents through overt instruction, example, and child-rearing practices, this is not the case in a lower-class situation. Thus, the influence of the home can strengthen or weaken the effects of the school. Somewhat the same thing seems to be true at a psychological level. Children whose relationships with their parents, particularly their fathers, are unhappy may reflect this hostility in their attitude toward political authority structures. This displacement does not necessarily imply a rebellion against authority. Lane found that men who had experienced "damaged" relationships with their fathers tended to be less willing to criticize formal authority (suggesting the "authoritarianism" pattern discussed in Chapter 3).[13] Family relationships during early life can thus have an important impact on later patterns of political behavior.

WEAKNESSES OF CHILDHOOD POLITICAL SOCIALIZATION

Anyone who looks at the usual substance of the child's political world, as we have just outlined it, is immediately struck by its obvious difference from the real world. It requires neither great cynicism nor sophistication to see that the idealized and personalized view of politics often held by children at the end of elementary school is hardly sufficient for understanding the actual operation of the politi-

[12] Jennings and Niemi, "The Transmission of Political Values," investigate the degree of similarity between the attitudes of high school students and their parents on several issues and on evaluations of sociopolitical groupings. There is a degree of relationship, though it is not markedly strong and is significantly less than the degree of correlation between the party identification of parent and child.

[13] Robert E. Lane, "Fathers and Sons: Foundations of Political Belief," *American Sociological Review*, 24 (1959), 502–11, and *Political Ideology: Why the American Common Man Believes What He Does* (New York: Free Press, 1962), chap. 17.

cal process. Indeed, much that is inherently necessary for such understanding is simply left out of the precollegiate curriculum in American public education. While a great deal of instructional time is devoted to institutional description, little or no attention is given to such vital aspects of the political system as political parties and interest groups. Formal details of the electoral process are covered, but always in terms of a rather naïve form of democratic theory that emphasizes the importance of participation while assuming its unquestionable efficacy. Even when it comes to ideals, the results are hardly promising, for the "future citizens" produced by this socialization process fail to give overwhelming support to traditional values of freedom and equality. A committee report of the American Political Science Association suggests some eight goals of precollegiate education in politics; the evidence seems to be that none of them are presently being achieved to any significant degree by the educational system in the United States.[14] Among the sources of the problem suggested by the committee are curriculum, textbooks, and the pattern of interaction between school and pupil.

Whatever the sources of this situation, the situation itself clearly has some implications for the functioning of the political process. An obvious point is that even if one feels it would be good for members of the society to hold this idealistic view of their government, this is not the way to arrive at it. Children grow up and it is not too long before many have doubts as to whether all political leaders are good or whether the government always responds directly to the voters. The outlook gained from early socialization is simply too much at variance with reality to be carried over into adult life by most people. But to the extent that remnants of childhood socialization remain, these perceptions also have an effect upon the nature of political behavior. Perhaps it is the early tendency to personalize the government and identify it with the executive branch that leads Americans to view the president as the source of all policy—and to blame him for any problems that arise during his tenure.

What happens when one's sources of knowledge about the political world expand beyond the classroom? Given the disparity between the view encouraged in the early years and that which must result from information in the mass media, an almost classic situation

[14] "Political Education in the Public Schools: The Challenge for Political Science" (report of the Committee on Pre-Collegiate Education, American Political Science Association). This report, reprinted in PS, 4 (1971), 432–57, contains a lengthy analysis of the problem, its possible causes, and some suggested programs for improvement. Among the unfulfilled goals cited by the report are that precollegiate education should transmit knowledge about the "realities" of political life, transmit knowledge of behavior and processes rather than only of formal institutions, and develop the ability to make explicit normative judgments about politics.

for producing cognitive dissonance is created. Existing values and perceptions are brought into question by new information and ideas. As we have seen, various courses of psychological action are available to reduce the dissonance and restore cognitive consistency. The individual could attempt to deny the new information as false and therefore disregard it, though this is difficult when it comes unendingly from a variety of sources. He could avoid contact with politics so that the dissonance is muted. Or he could make a fundamental attitude adjustment and discard previous values and perceptions. All of these forms of behavior and others are probably manifested by young people who find themselves in this conflicted situation. Perhaps this stress has always been a problem in maturation, but with the increasingly unavoidable character of information on public affairs and an increasing level of educational attainment, it becomes more widespread. At any rate, a great deal of political socialization must occur between emergence from childhood and transition into established adult life.

GROWTH AND CHANGE

The idea that there is a distinct period between childhood and adulthood is a modern one. Not so long ago, most people went from being children to being adults with little time in between. Today, however, there is a continually lengthening period of intermediate status during the high school and college years before the individual fully enters the economic world and is considered as a full-grown and independent adult. This segment of life may end as early as seventeen or eighteen or it may extend into the middle or late twenties. It is a part of the life-cycle characterized by conflicts of role expectations. In part the individual is treated as a child, in part as an adult. Hence, the political socialization process in these years contains similarities to both earlier and later patterns, as well as some unique elements.

Relatively little attention has been given to the political socialization process among high school students. Nevertheless, many of the same comments that were made earlier about the content of the political education curriculum in the earlier grades can be applied to the high school curriculum. Again, a rather limited view of the political process seems to be the one most commonly presented. The results, however, do not seem to be the same; for the high school student, if he has any interest in the subject, has access to a much broader base of information than he did in grade school.[15] As a result,

[15] Given the usual high school curriculum, the student receives little direct instruction on material related to contemporary politics with exception of (at most) a one-

the idealized political world of childhood no longer is viable for him, but it is not replaced with anything of substance—at least not through the formal process of education. Some students, of course, are actively interested in politics and may begin participation at this point, but the stimulus for this minority comes from the family or from other sources outside the classroom. A basic point that should not be overlooked is that most high school students are simply not very much interested in politics or knowledgeable about public affairs.

The Effects of the College Experience.   The proverbial "man in the street" today knows that college must have an effect upon people; after all, college students run around expressing all kinds of strange and radical ideas. Even before the apparent changes in campus political behavior in the 1960s, one could point to differences in beliefs between people who had been to college and those who had not. Those with some college training express more liberal opinions on a number of noneconomic kinds of issues, particularly racial equality, tolerance of dissent, and internationalism. Does college attendance really have this kind of influence and, if so, how and why does it occur?

One of the earliest and most well-known studies of the effects of college on political opinion was done at Bennington College in the late 1930s.[16] It was found that the women at that school did express much more liberal beliefs on contemporary issues than their parents. The degree of liberalism also increased with each year—seniors were more liberal than juniors, and sophomores were more so than freshmen. Such findings have been replicated at other institutions in succeeding years with generally the same results. Not all college students are highly tolerant, unprejudiced, or generally liberal, but they tend to become more so as the length of their exposure to college increases. Public opinion polls today consistently reveal college students to be the most "liberal" of all educational-age categories.

What are the sources of this effect of college on beliefs? There are several logical possibilities, including: (a) liberal college professors indoctrinate students with liberal beliefs; (b) increased awareness of the world through education makes one more liberal; and (c) students are expected to be more liberal by their peers and therefore they are. The first explanation (often offered by conservative critics of higher education) does not seem to be justified. There seems to be little evidence that individual college instructors are able to force

---

semester civics course, and this appears to have relatively little impact upon political attitudes. See Langton, *Political Socialization*, pp. 90–100.

[16] Theodore M. Newcomb, *Personality and Social Change: Attitude Formation in a Student Community* (New York: Dryden Press, 1943).

their own views on students (assuming that they even try) with any lasting effect. Indeed, one study suggests that introductory political science courses are not even able to significantly increase student interest in political participation.[17]

There is some validity to the idea that the accumulation of knowledge increases liberalism. To the extent that "liberal" means to be less dogmatic, less prejudiced, more open and tolerant, college makes people more liberal. Since students are likely to enter college bearing more stereotypes and oversimplifications of a conservative than of a liberal bias, any "myth-breaking" effect is likely to liberalize. (One suspects that if students were to enter with a different load of intellectual baggage, the political reverse might occur.) There is no evidence, however, that the educational process inherently transmits liberal values.

It is the third alternative that seems to offer the most satisfactory explanation: students adopt liberal attitudes as part of the college life-style exhibited by other students. This seemed to be the case at Bennington. Those women who were most popular were liberal; some of their peers consciously adopted the same political beliefs for reasons of social acceptance. In a later study, Jacobs argues that this factor accounts for much of the observed change in attitudes during college. The basic value pattern seems to be set before college entrance, while during college, opinions are modified in response to new information and expectations of others. He concludes that ". . . college has a socializing, rather than a liberalizing impact on values. It softens an individual's extremist views and persuades him to reconsider aberrant values." [18] The changes that occur in college, therefore, do indeed seem to be the result of a socialization process —socialization into the college community.

An additional explanation of change during college should be noted. This is the idea that the prevailing view of the political world is always changing and that young people, particularly students, tend to acquire the newer view. The late 1930s of the Bennington study was a time of considerable change in American politics and values, and the current era is another. Hence, the student may simply be subscribing to the beliefs encouraged by a perception of his world rather than the world his parents grew up in. In this sense, the change is not due to college at all, though young people in college, being more removed from parental influences, may be more influ-

[17] Albert Somit et al., "The Effect of the Introductory Political Science Course on Student Attitudes Toward Personal Political Participation," American Political Science Review, 52 (1958), 1129–32.

[18] Philip E. Jacob, Changing Values in College: An Exploratory Study of the Impact of College Teaching (New York: Harper and Row, 1957), p. 53.

enced by the times than those who remain in their home communities and environments. Finally, it should be noted that college students tend to come from more affluent homes than other young people do and have parents who were more educated. Hence, those who attend college may enter with a predisposition toward more liberal social beliefs.[19]

Radicalism and Rebellion.   Perhaps the most striking characteristic of the American political scene in the late 1960s was the prevalence of protest demonstrations on a large number of college campuses, demonstrations that usually expressed some radical critique of the existing political, economic, and social structure and that sometimes culminated in some sort of violence. Such a pattern of rejection of the status quo poses a major challenge to the assumptions of the political system and seemingly represents a sharp discontinuity from the learned political values of the early socialization process. Does this pattern of student radicalism mean that we must discard our earlier conclusions about political learning—or can we explain the pattern as a logical outgrowth of earlier socialization?

We shall not attempt to deal with the whole subject of student radicalism and associated phenomena such as revolution and extremism, but rather shall concentrate upon some general theories as to why certain individuals tend to become active on the political Left.[20] Leaving aside the value-laden arguments of both Right (subversion by foreign agents bearing drugs) and Left (natural reaction to oppression by agents of the system), two main social-psychological explanations have been widely suggested. The first is that student radicalism is an outgrowth of rebellion against one's parents. In seeking to change or overthrow the existing political and economic structure of middle-class America, the radical is thought to be expressing a rejection of his own family relationships. The opposing argument is that radicals are usually those students who come from a family background of radical, or at least liberal, political behavior and that, far from rebelling against parental values, they are carrying those values to their logical conclusion. Keniston, in his study of a small number of participants in the "Vietnam Summer" project of 1967, considers these two hypotheses, the "Radical Rebel" and the "Red-Diaper-

[19] Kenneth P. Langton and M. Kent Jennings, "Political Socialization and the High School Civics Curriculum in the United States," *American Political Science Review*, 62 (1968), 852–67.

[20] The literature on this subject is both large and of uneven quality. For some of the more important studies and references to other sources, see Kenneth Keniston, *Youth and Dissent: The Rise of a New Opposition* (New York: Harcourt, Brace, Jovanovich, 1971); Jerome H. Skolnick, *The Politics of Progress* (New York: Simon and Schuster, 1969); and Charles Hampden-Turner, *Radical Man: The Process of Psycho-Social Development* (Garden City, N.Y.: Doubleday, 1971).

Baby," and finds the latter to be much more explanatory.[21] According to his and other findings, committed radicals tend to come from families that have always emphasized liberal values, particularly in the areas of peace and racial equality. Many of the parents in his study had been active in the socialist and pacifist movements of the 1930s or were at least ardent Stevenson Democrats in the 1950s. While the parents may not have approved of the particular radical actions of their children, the students often consciously expressed the notion that they were simply being true to the ideas they had learned from their parents. Many came from religious traditions that tended to reinforce their actions, particularly Reform Jewish, Unitarian, or Quaker backgrounds. In essence, no fundamental change in values accompanied the adoption of a radical perspective and behavior.

This explanation also stands in opposition to the argument offered by radical apologists that student rebellion often comes as a protest against the "multiversity," as a result of large classes, lack of attention by faculty to students, poor teaching, hostile administrations, etc. Such an argument does not hold up because it was precisely those institutions that offered the better instruction and the more liberal atmosphere in which protests first emerged, and it was those students who tended to have more access to the advantages of these elite institutions who were in the vanguard of protest. Indeed, until Vietnam supplanted local campus issues as the dominant subject of protest, rebellion was almost entirely confined to well-financed, prestigious, and highly selective institutions. In other words, rebellion occurred at the Berkeleys and Columbias, rather than at their less distinguished sisters, because the former tended to attract those students who were more inclined toward radicalism and protest. The same reasoning may be applied against the conservative argument that student war protests were a result of a desire to avoid military service. Again, it was those students who ran the least chance of being drafted who most quickly protested the war.

Such explanations as Keniston's, while well documented, are based upon observation of small groups of the student population who were actively engaged in radical activities and strongly committed. What of the much larger (though still minority) segment that gave the small groups sufficient support to make protest activities highly visible? Obviously, not all of the students who expressed agreement with at least some radical goals could come from Left-leaning families, though a sizable proportion might have at some colleges. A possible explanation here for the phenomenon of the larger, supporting segment might be that given for campus liberalism

[21] Kenneth Keniston, *Young Radicals: Notes on Committed Youth* (New York: Harcourt, Brace, and World, 1968).

in earlier decades. Just as support for the New Deal was a dominant trend among Bennington students in the 1930s, so was support for protest against the war, racial inequality, and college administrations typical of students generally in the 1960s. Since committed radicals tended to be successful in the academic world, there was a natural degree of attraction of the less committed. And since political radicalism was linked to the changing student life-style (particularly by the enemies of both), the counterculture attracted a significant number of students to at least marginal support of radical politics. In short, radicalism became an important social trend among college students in the late 1960s and therefore attracted considerable numbers of students purely because of its visibility and apparent popularity. In drawing this conclusion, we do not intend to cast aspersions on sincerity of beliefs or make any judgment as to their normative value. The point we are making is that there has not necessarily been any violent change in political values of most students.

Thus, the characteristic pattern of campus events in recent years demonstrates the importance of the political socialization process. As Keniston's work shows, committed radicals are often quite influenced by the values held by their parents. For the more typical student, childhood learning may also be important. A person who has entered the political world with an idealized conception of leaders and processes is likely to expect much of them. To the extent that the disparity between ideal and reality cannot be closed by cognitive mechanisms, dissonance can easily lead to a rejection of the prescribed modes of participation and utilization of more direct action. While one may not be able to move the status quo visibly closer to the ideal, his efforts and advocacy may at least serve the psychological function of removing the dissonance. Furthermore, some have suggested that media coverage of civil rights demonstrations in the early 1960s may have had the effect of disseminating the idea of protest as a legitimate form of political expression. Finally, the fact that some students support protest activities because their peers do illustrates the importance of interpersonal association, through both peer-group pressure and imitation of respected persons. This pattern of influence and transferral of beliefs from individual to individual is one that is important at all stages of development, particularly as one becomes socialized into a social role.

POLITICAL SOCIALIZATION
IN ADULT LIFE

Most studies of political socialization have been limited to childhood. However, as we have defined the process, it is lifelong, and our understanding of opinion formation would be incomplete if we did not take note of the role of interpersonal influences and expectations as sources of opinions. The major source of socialization for the adult is the influence of those persons with whom he interacts on a regular and personal basis. The adult learns political attitudes through communication with friends, family members, neighbors, and work associates.

The Effects of Personal Associations.   In an all-too-infrequent example of continuing social research, the authors of the Bennington study reinterviewed the same women twenty years later.[22] Not surprisingly, a considerable number had experienced change in their political attitudes, some in a conservative and some in a liberal direction. The source of explanation for both stability and change seems to lie in the nature of the interpersonal environment in which they were living, particularly as represented by their husbands. In those cases in which a woman's attitudes formed in college were supported by those of her husband, the attitudes tended to remain fixed. If there was a difference in attitude from that of the husband, then the attitudes of one (usually the wife) or both tended to be realigned. These findings demonstrate the basic idea that people are influenced by those with whom they interact—and that interaction is greatest between husband and wife. The same phenomenon can be observed for other kinds of associations. A 1948 election study by Berelson and others found that there was a strong relationship between the partisanship of both a person's friends and his co-workers and his own voting intentions (shown in Table 4-3). The influence seems to be slightly weaker for co-workers. This finding might be explained on the grounds that a person can choose his friends, but usually not his work associates. As the table also shows, the Republican party had a relative advantage wherever there was a lack of homogeneity. Berelson and his colleagues attributed this to the fact that the study was conducted in a heavily Republican town (Elmira, New York) and suggested the existence of a "breakage effect" (i.e., the idea that there is a tendency for individuals to conform to the pattern of the majority in the community). Again, the study shows that interpersonal associations seem to influence one's own opinions and behavior.

This finding of interpersonal influence is hardly a novel one and does not, in itself, allow us to predict what an individual's opinion will be. However, one thing is clear about the nature of interpersonal influence: *social relationships tend to occur between people of like*

[22] Theodore M. Newcomb *et al.*, *Persistence and Change: Bennington Students after 25 Years* (New York: John Wiley, 1967).

Table 4-3
The Voter's Strength of Conviction and the Political Affiliation of his Associates

Respondent's Vote Intention	Three Closest Friends			
	RRR	RRD	RDD	DDD
Strong Republican	61%	37%	23%	2%
Weak Republican	33	33	29	11
Weak Democrat	6	22	29	49
Strong Democrat	—	8	19	38
N	286	76	35	103

Respondent's Vote Intention	Three Closest Co-workers			
	RRR	RRD	RDD	DDD
Strong Republican	59%	44%	21%	4%
Weak Republican	29	37	31	13
Weak Democrat	9	14	31	39
Strong Democrat	3	5	17	44
N	115	41	29	46

Source: Bernard R. Berelson, Paul F. Lazarsfeld, William N. McPhee, *Voting: A Study of Opinion Formation in a Presidential Campaign* (Chicago: University of Chicago Press, 1954), p. 99.

attitudes. Not only a person's spouse, but also his friends, co-workers, and other associates generally share his basic political beliefs and perceptions. Most political communication occurs between people who are already in fundamental agreement. There are several reasons for this. Most importantly, people tend to associate with others who share the same social characteristics—economic status, race, and often religion. Also, to the extent that people misperceive the political leanings of their associates, they tend to emphasize points of agreement, rather than disagreement. While interpersonal communication affects one's opinions, the result is generally to *reinforce* one's beliefs, not to change them. The consequence, therefore, is to strengthen the existing psychological barriers to opinion change that already exist. Not only will attempts to change an opinion pose a threat to one's own self-image, but also to the expectations of those who know one.

Opinion Leadership. If we ask the source from which most people get their day-to-day knowledge of public affairs, the likely answer would be: "from the mass media." After all, few of us have any first-hand knowledge of events in Washington or even of local government. A significant part of our information about the world, however, does not come directly from newsmakers and news media, but is mediated through other individuals. This phenomenon has been called the "two-step flow of communication." According to this theory, information and ideas flow from the mass media to certain individuals called "opinion leaders," who then communicate this material to others. These "opinion leaders" do not necessarily constitute any sort of elite. Rather, as the early voting studies demonstrated, they are simply individuals who (a) have a higher than average degree of interest in public affairs, and (b) are in a position or occupation that allows them to communicate with others quite frequently.[23] While teachers, clergymen, and civic leaders are more likely to act as opinion leaders than the average citizen, the proverbially talkative cab driver or barber may also perform the same function. To the extent that people receive their information at second-hand, it is likely to be altered in content. Not only is the information subject to distortion and interpretation by the ultimate recipient, it also is likely to be changed in some way by each intermediate source. Our knowledge of individual psychology suggests that the alterations that occur will generally be in line with the preconceptions of the individuals involved. Personal interaction is therefore important even in those areas of concern where the main information sources are the mass media.

THE SOCIALIZATION PROCESS AND OPINION FORMATION

While the subject of political socialization is interesting in itself, our purpose in investigating it here has been to gain a greater understanding of how and why individuals hold their opinions. We can think of political socialization in two ways: as a *source* for an individual's opinions and as an ongoing *process* by which his opinions are formed. Thinking of the socialization process as a source gives us some notion of where the individual's existing opinions came from in the first place. Basic political values and orientations—such as affiliation with a political party, expectations about government, or attitudes toward other social groups—may represent values learned in childhood. More precise opinions on contemporary issues may represent a combination of these early values with the prevailing values of the social group that have been adopted by the individual through an informal learning process. Hence, an individual's opinions have their roots in his associations with others, past and present.

[23] We are following Lazarsfeld *et al.*, *The People's Choice*, 3rd ed. (New York: Columbia University Press, 1968), chaps. 5 and 12, in the use of the term "opinion leader" to refer to anyone who initiates political conversations. This term should not be confused with similar terms used to refer to government officials or other policy-making elites.

As a learning process occurring throughout the life-cycle, socialization provides an explanation of attitude stability and change. Through personal contact, whether with a parent, teacher, or peer, the individual learns what kinds of attitudes and behavior patterns are expected of a particular social role. Certain attitudes and behaviors are rewarded—and thus reinforced—others are not and therefore tend to be extinguished. While this process may happen in an overt manner in the classroom, it may also come about through informal and even subconscious repetition of interactions. An individual may face some degree of incongruity in adult life between his past values and those expected of a person in his current social role. Such would be the case for someone experiencing an unusual degree of social mobility (e.g., growing up in a lower-class culture and then achieving high occupational status). In such a situation, a "re-socializing" process may take place, and the accompanying cognitive changes that are required may create some psychological conflicts with behavioral consequences. For most people, however, there is little conflict between the values learned in childhood and those expected of them in their adult roles. The typically homogeneous social environment is likely to be made up of others who, because of similar social background, have undergone a similar socialization pattern.

The socialization process has important implications for the likelihood of opinion change. In most instances, the effects of socialization are to *reduce* the probability that new stimuli will cause change. This effect operates at two levels. First, to the extent that orientations toward political attitudes are internalized as a result of the learning process, they become a part of the individual's conception of himself and his place in society. A change in opinion, therefore, would require a change in self-image and role-perception, and these elements have roots far back in time. Secondly, since an individual tends to interact with others of like background and opinions, a basic attitude change requires an adjustment in his attitude toward them and a reevaluation of the perceived utility of being in a state of agreement with these associates. At both a psychological and a social level, the consequence of the socialization process is to *reinforce* existing opinions and to erect barriers against opinion change.

As should be clear from the preceding discussion, the process of political socialization is quite consistent with the approach of psychological functionalism presented in Chapter 3. This approach states that an individual's opinions fulfill certain psychological needs and that since they are bound up with his self-image, they must be defended against attack. It is because opinions and attitudes are acquired over time as a part of the process by which one learns his social role that they occupy such a central position. Opinions may be learned at an adjustive level, but with time and reinforcement, they become internalized until they perform an ego-defensive function. Thus, the strain for cognitive consistency involves not merely the logical relationship between abstract political objects, but more importantly, the whole pattern of experiences of an individual's life.

The Sociology of Public Opinion

5

When it comes to knowing how different social groups vote or what kinds of opinions they hold, most people feel that they understand public opinion. Practicing politicians and amateur pundits are always willing to offer generalizations about the "Catholic vote," the ideology of the blue-collar worker, or the mood of the black community. While such statements may be unsupported stereotypes, they usually have some basis in fact. There are some observable and regular differences between social groups in their beliefs about public affairs. In this chapter we shall investigate the extent of these regularities, the reasons for them, and their implications.

In order to get a rough idea of the relative importance of various social cleavages and to provide an initial test of some popular stereotypes, we can utilize some simplified data such as that in Table 5-1. This shows the reported voting patterns of various social groups in presidential elections over the past twenty years.[1] Simply knowing the proportion of a group voting a certain way does not tell us much about the political importance of the characteristic defining that group unless we can compare the group with the rest of the population. For instance, the fact that 56 percent of Catholics voted Democratic in 1952 says little about the relationship of religion and partisanship until we compare it with the figure of only 37 percent Democratic for Protestants. It is for this reason that Table 5-1 also includes a "difference" figure for each pair of groups in each election. This figure simply represents excess in support for the Democratic candidate by the second of the groups in each pair over that given by the first. Thus, the difference between religious groups in 1956 was +19, a fairly sizable figure. This difference may be taken as an indication of the relative importance of different social characteristics in voting behavior.[2]

[1] Table 5-1 is oversimplified and incomplete, as it excludes some members of the population (e.g., Jews, farmers) and does not take account of the sizable vote for Wallace in 1968.
[2] This "difference" figure is the same measure as Alford's "index of class voting." See Robert R. Alford, *Party and Society: The Anglo-American Democracies* (Chicago: Rand McNally, 1963), pp. 79–86.

Table 5-1

Group Voting Patterns in Presidential Elections, 1952–1972

(Percentage of each group voting for the Democratic candidate and difference between groups)

		Presidential Elections											
		1952		1956		1960		1964		1968		1972	
Variable	Group	% Dem	Dif	% Dem	Dif	% Dem	Dif	% Dem	Dif	% Dem	Dif	% Dem	Dif
Sex	Men	47		45		52		60		41		37	
	Women	42	−5	39	−6	49	−3	62	+2	45	+4	38	+1
Race	White	43		41		49		59		38		32	
	Black	79	+36	61	+20	68	+19	94	+35	85	+47	87	+55
Occupation	White-collar	40		37		48		57		41		36	
	Manual	55	+15	50	+13	60	+12	71	+14	50	+9	43	+7
Religion	Protestant	37		37		38		55		35		30	
	Catholic	56	+19	51	+14	70	+40	76	+21	39	+4	48	+18
Total Electorate		45		42		50		61		43		38	

Source: Gallup election surveys, as reported in *Gallup Opinion Index*, no. 102 (December, 1973), 30.

The figures on presidential voting in Table 5-1 illustrate several characteristics of the impact of social groupings. First, the alignment of different groups is relatively stable. Catholics, blacks, and manual workers always appear somewhat more Democratic than their social opposites. Only for the sexes is there a reversal in the pattern of support for the parties, and that only of small magnitude. At the same time there is evidence of change. Religion becomes the most important correlate of voting in 1960, but then drops off in importance to almost nothing in 1968. Thus, while patterns of opinion distribution within social groups are relatively stable, groups may respond differently to the stimuli of events and political campaigns. Finally, it appears that, contrary to what one might expect, race and religion are the most important attributes in relation to voting in recent years— not economic status. This analysis is necessarily oversimplified; it obscures some important relationships and ignores others. Nonetheless, it does make the point that there are sociological regularities in political behavior and that these are sometimes complex and in need of close investigation.

THE QUESTION OF SOCIAL INFLUENCES

The association between social attributes and political behavior sometimes appears to be so strong that observers are tempted to advance the idea of *social determinism*. This was the case in the first scientific, survey-based voting study, *The People's Choice*.[3] Having found that in the Ohio community being studied Protestants, rural residents, and those in upper economic brackets tended to be more Republican, while Catholics, urbanites, and those of lower status tended to be more Democratic, the researchers constructed an "index of political predisposition" (IPP). Shown in Table 5-2, this index runs from a score of 1 (most Republicans) to 7 (most Democrats). Though obviously a rather crude measure, the index did distinguish fairly well between Republican and Democratic voters, as shown in the table. Affluent rural Protestants voted almost three-fourths Republican, while those at the opposite end of the scale— poor Catholics—voted Republican only about one-sixth of the time. On the basis of this sort of evidence, the authors argued that "social characteristics determine political preference." [4]

As is often the case when a thesis of strict social determinism is

[3] Paul Lazarsfeld *et al.*, *The People's Choice: How the Voter Makes Up His Mind in a Presidential Campaign*, 3rd ed. (New York: Columbia University Press, 1968; first published in 1944).

[4] *Ibid.*, p. 27.

Table 5-2
The Index of Political Predisposition and Its Relationship to Voting, Erie County, Ohio, 1940

Economic Level	Construction of the Index				The IPP and Voting Behavior	
	Protestant		Catholic			
	Rural	Urban	Rural	Urban	IPP Score	% Voting Republican
A or B	1	2	3	4	1	74
C+	2	3	4	5	2	73
C−	3	4	5	6	3	61
D	4	5	6	7	4	44
					5	30
					6 or 7	17

Source: Paul Lazarsfeld *et al.*, *The People's Choice: How the Voter Makes Up His Mind in a Presidential Campaign*, 3rd ed. (New York: Columbia University Press, 1968), pp. 26 and 174.

argued, there are significant weaknesses here. First, social character-istics did not appear to *determine* partisan choice; rather they offered an imperfect prediction. The IPP was able to explain statistically why some people voted as they did, but not why others failed to fit the pattern. In the data presented, some 26 percent of the affluent rural Protestants voted for Roosevelt, while 17 percent of the poor Catholics voted Republican. For those rather considerable segments of the population, social determinism failed to determine political preference.[5] While the measurement techniques used in this particu-lar study were less than precise (economic status was measured by the interviewer's appraisal of the respondent's home), the degree of explanation achieved by social characteristics in other studies is gen-erally of the same order. Membership in social groupings may be more or less related to preferences, but it is rare that the relationship is so strong as to justify a conclusion of social determinism.

Aside from the empirical weaknesses of a social determinism argu-ment, another problem to be considered is the more philosophical one of causation. The fact that a man is possessed of a certain set of attributes, such as Catholicism and a working-class occupation, and also favors the Democratic candidate, offers no inherent basis for concluding that one fact *caused* the other. Any attempt at demon-strating causation would require some reference to psychological processes that might account for the observed association between

[5] As Pomper points out, the use of such social attributes to predict voting behavior sometimes yields results little better than prediction by random guessing. Gerald M. Pomper, *Elections in America: Control and Influence in Democratic Politics* (New York: Dodd, Mead, 1968), p. 81.

group membership and political preference. A related problem in attempting to explain behavior by reference to social attributes is that, as in the case cited, such attempts are essentially ad hoc (i.e., they simply focus on the best-fitting pattern of group and response, even though that relationship may occur simply by chance). Patterns of explanation resulting from this process will not necessarily be applicable to other populations or under other conditions. The IPP from an Ohio county in 1940, for instance, would have been of little use in explaining voting in the South in that year. Again, to argue that a meaningful relationship exists between social characteristics and human responses demands reference to psychological reasons for the linkage.

We have raised this issue of social determinism in some depth because it is linked with some fundamental questions of democratic theory. To the extent that political behavior does result from membership in social categories, what is the implication of this for the political process? Does it suggest that public opinion will have more or less meaning for governmental action? In theory, there are two very different answers to this question. On one hand, it has been argued that an individual's interest basically is that of the groups to which he belongs. If this is the case, then we should expect opinions and votes to divide largely along the lines of social characteristics. In this sense, the individual is acting quite rationally when he votes for parties and candidates that will act to favor the interests of groups to which he belongs. This argument is most clearly advanced with reference to economic interests, but could be made for religious, ethnic, or other types of groups as well. From one standpoint, social determinism would facilitate citizens' acting in their own best interests and promote governmental responsiveness to public opinion. The counter argument denies that individual interests are identical with those of social groupings. Sociological regularities in preference are attributable to habit, group pressure, and the like, rather than to any conscious awareness of advancing one's own interests. While it is possible that group consensus might be based on group advantage, many such political patterns bear little relationship to current questions of public policy. Thus, it can be argued, to the extent that people act along group lines, they are failing to communicate their preferences to government and are thereby reducing the extent of democratic responsiveness.

In part the difference between these two perspectives lies in philosophical disagreement as to what constitutes one's "interest," but it also involves empirical questions about group orientations on specific types of issues and the reasons for them. As we examine the actual extent of the relationship between social characteristics and opinions, it is well to keep these ideas and their implications for the political process in mind.

CLASS AND STATUS

When we start to enumerate various social characteristics that we suspect are related to public opinion, the prime candidate always seems to be some form of economic status, whether we label it "social class," "wealth," "occupational prestige," or whatever. All of these terms, and others, suggest possible ways of measuring an individual's position on the economic dimension. We suspect that a person's economic position may be a determinant of some of his preferences both because that position determines many other attributes of his life (such as the neighborhood he lives in) and because so many issues of public policy seem to involve the allocation of advantages and disadvantages to different economic groups. Indeed, most who would argue a general position of social determinism would point to economic status as the major, if not the only, relevant social characteristic.

How can an individual's position on this economic dimension be measured? There are a number of possible variables that would seem to be indicators of this concept: income, type of occupation, degree of education attained, and self-identification with a social class, to name the more important. Of these, occupational status seems to be the most promising for both theoretical and practical reasons. First, the occupation of a person in contemporary American society seems to be the criterion by which his success is most commonly judged—by himself as well as others. Occupational status, or prestige, can be assigned to particular jobs in various ways, ranging from a simple blue-collar/white-collar dichotomy (such as in Table 5-1) to the assignment of a number on a one-hundred-point scale, based upon the job's particular rating in surveys of the desirability of occupations.[6] Using the latter method, it has been found that occupational status tends to be a function, first, of the education typically achieved by individuals who hold a particular job and, second, of their income.[7] Thus, occupation seems to be a good summary measure of social status.

The approach of asking a person which social class he identifies

[6] Such ratings seem to be relatively stable over time and even across national boundaries. See Robert W. Hodge et al., "A Comparative Study of Occupational Prestige," and Robert W. Hodge et al., "Occupational Prestige in the United States: 1925–1963," in Class, Status, and Power: Social Stratification in Comparative Perspective, ed. Reinhard Bendix and Seymour Martin Lipset, 2nd ed. (New York: Free Press, 1966), pp. 309–21 and 322–34.

[7] Otis Dudley Duncan, "A Socio-Economic Index for All Occupations," in Occupations and Social Status, ed. Albert J. Reiss, Jr. (New York: Free Press, 1961).

with would seem to reach the psychological implications of social status closely. There is a practical problem, however, in terms of the usual pattern of distribution of responses. Only a tiny minority of the population is willing to classify itself as being in the "upper class" or the "propertied class," and only a slightly larger number identifies with the "lower class." The alternatives of "middle class" and "working class" account for the great bulk of all respondents, who somewhat more favor "working" than "middle." Self-identification, therefore, provides a dichotomous measure at best and that a somewhat suspect one; for persons who fit a middle-class stereotype by any objective measure of occupation and income sometimes report that they are "working-class" people, apparently on the not illogical grounds that they do, after all, work for a living. This illustrates the fact that the working-class/middle-class dichotomy is basically derived from European society of an earlier day when affluent people indeed did not engage in "work," but rather derived their livelihood from accumulated wealth.

This last observation brings up the question of whether the idea of social class is indeed applicable to contemporary America. The arguments on this point are many and tangled, but the weight of evidence would seem to indicate that it is not. If by the term "class" we are implying the existence of definite, observable social lines that separate individuals into discrete economic groups, then it does not seem wise to use that term in describing the American public. There is economic inequality, to be certain, but there do not seem to be rigid lines separating the public into upper, middle, and lower classes. Instead, the idea of a dimension of *status*, containing a great many possible positions between top and bottom, seems much more feasible. In the following discussion of economic status and public opinion, there is no intention of implying any inherent rigidity of categories or unity within them. The occupational or other groupings that will be used are simply convenient ways of categorizing large segments of the populations for easy comparison.

Opinions on Economic Issues. One would logically suppose that economic status would have its greatest impact on opinions about economic issues. The validity of such an hypothesis is easily demonstrated. Table 5-3 presents breakdowns by several different status variables of Free and Cantril's "operational liberalism" scale. This scale is based on five questions of public policy, each dealing with domestic spending for social welfare purposes, such as federal aid to education and medicare.[8] Respondents who favored all proposals were classified as "completely liberal"; those who opposed all, as

[8] Lloyd A. Free and Hadley Cantril, *The Political Beliefs of Americans: A Study of Public Opinion* (New York: Simon and Schuster, 1968), pp. 13–15 and 207–08.

Table 5-3
Operational Liberalism* and Social Status, 1964

	Completely Liberal	Predominantly Liberal	Middle of the Road	Predominantly Conservative	Completely Conservative
Occupation					
Professional & business	33%	21%	22%	11%	13%
White-collar	39	20	29	5	7
Blue-collar	51	23	18	5	3
Farmers	34	24	21	12	9
Income					
$10,000 & over	32	21	25	10	12
$5,000–$9,999	41	21	24	7	7
Under $5,000	52	21	16	6	5
Education					
College	32	21	25	10	12
High school	42	23	22	6	7
Grade school	54	21	16	6	3
Class Identification					
Propertied class	20	20	34	12	14
Middle class	36	21	24	10	9
Working class	50	24	17	5	4
% of Total Sample N = 3,041	44	21	21	7	7

Source: Lloyd A. Free and Hadley Cantril, *The Political Beliefs of Americans: A Study of Public Opinion* (New York: Simon and Schuster, 1968), p. 216.
* Operational liberalism scale based upon responses to the following items dealing with approval/disapproval for (a) "Federal grants to help pay teachers' salaries"; (b) "medicare program financed out of social security taxes"; (c) "Federal Government making grants to help build low-rent public housing"; (d) "Federal Government making grants to help rebuild run-down sections of our cities"; and (e) "the Federal Government has a responsibility to try to reduce unemployment."

"completely conservative," with less unanimous degrees of opinion making up the intermediate categories. As the data show, there is a definite trend for those of lower status on each of the indicators to be more liberal (i.e., supportive of governmental action) and for those of higher status to be more conservative. The relationship is far from a perfect, deterministic situation, for there is considerable heterogeneity of opinion in all economic groups. However, the relationship is undeniably there and holds true for almost all issues of this type. Such issues would include not only federal aid and government spending generally for most domestic purposes, but also government regulation of the economy and labor-management relations.

This relationship of social status to opinions on economic issues is just as one would expect. Those who have less are more likely to support public action that would tend to benefit them; those who have more are less likely. This does not mean that lower-status Americans generally oppose capitalism and favor socialism any more than it means that the upper half of the population would endorse a completely laissez-faire economy and oppose any governmental intervention. The influence of economic position seems to extend only to those specific questions that bear a more or less direct relationship to the individual's own fortunes. On issues of financing programs from which individuals would benefit the expected patterns are present, but on issues such as federal revenue sharing with the states, which would not directly and clearly have an impact on most people, there is little relationship of status to opinion.

Nevertheless, even where it may appear to the observer that the self-interest of particular segments of the population would be directly affected by some proposed policy, people often fail to "vote their pocketbooks." Referenda for local bond issues often fail in lower-class neighborhoods, even though residents there would pay proportionately less of the cost. Some business groups in the early 1960s opposed the Kennedy administration's proposals for tax reduction, even though it was their taxes which would be lowered. Examples like these seem to contradict the idea that people are rational on even strictly economic matters. There are several reasons why people sometimes seem to oppose their own interests in public policy. One is a lack of sophisticated knowledge. The argument that tariffs must be raised in order to protect American workers from foreign competition may be persuasive to a factory worker who lacks enough knowledge of economics to realize that the industry he is in would benefit from an overall expansion of foreign trade. Second, any individual is subject to many other influences and considerations aside from his economic position. His membership in religious or ethnic groups may override his economic position as an influence on his opinions. Then too, an individual's opinions are interrelated, and his other beliefs about public affairs may take precedence. In the case of the business interests' opposing the Kennedy tax proposals, it appears that, in the minds of some, firmly held beliefs about economic stability and the importance of a balanced budget tended to outstrip the possibility of short-term financial gain. Finally, in generalizing about whether or not people are acting in their "own" interest, one must be careful to avoid attributing preferences to them that they do not have. Even if poorer people would bear less of the burden of some proposed public facility or program, this would not make the program in their interest if, indeed, they had no desire to partake of it. It is sometimes well to recall that a great many public programs that would generally be classed as being for liberal, social welfare purposes, such as higher education and recreational facilities, often benefit the middle class rather than the lower class. As was pointed out earlier, economic levels in the United States are broad ranges more than unified classes, and aggregates such as "white-collar workers" or "working people" are composed of individuals with heterogeneous interests and desires.

Opinions on Noneconomic Issues.   The pattern of social status and opinion on domestic economic matters was predictable, if not as regular as one might have expected. What about those issues that do not involve dollars and cents? Does the tendency still hold for lower-status persons to be more liberal and higher-status persons to be more conservative when the issues are not those of monetary advantage to economic groups? In particular, what about foreign policy?

Table 5-4 shows breakdowns of Free and Cantril's "international patterns" scale by several measures of social status.[9] Assuming that the "internationalist" position is the more liberal one and that "isolationism" represents conservatism,[10] then the social pattern is completely reversed. Lower-status groups display the least internationalism and upper-status groups the most. Nor is this reversal limited to international affairs. On many noneconomic questions, including ones of racial equality and protection of civil liberties, upper-status persons seem to be more supportive of what is usually identified as the "liberal" side of the issue. Conversely, lower-status persons seem to be the least supportive of these liberal ideals.

The most important reason for this phenomenon of lower-class conservatism seems to be the interrelationship of *education* with other indicators of social status. Much of the observed relationship between status and opinion on these noneconomic controversies is really due to the obvious fact that lower-status people are also less educated people. The internationalism data show this principle; the greatest group differences come when the scale is cross-tabulated with educational level. This effect of education is shown in Table 5-5 for a number of these kinds of issues. In each case, the more educated segment of the population expressed the most liberalism and, on each issue, education generally proved to be more strongly related to opinion than almost any other common sociological variable.

Why should education make this much difference? We can cite two general reasons. One is that the educational experience, particu-

[9] *Ibid.*, pp. 211–12.
[10] An assumption that is generally valid through the 1964 election; from the period of greater involvement in Vietnam shortly thereafter, it has become increasingly difficult to use such terms with any objectivity.

Table 5-4
International Patterns* and Social Status, 1964

	Completely Internationalist	Predominantly Internationalist	Mixed	Predominantly or Completely Isolationist
Occupation				
Professional & business	42%	31%	23%	4%
White-collar	35	35	24	6
Blue-collar	27	37	27	9
Farmers	25	39	28	8
Income				
$10,000 & over	45	32	18	5
$5,000–$9,999	32	35	27	6
Under $5,000	23	36	29	12
Education				
College	47	30	19	4
High school	30	38	26	6
Grade school	19	34	34	13
% of Total Sample N = 2,941	30	35	27	8

Source: Lloyd A. Free and Hadley Cantril, *The Political Beliefs of Americans: A Study of Public Opinion* (New York: Simon and Schuster, 1968), p. 227.

* Internationalism/isolationism scale based on agreement/disagreement with the following statements: (a) "The U.S. should cooperate fully with the United Nations"; (b) "In deciding its foreign policies, the U.S. should take into account the views of its allies in order to keep our alliances strong"; (c) "Since the U.S. is the most powerful nation in the world, we can go our own way in international matters, not worrying too much about whether other countries agree with us or not"; (d) "The U.S. should mind its own business internationally and let other countries get along as best they can on their own"; (e) "We shouldn't think so much in international terms but should concentrate more on our national problems and building up our strength and prosperity here at home."

larly at the college level, has an overall liberalizing effect, at least in terms of styles of political thought. (This argument was developed in Chapter 4.) The other reason is that many of these noneconomic issues involve various types of real or imagined personal threats, such as those from racial violence or crime in general. It is precisely those individuals who are both uneducated and of lower economic status to whom such threats are of the greatest practical reality. This argument will be developed more fully in Chapter 12. The point here is that noneconomic questions can have a different impact on individuals because of their education or economic status. A somewhat related psychological explanation can also be offered. It is sometimes observed that persons near the bottom of the social scale do not advocate egalitarian measures, but rather tend to oppose

Table 5-5

Education and Opinions on Noneconomic Issues

(1) *United Nations:* "Do you think that Communist China should or should not be admitted as a member of the United Nations?" (1970)

	Should	Should Not	No Opinion
College	52%	40%	8%
High school	32	53	15
Grade school	26	49	25

(2) *Prayer in Schools:* "The U.S. Supreme Court has ruled that no state or local government may require the reading of the Lord's Prayer or Bible verses in public schools. . . . Do you approve or disapprove of this?" (1971)

	Approve	Disapprove	No Opinion
College	45	51	4
High school	21	73	6
Grade school	22	70	8

(3) *Marijuana:* "Do you think the use of marijuana should be made legal, or not?" (1972)

	Yes	No	No Opinion
College	30	66	4
High school	14	82	4
Grade school	4	93	3

(4) *Abortion:* "Would you favor or oppose a law which would permit a woman to go to a doctor to end a pregnancy at any time during the first three months?" (1969)

	Favor	Oppose	No Opinion
College	58	34	8
High school	37	53	10
Grade school	31	57	12

(5) *Open Housing:* "Do you favor or oppose 'open housing' laws?" (1968)

	Favor	Oppose	No Opinion
College	61	31	8
High school	41	39	20
Grade school	31	36	33

(6) *Birth Control:* "Do you think birth control pills should be made available free to all women on relief of childbearing age?" (1970)

	Yes	No	No Opinion
College	61	30	9
High school	54	35	11
Grade school	42	38	20

Source: Gallup polls, as reported in *Gallup Opinion Index,* (1) no. 65 (November 1970), 9; (2) no. 77 (November 1971), 25; (3) no. 82 (April 1972), 20; (4) no. 56 (December 1969), 19; (5) no. 4 (October 1968), 31; and (6) no. 57 (March 1970), 15.

them. The reason for this may be that everyone likes to feel superior to someone; hence, the man who has little would not necessarily see his neighbor who has even less be made equal to him. Also, it may be possible for the lower-status individual to feel at least morally superior; hence, a tendency toward rigid censure of the life-styles of upper-status individuals (e.g., college students).[11] The roots of what appears to be a lower-class conservatism may lie therefore in the consequences of both the economic process and the educational.

For most people, the various elements of status—family background, occupational prestige, education, income—are quite consistent. However, some people experience a degree of inconsistency in these elements. This may result from social mobility. For example, a person from a lower-status background might attain a high degree of economic success in later life. Or a person's ascribed status (such as racial or ethnic group membership) can lead to a different social ranking from his economic or educational status. There have been a number of arguments advanced that persons who experience status inconsistency of one type or another tend to be more susceptible to political extremism, particularly of the right-wing variety.[12] Such generalizations almost always fail when subjected to empirical testing. Lenski, for instance, has found some tendency for persons with a lack of status consistency, or "crystallization," to hold more liberal attitudes and display more pro-Democratic voting tendencies than those who are consistent.[13] In *Social Mobility and Voting Behavior*, Barber examines the behavior of persons who have been upwardly mobile economically and finds that they tend to display attitudes between those of the lower-status group they have left and those of the higher group they have entered.[14]

To summarize the effects of social status on public opinion, one would have to say that it has a definite, but limited, impact. On economic issues, higher status is related to a conservative position, while on many noneconomic questions, the reverse is true. Both of these relationships seem to have a logical basis. The important point is that all of these findings show a relatively small influence of status on preferences. Social "classes" in America are only convenient

[11] Some of these ideas are presented in Robert E. Lane's work on "the fear of equality." See his *Political Ideology: Why the American Common Man Believes What He Does* (New York: Free Press, 1962), chap. 4.

[12] For a summary and incisive critique of these arguments, see Nelson W. Polsby, "Toward an Explanation of McCarthyism," *Political Studies* (1960), pp. 250–71; reprinted in Nelson W. Polsby *et al.*, *Politics and Social Life: An Introduction to Political Behavior* (Boston: Houghton Mifflin, 1963), pp. 809–24.

[13] Gerhard Lenski, "Status Crystallization: A Non-Vertical Dimension of Social Status," *American Sociological Review*, 19 (1954), 405–13.

[14] James Alden Barber, Jr., *Social Mobility and Voting Behavior* (Chicago: Rand McNally, 1970).

ranges on an economic dimension, not self-conscious social group-ings. As such, their explanatory power is relatively weak. Therefore, in seeking to understand the impact of social characteristics gener-ally on public opinion, we must turn to an examination of other kinds of sociological variables and their relationship to public opinion.[15]

RACE

If one had any doubts, then the voting data in Table 5-1 should have indicated that race constitutes the greatest social cleavage in America, at least as far as political opinions are concerned. The 47 percentage point difference in support for the Democratic party be-tween the races in 1968 is as great or greater than the difference be-tween economic groups in the most class-oriented European party system. This same racial gap is manifested in opinions on a range of issues as well. For instance on Free and Cantril's "operational liber-alism" scale (which deals with social welfare issues), 79 percent of all blacks fall into the "completely liberal" category, with an addi-tional 13 percent being predominantly so.[16] In terms of self-iden-tification, blacks are overwhelmingly liberal and almost none report identification with the Republican party. On some of the noneco-nomic issues of the type reported in Table 5-5, the differences be-tween white and black are much less striking, but even in these cases blacks almost always tend toward the liberal side of the ques-tion. Clearly, blacks seem to constitute generally the most liberal of the major demographic groupings in American politics today.

This pattern is not due solely to the effect of economic status. While it is true that the black population has less income and educa-tion than the white, this fact does not explain the pattern of opinion among blacks, for middle-class blacks generally display economic at-titudes that are just as liberal as those of lower-class blacks. What, then, can be offered as possible reasons for this black liberalism? One fact is that most blacks are poor, naturally leading to economic liberalism, and it may be that middle-class blacks continue to iden-tify with the problems and aspirations of the rest of the black com-munity to a greater extent than upwardly mobile whites do with the community they leave behind. Another factor is that blacks have more reason to be more enthusiastic about the efficacy of govern-mental action, particularly at the federal level, for it is in the public

[15] Social class seems to be of greater political importance in some other nations (such as Great Britain) for a number of reasons, among them the existence of a more rigidly defined class system and the lack of other cross-cutting political cleavages. See Robert R. Alford, *Party and Society: The Anglo-American Democracies* (Chicago: Rand McNally, 1963).

[16] Free and Cantril, *The Political Beliefs of Americans*, p. 217.

arena that some of their gains have come. Finally, the holding of liberal opinions involves rejection of some traditional values, and these values may be perceived as norms of white society. Hence, there is less tendency for blacks to cling to them.

For whatever reason, the difference between black and white opinions on issues is the greatest of any social cleavage. This cleavage in opinion is reinforced by several factors. Individuals are aware of being black or white (as they may not be in the case of social classes) and, what may be more important, they know that others are aware. Social interaction generally takes place within these self-conscious groups, rather than between the races. And the whole pattern of society tends to reinforce these attitudinal differences, not only through the racial pattern of economic distribution, but also through the whole thrust of American history.

RELIGION

A source of social cleavage that has proved to be important in many political systems is that of religious affiliation. While the United States has not had as much bitter religious conflict as many European nations, it sometimes appears that religion has played a part in political issues. In examining the effects of religion on public opinion in America, we will be doing so only in the context of religious affiliation as an attribute separating the population into groups. We are not assuming anything more than simple identification with a major religious grouping on the part of individuals, nor are we investigating the possible role that organized religious bodies acting as interest groups have played in the political process.

If we use a broad division of the population into Protestant, Catholic, and Jewish, then some regularities in opinions occur. Table 5-6 shows the effect of religion on several types of issues. On the economic "operational liberalism" scale, Catholics are more liberal than Protestants, and Jews are the most liberal of all. The same sort of relationship obtains for political party identification, Jews and Catholics being decidedly more Democratic. Moreover, the effect of religion here seems to be somewhat greater than was that of the social status measures examined earlier. However, when we move to specific noneconomic issues, several of which are shown in Table 5-6, there appears to be little systematic difference between Protestant and Catholic. The surveys cited included too few Jews to allow any precise breakdowns of their opinions, but there is a wealth of data indicating that they are the most liberal religious group on almost all issues.

Table 5-6
Religion and Opinions

(1) *Operational Liberalism (1964)*

	Completely Liberal	Predominantly Liberal	Middle of the Road	Predominantly Conservative	Completely Conservative
Protestant	38%	22%	22%	9%	9%
Catholic	55	22	17	3	3
Jewish	69	21	7	0	3

Source: Lloyd A. Free and Hadley Cantril, *The Political Beliefs of Americans: A Study of Public Opinion* (New York: Simon and Schuster, 1968), p. 216. (See Table 5-3 for a description of scale items.)

(2) *United Nations:* "Do you think Communist China should or should not be admitted as a member of the United Nations?"

	Should	Should Not	No Opinion
Protestant	32	52	16
Catholic	38	48	14

Source: Gallup Opinion Index, no. 65 (November 1970), 9.

(3) *Racial Problems—Looting:* ". . . a mayor of a large city has ordered the police to shoot on sight anyone found looting stores during race riots. . . . Do you think this is the best way to deal with this problem?" (1968)

	Best Way	Better Way	No Opinion
Protestant	54	41	5
Catholic	55	42	3

Source: Gallup Opinion Index, no. 37 (July 1968), 17.

(4) *College Disturbances:* "Do you think college students who break laws while participating in campus demonstrations should be expelled or not?" (1969)

	Yes	No	No Opinion
Protestant	84	9	7
Catholic	81	13	6

Source: Gallup Opinion Index, no. 46 (April 1969), 9.

(5) *Pornography:* "What about the magazines and newspapers sold on newsstands. Would you like to see state and local laws on such literature, or not?" (1969)

	Yes	No	No Opinion
Protestant	77	16	7
Catholic	77	15	8

Source: Gallup Opinion Index, no. 49 (July 1969), 19.

The distribution of opinion among religions is likely to be affected by other variables that might account for the observed relationships. One is obviously social status. In particular, Catholics have tended to be concentrated in blue-collar occupations. Though this is less true today than it was a few decades ago, it is still true enough to account for some Catholic tendency to be more in favor of governmental social welfare activities. Race is also a complicating factor, since almost all blacks expressing a religious preference are Protestant. Thus, if we control for race, the tendency for white Protestants to be more conservative is increased. Finally, geographic area enters in. Rural areas of the country and particularly the southern region are much more Protestant than urban and nonsouthern parts. This geographic factor increases the observed level of conservative opinion among Protestants, particularly on racial questions.

Relationships are also clouded by the fact that survey analyses usually lump all Protestants together into a single category, which obviously encompasses an almost infinite variety of theologies. Breaking the Protestant group into smaller segments can increase the apparent impact of religious membership somewhat, particularly since denominations tend to be concentrated at certain levels of social status. If we categorize denominations by the economic status of their members, we would come out with a list something like this— higher status: Congregational, Episcopalian, Presbyterian, etc.; medium status: Methodist, Lutheran, etc.; and lower status: Baptists, Disciples, and various smaller fundamentalist sects. Not surprisingly, the higher status denominations are more conservative on domestic economic issues, while the reverse is true for noneconomic questions, though the differences are not tremendous.

This interrelationship between religion and other relevant sociological characteristics makes it difficult indeed to generalize about the effects of religion on opinion, particularly given the small number of members of particular denominations who will appear in any sample survey. With these problems in mind, a few generalizations will be advanced. Clearly, Jews tend to be liberal across the range of issues, and this cannot be attributed to any nonreligious variables. Catholics tend to be economically liberal beyond the extent indicated by their social status. This is commonly attributed to the effects of Catholic theology, but a history of upward mobility from lower-class ethnic status in previous generations for many Catholic families may also play a part. For white Protestants, few generalizations can be offered. Most of the denominational differences could be attributed to the effects of other factors. Lenski does find some relationship between *religious* liberalism and attitudes toward freedom of speech issues, but this does not seem to hold true for other types of issues.[17]

There are some specific issues on which certain religious groups take strong positions that we would expect members to follow. This hypothesis can be confirmed, as Protestants seem to be more opposed to the things their churches oppose (e.g., drinking, gambling), while Catholics are more opposed to divorce, birth control, and abortion.[18] Yet, even on these "moralistic" questions, the influence of organized religion seems quite imperfect. For instance, over one-third of the Catholics favor legalizing abortion, and almost half would approve of free distribution of birth control pills to women "on relief," proportions only slightly below those for the population as a whole.[19]

OTHER SOCIAL CHARACTERISTICS

The variables of status, race, and religion seem to be the main social groupings related to opinion. A few other characteristics deserve brief mention. One such attribute is sex. Simply stated, there do not appear to be significant differences between the opinions of men and women on most issues. Differences of a percent or two appear in most surveys, but this could be attributed to random error. Through the 1960 election, there was a slight tendency for women to vote more Republican than men in presidential elections. Some observers attributed this to an inherent conservative ("Church, Children, Kitchen") tendency among women that appears much more strongly as a factor in European politics. However, this trend has reversed since 1964, perhaps as a result of issues involving war and peace. (See Chapter 11 for a discussion of sex differences and opinions on Vietnam.) At any rate, the difference in opinion between men and women is almost always small enough to make virtually no difference in the total picture. Presumably, this similarity in opinions between the sexes is due to the fact that the distribution of almost all other social variables is virtually the same for men and women; hence, they have no difference in "interests." Interestingly enough, issues such as those raised by Women's Liberation receive about the same support from men as from women—and sometimes even more.

Another sociological variable often overlooked is that of age. As far as economic issues are concerned, there is little general relationship

---

[17] Gerhard Lenski, *The Religious Factor: A Sociological Study of Religion's Impact on Politics, Economics, and Family Life,* rev. ed. (Garden City, N.Y.: Doubleday, 1963), p. 211.

[18] *Ibid.,* pp. 164–69.

[19] *Gallup Opinion Index,* no. 57 (March 1970), 15, and no. 92 (February 1973), 22.

of age to opinion. On some kinds of noneconomic issues, however, there are significant differences, and on these issues the younger age groups are the more liberal. When an issue seems to involve style rather than substance, the age gap is greater. Thus, on issues of crime there is very little difference between old and young; when the question is one of "morality" (e.g., marijuana, birth control, pornography, etc.) the difference is likely to be considerable. The most basic reason for such differences is presumably the fact of socialization at very different points in time. One should also not forget the factor of education: young adults today have experienced considerably more years of formal instruction than the older segments of the population.[20] Yet, for all the evidence of youthful liberalism, the point should not be overdrawn. It is well to keep in mind, for instance, that the 1968 candidacy of George Wallace received more support from voters under thirty (13 percent, outside the South) than from those over seventy (only 3 percent).[21] This youthful support may be attributed to less reluctance on the part of younger voters to deviate from established parties, but it is important to remember that such deviation can be to the political Right as well as to the Left. In general, while young people today are somewhat less accepting of some traditional values than their parents, a definite majority are still in agreement with the beliefs of the previous generation.[22]

One other type of sociological variable that seems to have an impact on opinion is geography, both in terms of rural versus urban residence, and in terms of geographic region of the country. The geographical variable will be considered in a slightly different context in the next chapter and so will not be dealt with here.

THE PSYCHOLOGICAL BASIS
OF SOCIAL INFLUENCES

As was pointed out earlier in this chapter, people do not hold opinions simply because they fall into some social category. Being black, poor, Catholic, young, female, or any combination thereof does not, in itself, force a person to be a liberal who votes for Democratic candidates. But there are statistical relationships between such at-

[20] As of 1967, almost 60 percent of those people sixty-five and older had no more than an eighth-grade education as compared to well under 10 percent in the group between twenty and twenty-four years of age. Computed from figures in U.S. Bureau of the Census, *Statistical Abstract of the United States* (1968), p. 211.

[21] Philip E. Converse *et al.*, "Continuity and Change in American Politics: Parties and Issues in the 1968 Election," *American Political Science Review*, 63 (1969), 211.

[22] For a comprehensive comparison of the beliefs of young people and their parents, see Robert Chandler, *Public Opinion: Changing Attitudes on Contemporary Political and Social Issues* (New York: R. R. Bowker Co., 1972), pp. 52–92.

tributes and opinions, and these are regular enough to suggest that there is some degree of causal influence. What kinds of social and psychological mechanisms can account for these linkages between social position and opinion?

Perception of the Environment.   The simplest explanation of why rich and poor, black and white have different policy preferences is that their actual physical and social environments differ, and, consequently, their personal needs for governmental action vary along these social lines. In the case of an economic policy that would benefit a particular group, this principle may operate in a very rationalistic, self-interested manner for many individuals. Other policies may be more symbolic, and support for or opposition to them by voters may be more related to psychological needs and satisfactions. At any level, the relationship between environment and need is never perfect because it is not the actual environment, but the perception of it by the individual, that affects his action—and perceptions are always subjective. A man may be poor, yet still identify himself as middle class because his self-image demands it; his opinions will respond to his perceived economic position rather than that of objective reality. The functional nature of perceptions and opinions affects, and often weakens, the link between environment and opinion. But the linkage does exist because perception is not totally subjective. The more forcefully an issue affects an individual (as a question of dollars and cents in the immediate future), the clearer the perception and the more direct the response to the environmental stimuli.

Group Interaction and Socialization.   Another reason for opinion regularities within social categories is that members of those categories may interact with each other. As was pointed out in the last chapter, people tend to communicate with others like themselves, thus tending to reinforce existing beliefs. This is more true for some kinds of social groupings than others. Some sociological categories are only statistical aggregates whose members may have little else in common and no particular pattern of interaction with each other; examples would be high school graduates, people with incomes between five and fifteen thousand dollars per year, or "Protestants" as a general category. Such groups are not likely to display much uniformity of opinion. On the other hand, some groups represent actual patterns of personal interaction. This is true of more identifiable religious groups—such as Jews, Catholics, and smaller fundamentalist Protestant denominations—and of particular racial and ethnic minorities. For many members of such groups, interpersonal communication is likely to occur almost entirely within the group, and group interests in public policy are more likely to be perceived.

When these sociological categorizations represent actual patterns of interaction and awareness, there is likely to be a considerable degree of homogeneity of opinion, a generalization that is borne out by the type of data presented throughout this chapter.

Identification with the Group.   A related factor that we have not yet discussed is the extent to which an individual identifies himself as the member of a particular social grouping. If one does not see himself as belonging to a group, then the group will have less influence on his opinions despite his objectively defined membership in it. Angus Campbell and his colleagues tested this notion and found that for Jews, Catholics, blacks, and union members, there was a tendency for those who identified more with the group and who perceived the group's involvement in politics to be legitimate to vote more heavily for Democratic candidates.[23] This same pattern held true in the 1960 election, when there was a strong tendency for Catholics and Protestants who were regular churchgoers to deviate from party identification to vote along religious lines.[24] Union members in the United States are generally more heavily Democratic in their voting behavior than are blue-collar workers as a whole, even though the members are often more affluent than the nonmembers. Thus, the influence that a social characteristic has upon preferences is largely a result of the extent to which people consider themselves as members of the group defined by that characteristic. This influence is likely to be the greatest for those groups in which the fact of membership is reinforced either by some formal organization (e.g., unions, the Catholic church) or by the obvious social differentiation accorded to the members by the rest of the population (e.g., blacks).

THE POLITICAL IMPLICATIONS OF SOCIAL INFLUENCE

To summarize the overall effect of social characteristics on public opinion in America, one would have to say that their influence is, at best, uneven. For *some* social groups on *some* issues, the relationship to opinion is great. For most individuals, on most issues, the effect is slight, or even missing. As we have suggested, the fact of group membership is most salient for those who find themselves in what are usually called "minority" groups; for the vast, less differentiated, majority, stimuli come from less identifiable sources.

[23] Angus Campbell *et al.*, *The American Voter* (New York: John Wiley, 1960), chap. 12.

[24] Angus Campbell *et al.*, *Elections and the Political Order* (New York: John Wiley, 1966), chap. 6.

How does this finding relate to the issue of rationality that was raised at the outset of this chapter? Basically, public opinion shows a tendency at least toward rationality. Economic opinions seem to follow economic lines of group interest, though the correlation is sufficiently imperfect to allow the cynic to feel justified in holding a low view of the public's competence. Opinions on noneconomic issues as a whole seem to be much less subject to group influence, except, of course, when the issue revolves around the group itself (e.g., blacks and racial equality policies). The relative lack of social influences in America is best illustrated by comparison to other political systems, such as those of western Europe, in which social cleavages have strong political repercussions. Figure 5-1 illustrates a characteristic pattern in which there is not only a socioeconomic cleavage, but also some sort of cultural division, most commonly a religious one.[25] The crucial implication of such a situation is that each of the quadrants is capable of generating at least one political party that would represent the interests and receive the votes of only that segment of the population. Quadrant II, for instance, might represent a typical conservative party, such as the Christian Democrats in Italy. Such a pattern does not hold for the United States, for American parties have generally been able to cross economic lines as well as other lines of cleavage, such as those of race and religion. The Democratic party has historically been able, more or less, to unite diverse social groups, such as southern whites, rich, poor, blacks, Catholics, etc., though this

Figure 5-1
Typical European Pattern of Multiple Political Cleavages

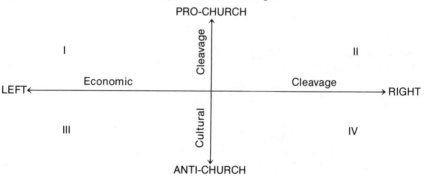

[25] This diagram is adapted from that presented by Giovanni Sartori, "European Political Parties: The Case of Polarized Pluralism," in *Political Parties and Political Development,* ed. Joseph LaPalombara and Myron Weiner (Princeton: Princeton University Press, 1966), pp. 137–76. Such a pattern of crosscutting cleavages might be applied to Italy, France, Belgium, Holland, and the Scandinavian countries throughout the period since World War II.

seems to be becoming increasingly difficult. The reasons why the United States has a two-party system, rather than a system made up of many smaller parties, go far beyond the nature of the cleavage structure, but the relative lack of correspondence between social group and political preference is a very basic factor. Actually, in most of American history, political cleavages have been a product of geographic regionalism, an aspect that will be more fully discussed in the next chapter.

One final implication of this sociological analysis for the nature of public opinion ought to be noted. As we have seen throughout the analysis, there are very different patterns of opinion distribution for economic and noneconomic issues. This difference in types of issues is a very important one, and it will be systematically dealt with in Chapter 9.

Political Culture: The Role of History and Geography

6

Some years ago, V. O. Key and Frank Munger pointed out a weakness in the social determinism of the early voting studies: the distribution of social attributes could not explain persistent geographic patterns of voting behavior.[1] The problem that stimulated their attention was the distribution of the vote in presidential elections in Indiana counties. They found that there was a high degree of similarity in the division of the vote between the election of 1868 and those of 1900, 1920, and even 1948. This persistent pattern is immediately evident if we look at maps such as those in Figure 6-1.[2] Statistically, there is a substantial correlation in the vote by counties in Indiana (and other states) between pairs of elections widely separated in time.

Such a finding is interesting, for it was obviously a different set of voters in each county who determined the outcomes of the 1868 and 1920 elections. This persistence challenges the notion of determinism by social and economic characteristics, for it does not appear that the distribution of these can account for the regularities. In states such as Indiana, one finds rural farm communities that are heavily Democratic in their voting habits and urban areas that are heavily Republican, as well as areas that fit the usual generalization that farmers vote Republican and city dwellers Democratic. As Key and Munger explain, the roots of the phenomenon of persisting patterns of partisanship lie far back in local history. Counties adopted

[1] V. O. Key, Jr., and Frank Munger, "Social Determinism and Electoral Decision: The Case of Indiana," in *American Voting Behavior*, ed. Eugene Burdick and Arthur J. Brodbeck (New York: Free Press, 1959), pp. 281–99. See also Frank J. Munger, "Two-Party Politics in the State of Indiana" (unpublished Ph.D. dissertation, Harvard University, 1955). This degree of geographical voting stability is further documented in William R. Shaffer and David A. Caputo, "Political Continuity in Indiana Presidential Elections: An Analysis Based on the Key-Munger Paradigm," *Midwest Journal of Political Science*, 16 (1972), 700–11.

[2] The elections depicted in the three maps were chosen because in Indiana they were all quite close, and therefore a relatively equal number of counties were carried by each party.

Figure 6-1

The Presidential Vote in Indiana Counties: 1868, 1916, 1948

(Shaded areas represent counties carried by the Democratic candidate.)

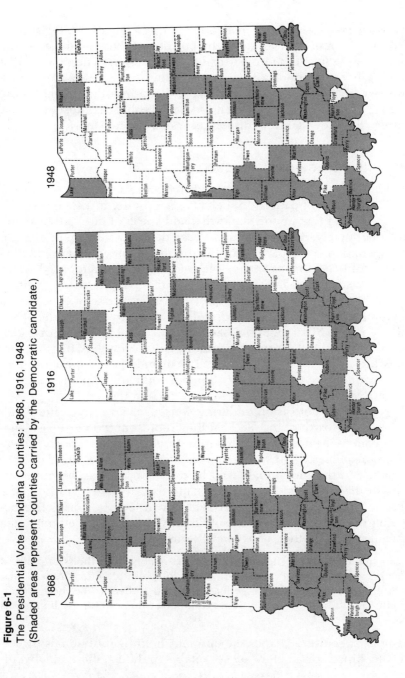

their party perferences because of Civil War sympathies, because of the original ethnic and religious composition of those who settled the area, and for a host of more particular local reasons. The point is that many basic orientations, of which party loyalty is the most obvious, were established long ago and have been passed down to the present. This historical factor and its geographic manifestations are vital for the understanding of political behavior in America.

THE CONCEPT OF POLITICAL CULTURE

The idea of culture is widely used in modern social science to refer to a wide variety of patterns of behavior and belief in a social system. We can restrict that notion somewhat and speak of the "political culture" of a society. As Almond and Verba define it, "The political culture of a nation is the particular distribution of patterns of orientation toward political objects among the members of a nation." [3] At its root, political culture consists of the way that people look at politics, the way they conceptualize the process, and what they expect from government. Political culture therefore goes far beyond the usual realm of public affairs into the basic attitudes that members of a society hold toward authority. The idea of culture implies that the elements are more fixed and universal than individual opinions. Cultural attributes are those held by the great bulk of the population and remain relatively constant over long periods of time.

The fact that there is an enduring consensus on such cultural values is an outgrowth of the fact that they represent the most basic elements communicated from generation to generation through the socialization process. Thus, the sources of these values lie mainly in the past, and the individuals who hold the values may be quite unaware of their origins. But cultural patterns can have a considerable impact on political opinions and behavior in today's world. The political culture of a society does not directly *cause* public opinion on a particular issue. Rather, as Daniel Elazar says,

. . . its influence lies in its power to set reasonably fixed limits to political behavior and provide subliminal direction for political action in particular political systems; limits and direction all the more effective because of their antiquity and subtlety whereby those limited are unaware of the limitations placed upon them.[4]

The political culture shapes the opinions held by individuals by setting the broad parameters of acceptable public policy and by in-

[3] Gabriel A. Almond and Sidney Verba, *The Civic Culture: Political Attitudes and Democracy in Five Nations* (Boston: Little, Brown, 1965), p. 13.

[4] Daniel J. Elazar, *Cities of the Prairie: The Metropolitan Frontier and American Politics* (New York: Basic Books, 1970), p. 257.

fluencing the way in which political action is viewed. It is thus an important element in the process of individual opinion formation and should not be neglected.

To deal completely with the subject of political culture in America, the whole pattern of traditional American political beliefs and orientations should be investigated.[5] Some material along these lines will be presented in Chapter 9. Our purpose at this point, however, is to understand why some Americans hold one set of opinions and others do not. To the extent that there is a single American political culture, this will tend to produce a uniformity of opinion. Yet, while some cultural elements are common to almost all segments of the population, there are some important variations in the way that people look at politics within the United States. Like cultures generally, political *subcultures* have identifiable historical antecedents and tend to be sufficiently concentrated in specific geographic areas that they can be identified. It is the purpose of the discussion in this chapter to describe the most important sources of subcultural political values in America and to show their importance for the formation of public opinion.

SOURCES OF AMERICAN POLITICAL SUBCULTURES

To catalog all of the varieties of political subcultures that have developed in the course of American political history would require a far more extensive treatment than is possible here. We shall limit the discussion to several important sources of cultural variation that have had a continuing impact on the patterns of political behavior of large segments of the population.

Region. The most important political cleavages throughout most of American political history have been regional. In the early part of the nineteenth century, the division was largely on an East-West basis, pitting the developing frontier against the established, more urbanized coastal areas. With the growth of controversy over the question of slavery, the cleavage became primarily one of North versus South, culminating in a post-Civil War alignment of Democratic "solid South" and a less solidly Republican North. This North-South cleavage persisted until the period of political change now in evidence, with occasional tendencies toward revival of an East-West, industrial-agrarian pattern, such as that during the Populist period in the 1890s. These cleavage patterns were never limited to political

[5] For a thorough examination of American political culture based upon survey data, see Donald J. Devine, *The Political Culture of the United States: The Influence of Member Values on Regime Maintenance* (Boston: Little, Brown, 1972).

partisanship; they also reflected more fundamental patterns of opinion. Since the most important regional cleavage in opinion today is that of the South and non-South, we shall focus our attention upon it. There are minor regional variations among the Northeastern, Midwestern, and Pacific areas, but these are small and irregular compared to their contrast with the South.

The politics of the South has always been the politics of race. As V. O. Key points out,

> In its grand outlines the politics of the South revolves around the position of the Negro. It is at times interpreted as a politics of cotton, a politics of free trade, as a politics of agrarian poverty, or as a politics of planter and plutocrat. Although such interpretations have a superficial validity, in the last analysis the major peculiarities of southern politics go back to the Negro.[6]

For white southerners, then, the most crucial issue has been the question of racial supremacy; other issues have arisen, but all are subordinate to that of race and tend to be evaluated on the basis of their impact on race relations. For example, the issue of federal aid became a question of whether or not that would increase pressures for integration. This emphasis on race has never been true of all white southerners, but it has been sufficiently widespread to dominate the politics of much of the South and to give it a distinctive character.

Table 6-1 demonstrates this deviation of southern whites from the pattern of opinion distribution in the rest of the country on racial issues.[7] On the issue of school integration, even by 1964, the South was opposed by about three to one, whereas the rest of the country gave at least slight support. This pattern holds true for other issues of public policy dealing with race, such as questions of discrimination in employment, handling of racial violence, and so on. To be sure, the South has progressed considerably since *Brown* v. *Board of Education* in 1954 in the extent to which it will acquiesce in integrationist policies. At the same time, questions of racial equality have come to northern cities in the form of controversies over busing, open housing, and employment; in some cases producing an antiblack backlash. Such trends tend to lessen the gap in attitudes between whites of North and South. Still, it is region that exercises a powerful influence on the attitudes of white toward black.

While the South has obviously been on the antiliberal side of racial questions for two centuries, its reputation as a bastion of conser-

[6] V. O. Key, Jr., *Southern Politics in State and Nation* (New York: Random House, 1949), p. 5.

[7] In this discussion of attitudinal differences between North and South, we shall deal only with the white population, as it is for them that the regional differences are most important.

Table 6-1
Region and Opinion: School Integration and Medicare, 1964
(White sample only)

	Region *			
	Northeast	Midwest	West	South
School Integration				
Favor	55%	39%	44%	21%
Against	26	37	38	61
No opinion	19	24	19	17
Medicare Program				
Favor	57	42	45	41
Against	23	36	32	32
No opinion	20	22	23	28
N	298	419	218	356

Source: Data computed from Survey Research Center (University of Michigan) 1964 election study.

* Regional categorizations as follows: Northeast—New England and Middle Atlantic; Midwest—East North Central and West North Central; West—Mountain and Pacific; South—Border and "Solid South."

vative opinion on all political issues is not justified by the facts. On issues that are nonracial and noneconomic in nature (such as those in Tables 5-5 and 5-6 in the previous chapter) there is a tendency for the South to be less liberal than other regions, but the difference is relatively slight. In part this tendency toward social conservatism may be traced to the fact that the South is more rural and less afflu- ent than the other regions; it may also represent some spillover effect from opinions on race. On economic issues, however, there is no such deviation. As the data on the medicare question illustrate, the South is as eager for domestic social welfare legislation as the Mid- west and West. At many points throughout American history, the South has been on the liberal side of economic issues. This di- vergence of reality from the popular image of the South reflects an old division in southern politics. In several Deep-South states, there is an enduring tension between the "hills and the delta" (i.e., be- tween the poor agricultural areas that favor populist economic poli- cies and the conservative delta plantation areas allied with business interests).[8] That the South has a reputation for overall conservatism is mainly due to its congressional representation, which customarily includes a good number of members who hold notably conservative ideologies. That the South has not been better able to promote its economic preferences is a result of a one-party Democratic system

[8] The phrase is that of V. O. Key. See his discussion of this cleavage in Mississippi in *Southern Politics*, pp. 229–53.

which, in turn, is largely a result of emphasis on the politics of race.

The idea of region as a *cultural* phenomenon transcends the simple state groupings of the type used in Table 5-1. Geographical patterns of historically developed political subcultures in America are infinitely more complex. The "South," for example, is not a single entity. Several distinct regions can be distinguished in it: the historical border states (Maryland, West Virginia, Kentucky, Missouri, Oklahoma); the outer South (Virginia, Florida, Tennessee, North Carolina, Arkansas, Texas); and the deep South (Louisiana, Mississippi, Alabama, Georgia, South Carolina). It is the last—from Louisiana through South Carolina—that we typically associate with a southern stereotype. This deep-South region is largely coterminous with the "black belt," the area which, due to agricultural patterns before the Civil War, contains the highest proportion of black population. It is in this area that whites have always displayed the most hostility toward blacks, the most single-minded attention to the politics of race, and the most support for third-party candidates, such as Strom Thurmond in 1948 and George Wallace in 1968. In the outer South, there has been less emphasis on racial questions and a consequent tendency to give support to Republican candidates as far back as the 1920s on the basis of economic issues. There is also the mountain South of the Appalachian and Ozark plateaus which, because of its opposition to secession, adopted and has maintained strong Republican voting patterns for over a century.

While the South is not uniformly "southern," its cultural influence flows far beyond the Mason-Dixon line. Large areas outside the southern and border states were settled by migrants from those areas, and the effects are still visible. This settlement was particularly important in Ohio, Indiana, and Illinois, many of whose original inhabitants came from Virginia, Kentucky, and the Carolinas.[9] This fact largely explains the pattern of partisan distribution in Indiana that was shown in Figure 6-1. The basic geographical strength of the Democratic party in Indiana lies in the southern half of the state in the area of heaviest southern settlement, which is also the more rural and less industrialized part. The same is true in Illinois, though the concentration of Democratic votes in the city of Chicago often masks the fact. That such areas of southern origin are Democratic is not to say that they are liberal in their beliefs, for the reverse is true. It simply illustrates the point that partisanship, derived originally from Civil War attitudes, persists over several generations. Much the same pattern of settlement and politics can be seen in other states; Arizona and New Mexico were southern settled and have had conservative

[9] For a concise description of these influences, see V. O. Key, Jr., *American State Politics: An Introduction* (New York: Alfred A. Knopf, 1956), pp. 218–29.

Democratic tendencies throughout most of their history. Somewhat the same influence also passed into southern California. Southern influence also has a contemporary aspect: large numbers of whites from the South have migrated to northern and western cities in the last several decades. Such migrants tend to keep their previous political values in their new environments.[10] Thus, political values in America often depend upon the particular regional subculture in which one grows up, and understanding this fact can greatly aid in comprehending the nature of political behavior.

Religion and Immigration. In thinking of the role played by religion and national origin in American political history, we tend to think in terms of the dichotomy between Catholic immigrants in urban areas and native rural Protestants. The patterns of ethnic and religious cleavage that were established as much of the country was settled throughout the nineteenth century are somewhat more complex than this. First, it is important to realize that a great part of the foreign immigrants until about 1890 settled in rural, frontier areas, rather than concentrating in large cities as the later immigrants from eastern and southern Europe did. Thus, significant parts of the Midwest and mountain states were settled by people of recent English, Irish, German, and Scandinavian extraction. Second, these immigrant groups were both Catholic and Protestant in makeup: English and Scandinavians being Protestant, Irish being Catholic, and Germans being split between Lutheran and Catholic. Finally, the religious division was not necessarily along Catholic-Protestant lines; it is better described as between "pietists" and "ritualists." [11] The pietists, following a Calvinist emphasis on "right action," included the evangelical Protestant denominations and Scandinavian Lutherans, while the ritualists were not only Catholic but German Lutheran. In addition to historical antipathies between Protestant and Catholic, native and immigrant, political conflict along religious lines was further heated by the presence of issues such as prohibition and parochial schools.

These cleavages were strong enough to have a major impact on the politics of the nineteenth century, perhaps influencing it more than economic class. Catholics, along with native Protestants of southern extraction, tended to vote heavily Democratic; pietistic Protestants were staunchly Republican. German Lutherans tended to be torn be-

[10] In 1968, George Wallace received twice the proportion of votes from southern migrants that he did from other northern whites. See Philip E. Converse *et al.*, "Continuity and Change in American Politics: Parties and Issues in the 1968 Election," *American Political Science Review*, 63 (1969), 1102.

[11] See Paul Kleppner, *The Cross of Culture: A Social Analysis of Midwestern Politics 1850–1900* (New York: Free Press, 1970), chap. 2.

tween the two parties, having a tradition of anti-Catholicism, but also not agreeing with many of the social policies, such as prohibition, advanced by the pietists. Thus, the German Protestant held the balance of political power in a number of states in the late nineteenth and into the twentieth century. As Lubell has pointed out, isolationist attitudes in the Midwest were a product of German and Scandinavian ethnicity, rather than physical insularity.[12] Old religious patterns still have an observable impact upon voting behavior. For example, DuBois County, a rural area in southwestern Indiana, has been the most heavily Democratic county in the state in most elections over several decades, a fact that would be hard to explain unless one knew that a substantial majority of its population are Catholics of German descent.

Other Sources of Cultural Variation.   We have given specific attention to the North-South and pietist-ritualist cleavages because their effects are both widespread and easily documented. Certainly there are many other subcultures in America that involve smaller numbers of people and exercise an important effect on attitudes toward public affairs. The various nationality groups in cities throughout the country (e.g., Poles, Italians) represent aggregates with enough self-awareness and interaction to be labeled as subcultures with particular patterns of opinion and behavior. Some of the distinctive social groups whose opinions were investigated in the previous chapter actually form particular subcultures, the Jewish and black communities being prime examples. One final sort of geographically related cleavage is that of rural versus urban residence. The old stereotype that people in rural areas are more conservative has some degree of validity across a range of issues. Actually, a better division would be metropolitan versus nonmetropolitan, for individuals in smaller cities and towns tend to be the most conservative of all. To some extent, rural conservatism may be real, though the observed difference is due in part to the fact that the less urban areas of the nation contain individuals who are more southern, older, less well educated, and less likely to be members of religious and racial minorities—all of which would tend to produce a less liberal pattern of opinion. Population movement and mass communications in modern society are tending to decrease the distinctiveness of opinion among all geographically based cultural groups today, but historically developed patterns of orientation still exercise greater influence on public affairs than we usually realize.

[12] Samuel Lubell, *The Future of American Politics,* 3rd ed. rev. (New York: Harper & Row, 1965), pp. 131–55.

MORALISM, INDIVIDUALISM, AND TRADITIONALISM

While findings on historical patterns of voting behavior and even geographical regularities in opinions aid our understanding of opinion formation, they really do not get at the basic idea of political culture as a "pattern of orientations toward political objects." Do people of different regions or religious heritage actually conceptualize the political world in different ways? We shall examine one particular theory that suggests an answer to this question and then examine the implications of that theory for contemporary politics.

Daniel Elazar has proposed a very broad and intriguing theory of the historical and geographic origins of political culture in America.[13] His analysis rests upon the idea of three streams of migration that settled the nation: the northern (or Yankee) stream from New England; a middle stream, principally from New York, New Jersey, and Pennsylvania; and a southern stream from the slave-holding colonies along the Atlantic coast. Each stream had its own pattern of religious, political, and social behavior. Furthermore, each stream tended to be reinforced by immigrants from particular European countries who shared many of the values of the native stream. For the sake of simplicity, these patterns are summarized in Table 6-2. The southern stream alone received little reinforcement from foreign sources, as there was little European migration into that region. Figure 6-2 gives a highly oversimplified picture of the areas of the country settled by the three streams.[14]

The settlement of the nation by these three streams is significant because each, according to Elazar, has its own characteristic political culture.[15] The northern Yankee stream carried with it what he calls the *moralistic* or "M" culture. This culture sees the political system as a "commonwealth" and political activity as a way of building a better society. The M culture favors a politics more issue-oriented and less concerned with personal and partisan gain. Many of the leaders of the nonpartisan and Progressive reform movements of the early twentieth century came from this tradition. Hence, areas dominated by the M culture tend to encourage widespread "amateur" participation in politics and government intervention in economic and social affairs.

---

[13] Elazar's theory is presented in *Cities of the Prairie* and in his *American Federalism: A View from the States*, 2nd ed. (New York: Thomas Y. Crowell, 1972), chaps. 4 and 5.

[14] No source is listed for the map in Figure 6-2 because it is based upon material from Elazar and a number of other sources, plus the author's own interpretation of historical data.

[15] The following description of the three cultures is drawn mainly from Chapter 6 of *Cities of the Prairie*. See also *American Federalism*, pp. 100–01.

Table 6-2
Characteristics of the Three Cultural Streams

	Native Stream	European Stream	Excluded Stream	Modal Characteristics
Northern (Moralistic)	Yankee (New England)	North Sea (English, Scottish, Welsh, Scandinavian, Dutch, etc.) Anglo-Canadian Jewish *		Calvinist Protestant. Communitarian. Entrepreneurial. Middle class. Republican. Fiercely loyal as a group to one party or fiercely independant.*
Middle (Individualistic	Middle Atlantic	English Continental (French, German, Belgian, etc.) Irish		Catholic or hierarchical liturgical Protestant. Individualist and Pluralist. Multiclass. Entrepreneurial. Mixed party loyalities.
Southern (Traditionalistic)	Southern	Mediterranean (Italian, etc.) Eastern European French-Canadian	Hispanic Afro-American	Single dominant religion or "color." Individualist but kinship oriented. Originally working class. Overt ethnic identity. Democratic.

Source: Daniel J. Elazar, *Cities of the Prairie: The Metropolitan Frontier and American Politics* (New York: Basic Books, 1970), p. 190; also see pp. 166–79.
* The Jewish stream deviates from these modal characteristics in several respects.

The middle stream carried with it what Elazar calls the *individualistic* or "I" culture. The I culture views the political process as a marketplace in which individuals can advance their own interests. It is more tolerant than the M culture of a reasonable degree of political corruption and places an emphasis on strong political parties manned by professionals. Since the I culture places high value on private activities, it tends to oppose governmental intervention and regulation, except for the purpose of stimulating the growth of business. Thus, areas in which the I culture is predominant tend to have party systems based more on the allocation of patronage than on issue orienta-

Figure 6-2
Generalized Pattern of Cultural Settlement in the United States

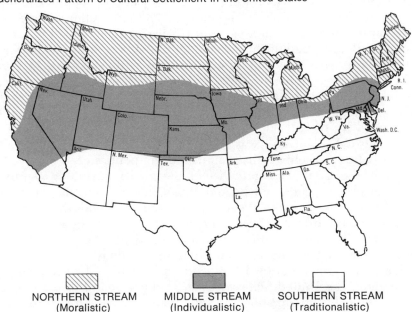

NORTHERN STREAM
(Moralistic)

MIDDLE STREAM
(Individualistic)

SOUTHERN STREAM
(Traditionalistic)

tions.[16] It is important to realize that the I culture is the dominant one in the American political system and that the prevalence of T or M influences in particular areas may only represent degrees of deviation from it.

The culture carried by the southern stream is the *traditionalistic* or "T" culture. In the T culture, the paramount purpose of government is to preserve traditional values. Political parties play little part in such a culture, for the open competition they engender is not valued. Family ties are much more important than in the other two cultures, and personalism seems to be extended to a politics that divides into factions headed by individuals, rather than enduring party organizations. Political leadership roles tend to be left to traditional political elites, the "leading families," the "best" people. Such a culture developed only in the American South with its almost feudal system of plantation agriculture and less industrial, more rural society. It was supplemented, Elazar says, by the two streams that were ex-

[16] This difference in the nature of political parties is illustrated by the contrast between the "job-oriented" parties of Ohio, Illinois, and Indiana, and the "issue-oriented" parties of Michigan, Minnesota, and Wisconsin. The former are predominantly I states, according to Elazar, and the latter are Yankee- and Scandinavian-settled M states. For a discussion of these states, see John H. Fenton, *Midwest Politics* (New York: Holt, Rinehart and Winston, 1966).

cluded from political life for so long, the Afro-American and the Hispanic (Chicano), which were assigned to subordinate roles in the T culture. Elazar also places the immigrants from southern and eastern Europe into this traditional stream because they tended to come from semifeudal, traditional societies in the old countries, emphasizing kinship ties and having little experience with mass participation in democratic government. The immigrants from these countries, however, did not settle in the traditionalistic southern culture, but rather settled in large cities that had generally been founded and populated by the M culture of the Yankee stream. The pattern of their cultural adaptation was often to form and support the great urban political machines that dominated the politics of so many cities from the Civil War until the middle of the twentieth century. Such machines, often run by individualistic Irish or natives, provided a measure of paternalistic support consistent with the expectations of the traditional culture from which the recent immigrants had just come. Thus many cities, originally moralistic, came to embody many of the aspects one associates with the I culture.

While we can describe broad patterns of cultural development throughout the United States, they are seldom found in their pure form. The paths of migration and settlement are tangled indeed, and one often finds that particular communities represent a unique blend of cultural influences.[17] Elazar suggests a *geological* analogy:

In the course of time, different streams of migration passed over the American landscape. . . . These streams, in themselves relatively clear-cut, have left residues of population in various places to become the equivalent of geological strata. As these populations settled in the same location, sometimes side by side, sometimes overlapping, and frequently on top of one another, they created hardened cultural mixtures that must be sorted out for analytical purposes, city by city and county by county from the Atlantic to the Pacific.[18]

Clearly, the historically developed political subcultures in the American system exercise an influence on patterns of opinion and political behavior. Elazar suggests several differences in policy—outputs of state governments that are explained in part by the dominant cultural heritage.[19] As we have seen earlier in this chapter, migration patterns of a century ago still exercise a strong impact on the partisan loyalties of local areas. Kevin Phillips, a Republican strategist writing in the aftermath of the 1968 election, has presented a theory of

[17] See the map of cultural types in local communities throughout the nation in Elazar, *American Federalism*, p. 107.

[18] *Ibid.*, p. 103.

[19] *Ibid.*, pp. 139–54. See also Ronald E. Weber and William R. Shaffer, "Public Opinion and American State Policy-Making," *Midwest Journal of Political Science*, 16 (1972), 683–99.

political realignment that seems closely related to Elazar's cultural theory, though expressed in different terms.[20] According to Phillips, there is a long-term trend for Yankee-settled moralistic areas (once the stronghold of the Republican party) to be changing to Democratic, while the middle (individualistic) and South (traditionalistic) states are moving heavily into the Republican camp. While some strong criticisms can be made on other grounds as to the validity of his conclusion that the Republican party will become a majority party, Phillips' thesis provides an excellent explanation of voting patterns in 1968, when almost all states and local areas carried by Humphrey were in the areas where the M culture was dominant. Also, the 1968 candidacy of George Wallace fits quite well into the theory: the areas where he did well were those that were southern settled, while in the areas of the northern stream, he received only a tiny fraction of the vote.[21] The 1972 election seems to fit this cultural pattern too; perhaps it was no coincidence that the Democrats nominated George McGovern, a man from the moralistic state of South Dakota, whose ideas and style seem to typify the ideals of the moralistic culture as it is manifested today. And Richard Nixon seems to embody the individualistic culture in many ways.[22]

Thus, we see that the political culture into which an individual is socialized seems to exercise a significant, if unnoticed, influence over his political behavior. We must beware of assuming direct correlations between culture and opinion, however. At the present time, it would appear that the moralistic culture is on the liberal side of most issues, but this has not always been so, and one can certainly find evidences of persons embodying M orientations who would advance an extremely conservative ideology. The cultural differences lie more in the broad expectations people have about the role of the political system rather than in their specific preferences, more in the style of the political action they desire than in its substance.

POLITICAL CULTURE AND OPINION FORMATION

We should make clear at this point that the effect that historical cultures have on a person's beliefs do not come through any automatic

[20] Kevin P. Phillips, *The Emerging Republican Majority* (Garden City, N.Y.: Doubleday, 1970).

[21] Elazar, *American Federalism*, p. 139. My own analysis of county voting results in Illinois reveals a substantial correlation between the vote for Wallace and southern antecedents of the population—as measured by a number of social and political characteristics of the counties of a century ago.

[22] See the excellent interpretation of Richard Nixon in relation to the nature of American culture in Garry Wills, *Nixon Agonistes: The Crisis of the Self-Made Man* (New York: New American Library, 1970).

"magical" transference of values. The distinctive aspects of any political culture are transmitted, as are all basic values—through the socialization process. These values are learned by the child from his parents, peers, and teachers. Throughout his adult life, he is likely to interact with people holding the same particular cultural values, thus reinforcing his beliefs. The political subsystem in which he lives has been shaped by these same cultural forces, and therefore his expectations about political parties, political leaders, and governmental action will be consistent with what he observes. Because subcultural patterns are maintained through this interpersonal socialization, increased geographical mobility tends to destroy distinctive section patterns. A person may keep his own values in a different cultural setting, but it will be much harder for him to pass them on intact to his children. Thus, cities in America, which have a mix of persons from different cultural types, tend to have less pure types of particular political cultures. In rural areas, however, where there has typically been little or no in-migration in the last century, the old cultural patterns may remain relatively undisturbed, except for the increasing impact of mass communications.

It has been the purpose of this chapter to demonstrate the importance of historical and geographic factors in influencing opinions. To offer simple and unqualified generalizations that can be easily proved by reference to public opinion data has generally not been possible. In part this is due to the fact that social science researchers have often neglected to measure this cultural aspect; certainly, such measurement on a large scale is difficult.[23] Yet the fact remains clear that patterns of opinion on the most contemporary issues are in part determined by events of decades and even centuries before.

[23] James Q. Wilson and Edward Banfield, "Public-Regardingness as a Value Premise in Voting Behavior," American Political Science Review, 58 (1964), 876–87, suggests a linkage between ethnicity and voting on local referenda, a conclusion disputed by Raymond E. Wolfinger and John Osgood Field, "Political Ethos and the Structure of City Government," American Political Science Review, 60 (1966), 320–26.

Opinion Manipulation: Media, Propaganda, and Political Campaigning

7

While we have thus far examined several different kinds of influences on individual opinion formation, we have neglected what is sometimes viewed as the most important—mass media and the possibility of using them to mold the opinions of the mass public. It is undeniably true that media play an increasingly important role in modern society, that the bulk of our information about public affairs is transmitted through them, and that considerable money and effort are expended in attempts to influence the public through these means.

Let us clarify the meaning of these terms. The idea of "media" comes from the expression "medium of communication" (i.e., something that *mediates* between the speaker and the listener). The word "media" is generally used alone to refer to the "mass media" (i.e., those media that are capable of directing the same message to large numbers of people, particularly television, radio, newspapers, and magazines). One should be aware that there are other more personalized media, such as letters and personal contact by an intermediary. Even traditional political campaign paraphernalia, such as buttons and bumper stickers, are media of communication. While we will be mainly concerned here with the role of the "mass" variety of media, we must keep in mind that politically relevant communications occur in an astonishing variety of ways.

There are a number of ways to consider the role of mass media in contemporary society, and most of them, unfortunately, are beyond the scope of this book. We shall concentrate upon two: media as a source of information about public affairs, and the possibility of using media to influence the opinions and behavior of the mass public.

MEDIA AS A SOURCE
OF INFORMATION

Nearly everyone in the mass public receives almost all of his infor mation about public affairs (at least indirectly) through the mass media. Very few of us are personal observers of governmental and political events, even in our own communities, let alone at the national and international levels. Since the electronic and printed media provide the information upon which opinions are based, we shall examine the extent of public reliance on different media, patterns of media usage in the population, and the question of bias in media coverage of the news.

Table 7-1 reports survey data on the reported use of various media for information about public affairs. In the last decade, television has clearly surpassed newspapers as the major source of news for most people, though much of television's gain since World War II has come at the expense of radio. About one-third of the population reports relying only on television, about one-fifth only on newspapers, and one-fifth on both, with other combinations and other media accounting for the remainder. These same patterns of usage emerge if people are asked which medium provides most of their information about national political campaigns.[1] This reliance on television is also confirmed by popular acceptance of its believability, also shown in Table 7-1. Less than 10 percent of the respondents surveyed by the Roper Organization in each of seven surveys over a twelve-year period felt that television was the "least believable," as against about one-fourth to one-third each for radio and newspapers.[2] The same studies show by an increasing margin over the years that the public, if forced to have only one news medium, would take television. A majority of the public uses television as its major source of information about public affairs, and a clear plurality believes that information to be worthy of acceptance.

While television seems to be a major information source for most people, there are some sociological differences in the audiences of different media. The use of print media is particularly subject to variation with education and social status. To use newspapers and magazines as an information source requires not only more education than does acquiring the same information from radio and television, but more desire for that information. Magazines are particularly subject to this effect; only a minority of the public regularly reads magazines

[1] Dan Nimmo, *The Political Persuaders: The Techniques of Modern Election Campaigns* (Englewood Cliffs, N.J.: Prentice-Hall, 1970), p. 116.

[2] Burns W. Roper, *An Extended View of Public Attitudes Toward Television and Other Mass Media 1959–1971: A Report by the Roper Organization, Inc.* (New York: Television Information Office, 1971), p. 4.

Table 7-1
Public Attitudes Toward the Media, 1959–72

". . . Where do you usually get most of your information about what's going on in the world today—from the newspapers or radio or television or magazines or talking to people or where?"

Source of Most News *	1959	1961	1963	1964	1967	1968	1971	1972
Television	51%	52%	55%	58%	64%	59%	60%	64%
Newspapers	57	57	53	56	55	49	48	50
Radio	34	34	29	26	28	25	23	21
Magazines	8	9	6	8	7	7	5	6
People	4	5	4	5	4	5	4	4
Don't know, etc.	1	3	3	3	2	3	1	1

"If you got conflicting or different reports of the same news story from radio, television, the magazines, and the newspaper, which of the four versions would you be most inclined to believe . . . . ?"

Most Believable	1959	1961	1963	1964	1967	1968	1971	1972
Television	29%	39%	36%	41%	44%	44%	49%	48%
Newspapers	32	24	24	23	24	21	20	21
Radio	12	12	12	8	7	8	10	8
Magazines	10	10	10	10	8	11	9	10
Don't know, etc.	17	17	18	18	20	16	12	13

Source: *What People Think of Television and Other Mass Media 1959–1972: A Report by the Roper Organization, Inc.* (New York: Television Information Office, 1973), pp. 2–3.
* Figures add to more than 100 percent because of multiple responses.

dealing with public affairs. There is not much reverse effect with the electronic media, however. While a stereotype exists that television is watched mainly by the poor and uneducated, this receives scant support from empirical findings. The Roper study reports that the number of hours per day spent watching television by both college educated and upper economic level individuals is only slightly less than the national average.[3] Some variations in reliance on electronic media have been reported—women spend somewhat more time with radio and television [4]—but none which seem of much practical significance. Truly, television has become a "mass" medium in every sense of the word.

Since television has become such a widespread information source and is believed by those who use it, an obvious question is whether

[3] *Ibid.*, pp. 5–6. See also Bradley S. Greenberg and Hideya Kumata, "National Sample Predictors of Mass Media Use," *Journalism Quarterly*, 45 (1968), 641–46.
[4] Greenberg and Kumata, "National Sample Predictors," p. 645.

or not television news coverage is biased. Sharp charges of slant and prejudice have come in recent years from former Vice-President Agnew and other conservative critics, [5] complaints have also come from groups on the Left and from the black community. To attempt to deal with this controversial subject in a few words is difficult, but a few points can be made. Edith Efron has presented the most well-documented charge of pro-liberal bias by network news.[6] Using a detailed content analysis of every word spoken on the three network news broadcasts during the closing months of the 1968 presidential election, she found that more than ten times as much "anti-Nixon" comment was aired as "pro-Nixon," while the balance was about even for Humphrey and even for Wallace. Favorable treatment was also reported for liberals generally, Vietnam war opponents, and black militants. No similarly documented rebuttal has come as yet from those who disagree with Efron's analysis. However, one point should be made. Inspection of the copious appendices in the book reveals that the great bulk of the negative material comes not from reporter opinion, but rather from other sources quoted or shown directly. Televised criticism by other politicians, protesters, foreign diplomats, or the "man in the street" are all counted in the analysis as negative material. Thus, if there was serious anti-Republican bias in television coverage of the 1968 election, it was in the *choice* of material, rather than in its presentation.

This last observation suggests something about the nature of biases inherent in television or any other news medium in American society. Television and radio stations, like newspapers and magazines in the United States, are business enterprises (some would say "show business") and are therefore dependent upon maximizing their number of customers and viewers. To do this, it is necessary to concentrate upon what is thought to be most interesting to the public. And what is "interesting" to the public seems to be scandal, disorder, and criticism, particularly when portrayed in a colorful way. American journalism gave considerable attention to student and antiwar protests in the late 1960s—until they lost their novelty and thereby ceased to be news.[7] Thus, news coverage very often seems to accentuate the negative aspects of the political process, a fact that

---

[5] E.g., Joseph Keeley, *The Left-Leaning Antenna: Political Bias in Television* (New Rochelle, N.Y.: Arlington House, 1971).

[6] Edith Efron, *The News Twisters* (Los Angeles: Nash Publishing, 1971). A less ambitious study of the 1972 election reported a definite pro-McGovern bias. See *"Liberal Bias" as a Factor in Network Television News Reporting* (Washington: The American Institute for Political Communication, 1972).

[7] There is some evidence that protests on college campuses did not decrease nearly as much in quantity or intensity after 1970 as news coverage of them would indicate. See *The Chronicle of Higher Education,* vol. 6, no. 6 (November 1, 1971).

is likely to bring charges of partisan or ideological bias from those offended by the implied criticism.

Just as journalistic businesses must seek that which stimulates the interest of the largest number of people, so must they be careful to stay fairly close to the values of the public. Newspapers, radio, and television, therefore, tend to stay generally in the political middle of the road, a fact that gains them no praise from ideological activists of either Right or Left. Because the public is also a white public, television depicts a white society, though in recent years network programmers have awakened somewhat to the existence of a large mass of black consumers. In many ways, a strong case can be made that American journalism in the second half of the twentieth century is lacking in forceful and opinionated journalism. While newspaper editors of earlier years used the front page as a pulpit, one must now turn to the editorial page in most daily papers to find anything but carefully worded wire-service stories on national affairs. In many ways, the information that Americans gain about public affairs is both homogeneous and bland.

The whole question as to whether the news Americans get from the media is seriously biased is a normative one in many ways, and we have certainly not resolved it here. One point is clear: the public had confidence in the media. The Roper study found that its respondents ranked media performance as generally better than that of schools or local government. Only 21 percent indicated that television was "not fair" in showing all points of view; 7 percent felt that it leaned too much to coverage of the political Left; and 2 percent felt that it leaned too much to the Right.[8] Whether or not any particular medium is actually biased in its reporting, the question still remains as to the ability of the media to influence the opinions of the public. It is that question which we shall now consider.

THE QUESTION OF MANIPULATION

The issue of whether or not the mass media can be used to effect some change in public opinion that would not otherwise occur is a controversial one of much current interest. Critics of bias in the news media presumably believe that the alleged bias has some impact on public opinion—if not, then they would be objecting on purely aesthetic grounds. Many voices have been raised in the last few years to protest that technological innovations in political campaigning are dangerous to the democratic process because they give unfair advantage to those with the considerable resources needed to purchase

[8] Roper, *Extended View of Public Attitudes*, pp. 13–15.

them. Reflecting this concern, the first new federal legislation in many years regulating campaign spending was passed in 1972. And, furthermore, a great many pages have been written exposing and explaining the "new politics" in which candidates are supposedly remolded according to the dictates of the "image makers." [9] While granting that important questions are raised by this literature, we can certainly not take its assumptions about the effects of media as valid without investigation, if only because of the purposes for which the assumptions are made. Much of the writing on the subject is that by journalists who have observed the process of "image making" from the inside with little or no information as to whether voters "bought" what was allegedly being "sold" to them. Other claims about the power of the "new politics" are made by people in the business of selling their services as practitioners thereof, and one would hardly expect them to downgrade the usefulness of their product. Denunciations of media campaigning come from unsuccessful partisans who would rather think that their side lost because the election was stolen from them than because the voters simply did not like their candidate or his positions. Clearly, the question of whether or not the communications media in contemporary America can be used to manipulate public opinion is both serious and complex, and requires a careful analysis of empirical findings.

One term that has frequently been used in discussions of the effectiveness of mediated communication is "propaganda." Lasswell defines propaganda as "the manipulation of symbols as a means of influencing attitudes on controversial matters." [10] While he and his associates were able to construct several "tests" (sufficiently precise to result in criminal convictions during World War II) for determining whether or not a particular communication was propagandistic, there are some severe and inherent weaknesses in the concept. There seems to be no clear point where "propaganda" stops and "advertising," "persuasive argument," or "education" begins. The concept of propaganda is basically normative; communications on behalf of our enemies are propaganda, but those of our allies are not. There may be, as Lasswell's definition suggests, some notion that propagandistic arguments make more appeal to emotions than those that are not so classified, but one would hesitate to label all opinionated

[9] To cite only a few of the catchier titles: James M. Perry, *The New Politics: The Expanding Technology of Political Manipulation* (New York: Clarkson N. Potter, 1968); Ray Hiebert *et al.*, eds., *The Political Image Merchants: Strategies in the New Politics* (Washington: Acropolis Books, 1971); Joe McGinniss, *The Selling of the President 1968* (New York: Pocket Books, 1970); and Gene Wyckoff, *Image Candidates: American Politics in the Age of Television* (New York: Macmillan, 1968).

[10] Harold D. Lasswell *et al.*, *Language of Politics: Studies in Quantitative Semantics* (Cambridge, Mass.: M.I.T. Press, 1965), p. 177.

statements using emotional appeals as propaganda. And what seems a matter of cold, hard logic to one man may be a soft-hearted emotional appeal to another of a different persuasion. Because of the problems with propaganda as a meaningful concept, one seldom finds it used in contemporary social science, and most references to it come from writings during or about World War II.

The remainder of this chapter will be devoted to an examination from several perspectives of the question of the efficacy of media for opinion manipulation. The discussion will be almost entirely about campaigning in American elections. The reasons for such concentration are several. First, most of the available empirical work deals with political campaigning. Second, while ideally we would wish to look at evidence as to whether opinions can be changed, rather than votes, one can logically assume that serious attempts to change attitudes on public affairs are ultimately designed to change the behaviors of the public, of which voting would seem to be one of the most important types. Finally, it seems proper to concentrate on the electoral process because of its obvious substantive importance and because of the volume of concern about electoral manipulation today.

BANDWAGON OR UNDERDOG?

One fear sometimes voiced by those who are suspicious of public opinion polling, computers, and political use of the media is that they will tend to sway public opinion by reporting the distribution of that opinion. The idea here is that people will jump on the proverbial bandwagon of the winning candidate simply because he is winning. This is certainly a logical idea and one used by advertisers of consumer products. Psychologically, there is some validity to the notion that people like to be with a winner and hate to be left out. A contrary argument that is sometimes advanced is that Americans like the underdog and will therefore flock to the camp of the trailing candidate. (Of course, both effects could be in operation simultaneously, thereby canceling each other out.) What evidence do we have on the question?

One way we can get at this question is simply to observe the performance of candidates in published polls over a period of time and see whether or not the leading candidate tended to increase his margin (a "bandwagon" effect) or do less well (an "underdog" effect). Figure 7-1 charts the proportion of the vote received by candidates in Gallup polls for the months preceding the 1968 and 1972 presidential elections. Clearly, in 1968 there was no Nixon bandwagon, for his percentages stayed relatively constant, though there might have been some underdog appeal by Humphrey. It is instruc-

Figure 7-1
Development of Presidential Preference as Reported by Gallup Polls, 1968 and 1972

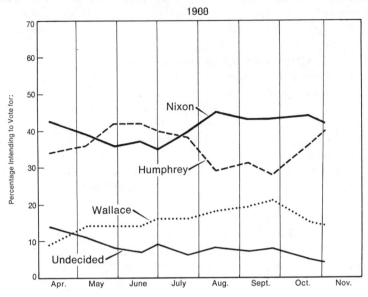

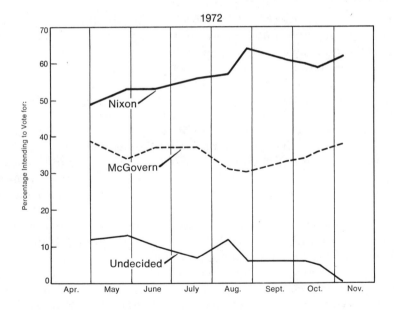

Source: Data from Gallup polls as reported in *Gallup Opinion Index,* no. 38 (September 1968), 6; no. 39 (October 1968), 9; no. 41 (November 1968), 9–10; and no. 89 (November 1972), 2–3.

tive to note that voters were aware of Nixon's leading position; in the two months prior to the election, the public, by a wide majority, thought that Nixon would probably be the winner in November.[11] In 1972, Nixon was far ahead at the outset, experienced some increase as a result of popular reactions to the two national conventions, and then maintained his margin over McGovern through the last months of the campaign. The data presented here are generally confirmed by evidence from other elections.[12] It can always be argued that candidates might have done better had it not been for the polls, but this is purely speculation. It appears that changes in presidential preference are much more easily explained by national and international events than by the published results of survey research.

If public opinion polls seem to have little or no net effect on voting behavior, perhaps this is due to a lack of awareness of them or a lack of confidence in their findings by many voters. Less easy for a voter to ignore are reports of actual votes cast by others in the election itself. Because of the different hours that polling places close throughout the country, the development of sophisticated computer projection systems has made it possible for television networks to broadcast election results from eastern states while many people in California have yet to cast their ballots. The possibility that the public in western states might be influenced, either by a bandwagon effect or by a feeling that the election has already been decided so that there is no use in turning out, has seemed serious enough to many that congressional investigations have been held to examine the topic.

Because of this concern, several large-scale studies were conducted at the time of the 1964 election. That contest, by chance, was such as to provide a clear test of the problem, for early returns favored Johnson enough to suggest to potential voters that the election had already been decided—whereas in 1960 and 1968 the election outcome was in doubt until the following day. Table 7-2 shows data from one of these studies. These figures demonstrate very clearly that exposure to election return broadcasts before voting had virtually no influence on the ultimate choice made, for the defection rate from earlier preference is no greater among those who had been exposed to broadcasts than among those who had not. Furthermore, there appeared to be no particular influence upon voter turnout.[13]

---

[11] *Gallup Opinion Index*, no. 40 (October 1968), 10.

[12] For a summary of the evidence on this point, see Harold Mendelsohn and Irving Crespi, *Polls, Television, and the New Politics* (Scranton, Pa.: Chandler, 1970), pp. 17–25.

[13] Harold Mendelsohn, "Election-Day Broadcasts and Terminal Voting Decisions," *Public Opinion Quarterly*, 30 (1966), 224.

Table 7-2
Intended Votes and Actual Votes for Those Exposed and Not Exposed to Prior Broadcasts of Election Results, California, 1964

Actual Vote	Intended Vote: Johnson		Intended Vote: Goldwater	
	Exposed to Election Broadcasts	Not Exposed to Broadcasts	Exposed to Election Broadcasts	Not Exposed to Broadcasts
Johnson	97%	97%	2%	—*
Goldwater	2	2	97	97
Refused to disclose vote	1	2	2	2
N =	94	635	58	425

Source: Harold Mendelsohn and Irving Crespi, *Polls, Television, and the New Politics* (Scranton, Pa.: Chandler Publishing Company, 1970), p. 203.
* —indicates less than 0.5%

The results of this and four other major studies were all the same: even the small segment of the electorate exposed to election returns before voting does not appear to behave differently from the electorate as a whole.[14] As Warren Miller testified before a Senate Committee, ". . . the net impact [of televised election predictions] is, insofar as one is able to provide appropriate statistical measurements, zero." [15]

The evidence of both sequential polls and studies of election return broadcasting suggests that fears of a bandwagon effect do not seem to have much basis. The relative success of a candidate in the polls may certainly have an impact on party leaders, campaign workers, and potential contributors, but this is irrelevant to our concern here. This lack of impact of polls certainly does not prove that mass media cannot be used in other ways to manipulate public opinion, though it hardly strengthens that case. It does suggest two conclusions about mass political behavior. One obviously is that people make their voting decisions on the basis of other considerations than who they think is going to win. The other is that while there may be some psychological tendency to go with the majority, the relevant public is probably perceived by most people to be those like themselves with whom they interact on a personal basis. Such an influence is, of course, largely beyond the control of the mass media.

[14] For a summary of the five studies and a general analysis of the problem, see Mendelsohn and Crespi, *Polls, Television, and the New Politics* chap. 4. See also Kurt Lang and Gladys Engel Lang, *Voting and Non-Voting: Implications of Broadcasting Returns Before the Polls Are Closed* (Waltham, Mass.: Blaisdell, 1968).
[15] Cited in Mendelsohn and Crespi, *Polls, Television, and the New Politics*, p. 236.

THE EFFECTS OF CAMPAIGNING:
EMPIRICAL FINDINGS

To directly assess the effect of political campaigning on election results is difficult. People sometimes try to draw conclusions based on a simple relationship between effort and results, producing statements of the form "Nixon must have sold his image successfully because he won," or "Money is useless in politics because the Republicans always have spent more in presidential elections but usually have lost." Such generalizations—and they actually are made—are meaningless because they cannot take into account all of the other variables that go into the determination of an election. Nixon might very well have won in 1968 without the particular campaign effort he used; for all we know, the Republicans might have been even less successful from 1932 to 1960 without their advantage in campaign funds. The problem is that we must find some way of comparing election results with and without the use of particular campaign tactics, and it is generally impossible to find actual sets of elections in which all of the relevant factors (e.g., candidates, conditions, voter opinions) are really comparable.

Interestingly enough, this same problem of assessing effectiveness occurs in the field of commercial product advertising. While great resources have been devoted to the investigation of advertising techniques and their results, there is still a relative lack of knowledge about the exact nature of the linkage between advertising and sales. For the most part, studies of advertising effectiveness have measured its success in *communication* (i.e., in achieving brand awareness, knowledge of the message, etc.), rather than in the actual *influence* of advertising on behavior as measured by sales.[16] Measures of communication, which are analogous to surveying the public to find out their familiarity with a candidate, are employed in preference to studies of sales influence because measuring familiarity is a much simpler task. A number of methods have been suggested for advertising research that would get at the actual effectiveness of a given method in producing sales, many of them experimental in nature, utilizing different stimuli for different audiences. Still, the field of product advertising, while its practitioners remain confident that "advertising works," cannot specify with any precision the actual effect of a particular amount of advertising on the behavior of the public. We bring up this point about the problems of advertising research since anyone who seeks to demonstrate the effectiveness of political campaigns faces the same problems on a much greater scale.

[16] Charles Raymond, "Measurement of Sales Effectiveness of Advertising," in *Handbook of Advertising Management*, ed. Roger Barton (New York: McGraw-Hill, 1970), chap. 22.

Many more variables affect an election outcome than affect consumer choice between competing brands of automobiles or detergents. Political events are unique—an electoral choice between the same two candidates occurring only once or twice. Nor can the most sophisticated, quasi-experimental techniques of research on effectiveness generally be applied in the political process. As a result, the evidence we can assemble about the effectiveness of political campaigning in America will hardly prove or disprove the possibility of manipulation. At best, the weight of the evidence may suggest what the likelihood of such media power may be.

Differential Exposure to Campaign Stimuli. While social researchers will probably never be able to vary the level of campaign stimuli in order to observe their effects in the way students of commercial advertising might, in some cases it is possible to compare groups of persons who have received differing amounts of a particular type of campaign communication. One such situation presented itself in 1952 when, in Iowa, some parts of the state received television broadcasts and others did not. Simon and Stern investigated whether television availability had an effect on either the rate of voting participation or on the partisan division of the vote.[17] Carefully controlling for the political tendencies exhibited by counties in the past, they found no discernible effort on either variable. If this particular experience was representative, one might conclude that television had no net effect on the 1952 elections (i.e., it would not have mattered if the medium had been in existence or not). Such a study cannot be replicated in later elections, unfortunately. Television has become so widely diffused throughout the population since 1952 that any areas or groups that do not receive it are likely to be so unusual in geographic remoteness, economic status, or life-style that they would not be comparable to those with television. This is the problem we face in looking at the effects of mass communications. Since those communications are received by virtually everyone, it is extremely difficult to verify the actual consequences.

One aspect of campaigning about which there is a body of information is that of personal contact, particularly that by party workers (this is "mediated" communication, but of an individual rather than a mass nature). This phenomenon offers more opportunity for study, as we can find party workers in specific geographic areas, representing a variety of social environments, who attempt to influence voters with different rates and types of campaign stimuli. Several research

[17] Herbert A. Simon and Frederick Stern, "The Effect of Television Upon Voting Behavior in Iowa in the 1952 Presidential Election," *American Political Science Review*, 49 (1955), 470–77.

projects have attempted to correlate the amount and type of effort reported by party workers with the electoral success of their party in their precincts, controlling for relevant characteristics of the voters.[18] In both the studies cited, there was a statistically significant relationship between effort expended by precinct workers and the success of their party. It appeared that the difference in expected division of the two-party vote was between 5 and 10 percent, comparing cases in which the Democratic worker performed well and the Republican did nothing, with situations in which the reverse was true. Hence, this figure of 10 percent of the vote that might be attributable to local campaign effort is only a potential one that would be valid if one party performed at maximum efficiency and the other refrained from all activity—and neither situation is likely to come about in any real election. Instead, parties tend to perform at roughly the same rates overall and therefore largely offset each other.

This question of personal campaigning has also been investigated by at least two experimental studies.[19] In each of these, researchers received agreement from party organizations to campaign in some parts and not in other parts of noncompetitive districts. In both instances, the effect upon voting behavior was small, amounting to only a few percentage points, coming in one case from an effect on turnout of voters favoring the party and in the other from an effect on voter preference. Again, the effect of personal campaigning, even under idealized and extreme conditions, was quite small. As an additional source of evidence on this point, and one that goes beyond the limitations of particular communities, we can point to Kramer's analysis of national surveys for several presidential elections.[20] Kramer looks at whether the voter can recall having been contacted by representatives of the political parties and then relates this answer to the voter's behavior, taking account of his previous political preference. His finding is that personal campaigning seems to have no particular effect on the voter's preference for a candidate, though there is a slight partisan advantage derived from increasing the rate of voting

[18] The best-known studies are those of Gary, Indiana, reported by Phillips Cutright, "Measuring the Impact of Local Party Activity on the General Election Vote," *Public Opinion Quarterly*, 27 (1963), 327–86, and Detroit, reported by Daniel Katz and Samuel Eldersveld, "The Impact of Local Party Activity Upon the Electorate," *Public Opinion Quarterly*, 25 (1961), 1–24. Similar findings for precincts throughout the state of Indiana are reported in Alan D. Monroe, "Political Party Activism: Causes and Consequences" (unpublished Ph.D. dissertation, Indiana University, 1971), chap. 9.

[19] J. M. Bochel and D. T. Denver, "Canvassing, Turnout, and Party Support: An Experiment," *British Journal of Political Science*, 1 (1971), 247–69, and John C. Blydenburgh, "A Controlled Experiment to Measure the Effects of Personal Contact Campaigning," *Midwest Journal of Political Science*, 15 (1971), 365–81.

[20] Gerald H. Kramer, "The Effects of Precinct-Level Canvassing on Voter Behavior," *Public Opinion Quarterly*, 34 (1971), 560–62.

participation by people already committed to a party. The evidence from all of these studies seems consistent. If one political party organization does a much better job than the other in reaching the voter, then it will gain a small advantage. This advantage apparently comes not from persuading anyone, but from simply getting out the vote. American parties, by and large, do not do a very good job of personally contacting voters; if both did, then they would still tend to offset each other and not change election results very much.

The Individual Voting Decision.   If we know little about the effects of mediated campaigning on voters, we have learned a great deal about voting behavior itself. The behavior of the American voter will be evaluated in Chapter 14. At this point, however, it is worthwhile to note some points about the electoral decision.

First, consider the point in time when voters decide how they intend to vote. As public opinion polls such as those reported in Figure 7-1 generally indicate, the proportion of voters who report themselves "undecided" in a presidential election is usually little more than 10 percent, even before one or both of the candidates have been nominated. A few of those who express a preference at one time may change their minds as the campaign continues, though most of these switchers are canceled out in the aggregate by people switching in the opposite direction.[21] The point is that most voters (60 to 80 percent) have decided how they will vote before the campaign itself even begins.[22] And by the closing days of the campaign, when parties customarily pour large sums of money into television saturation campaigns, only a very small proportion of voters have not already made their decision. Many voters change their party voting preference from election to election, but this occurs throughout the period between election years, presumably in response to events, conditions, and performance, rather than to any direct campaign stimuli.[23] Thus, what we know about *when* voters decide points out two things about their decision making: that they change their minds without the stimuli of campaigns and that only a minority are available for influence by the time the candidates have been nominated and campaigning really gets under way.

It is also interesting to consider the relative amounts of attention to

[21] For data on vote switching as found by panel studies done for the Nixon campaign in 1968, see Don Oberdorfer, "Political Polling and Electoral Strategy: The 1968 Election," in *Political Opinion and Behavior: Essays and Studies,* eds. Edward C. Dreyer and Walter A. Rosenbaum, 2nd ed. (Belmont, Calif.: Wadsworth, 1970), pp. 51–58.

[22] William H. Flanigan, *Political Behavior of the American Electorate,* 2nd ed. (Boston: Allyn and Bacon, 1972), p. 109.

[23] Paul Lazarsfeld *et al., The People's Choice: How the Voter Makes Up His Mind in a Presidential Campaign,* 3rd ed. (New York: Columbia University Press, 1968), pp. 101–05.

political communications by voters of varying predispositions. As almost everyone who has studied political behavior has found, persons who have strong political preferences are the most likely to expose themselves to all manner of campaign stimuli.[24] People who have weak preferences or none at all and who are generally uninterested in politics pay the least attention to the efforts of political parties to attract them. But, unfortunately for the campaigners, the strong partisans who are reached are the least likely to be affected by the campaign information, for their minds are made up, while the marginal voters who could potentially be persuaded are the hardest group with whom to communicate.[25] Furthermore, even when campaign communications do get through, the message that is received may not be the one that the sender intended. As we have already seen (in Chapter 3), the powers of the mass public to exercise selective perception and distort the content of communications that fail to reinforce existing beliefs and perceptions are considerable. The obvious combative nature of political campaigns and the ease of identifying messages that come from the opposite party suggest that the tendency to either distort or completely ignore messages designed to sway a person from his previous preferences will be particularly great. As a result of all this, much of the effort directed at persuasive communication falls only upon the eyes and ears of those who have already been persuaded.

To conclude this brief survey of how the voter decides, let us note the existence of a host of reasons why people vote the way they do other than what parties and candidates tell them. The most important influence on voting is that of party identification, a psychological loyalty that (a) is most commonly copied from one's parents and (b) tends to remain constant throughout adult life. As pointed out in Chapter 5, there are also a number of sociological correlates of partisan voting—race, religion, and economic status—and in the preceding chapter we saw that the historical context into which a person is socialized can have a significant impact on his vote. The purpose of recapitulating these factors is to point out that all of them are, for practical purposes, constant influences on the voting decision and far out of the reach of even the most sophisticated techniques of politics,

[24] See Lester W. Milbrath, *Political Participation: How and Why Do People Get Involved in Politics* (Chicago: Rand McNally, 1965), pp. 44–45, for a summary of the sources on this point.

[25] In fact, for those voters who are the most interested and involved in an election campaign, increased attention to the mass media tends to result in greater party regularity and less deviation in voting. See Philip E. Converse, "Information Flow and the Stability of Partisan Attitudes," *Public Opinion Quarterly*, 26 (1962), 578–99, and William Flanigan and David RePass, *Electoral Behavior* (Boston: Little, Brown, 1968), pp. 95–100.

old or new. They never determine the voting decision so completely that there is no room left for short-term influences, but they do indicate that persuasion must operate within rather narrow limits.

We cannot pretend that the evidence and arguments advanced in this section are capable of disproving the possibility of manipulation. Nevertheless, we would be justified in concluding that there is little or no empirical evidence for believing that voters in America are widely manipulated by political campaigns, and what empirical findings there are would tend to weigh against that possibility.

THE EFFECTS OF CAMPAIGNING:
A PSYCHOLOGICAL ANALYSIS

Because of a number of practical difficulties already mentioned, the kind of empirical evidence that would be required to precisely determine the nature of the effect of campaigns on voters does not exist. In lieu of that, let us take some principles of human behavior and attempt to apply them to the problem.[26]

We may take as given the idea that in order to change a person's vote, one must first alter the psychological factors that cause that decision. Voters have reasons for their voting intentions—though these may appear unconscious or weak or illogical to the outside observer—and the beliefs or perceptions that form these reasons must be affected to produce the desired behavioral change. This, of course, is what campaign communications are intended to do. Yet there are a number of inherent factors that can stop given stimuli from causing the intended response. This fact has been summarized in what has been called "The Law of Minimal Consequences": ". . . the short-run conversion potential of the media content is progressively reduced by the presence . . . of a host of intervening conditions, each one of which tends, . . . to minimize the likelihood of a response disjunctive with prior inclinations." [27]

What this means is that when the stimulus of a campaign message reaches a voter, certain barriers stand between that stimulus and any attitudinal change. It is possible that a given message may get through any given barrier, but there is a good probability that it will be turned aside and dealt with by the individual in some way that does not produce any change in his attitudes. Since there are several different types or levels of these barriers, the probability that a stimulus will get through all of them and bring about a change is not very great. This process is depicted in Figure 7-2. It is instructive to ex-

[26] The form of the analysis in this section is suggested by Chapter 5 of Nimmo, *The Political Persuaders*, though the substantive conclusions reached here are somewhat different.

[27] Lang and Lang, *Voting and Non-Voting*, p. 4.

Figure 7-2.
Barriers to Change by Campaign Communication

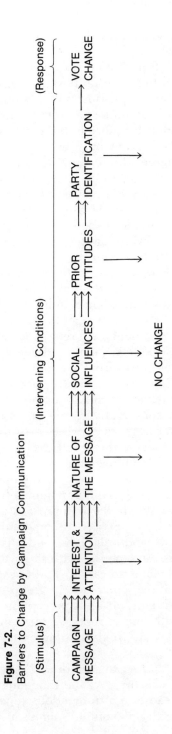

amine the nature of these various types of intervening conditions and we shall do so briefly.

The first barrier that an attempt to persuade faces is that people may not pay attention to it. While there is a considerable volume of campaign communication in various media in the months preceding a general election, campaigning still accounts for only a small part of all the stimuli received by most individuals. As we noted earlier, people tend to pay attention only to those communications with which they already agree. One countermeasure to this lack of attention is the widespread practice of using brief spot commericals on television that are unlikely to be avoided even by committed opponents. The nature of the message itself is the second barrier. An appeal that arouses a favorable response in one person may be meaningless to another and even counterproductive for a third. Yet the very use of the mass media means that the same message will be presented to all three. People vary in their receptiveness to different messages on a number of dimensions. One is simply the level of sophistication and knowledge. The candidate who wishes to make a case for the virtues of a protective policy in international trade must choose between an argument in terms of economic theory (which would go over the heads of part of his audience) or a simplified, emotional appeal to "save jobs from competition from foreign slave labor" (which would insult the intelligence of the more sophisticated). Television broadcasts reach both blacks and prejudiced whites, liberals and conservatives, businessmen and labor union members, thus any message that strikes a strongly responsive note with one group may alienate the other.

The everyday social influences on an individual produce a third barrier. As we saw in Chapter 4, most people operate within a politically and socially homogeneous environment, interacting with persons like themselves who hold similar opinions. In attempting to change an individual's attitude, a persuasive communication is competing with his family, friends, and neighbors, and it is likely that the individual has more stake in agreeing with them than with the distant source of a mediated communication. To the extent that an individual identifies with a particular social group—whether racial, religious, economic, or cultural—his perception of how this group stands on an issue will tend to reduce his receptiveness to attempts to persuade him to deviate from the opinion he believes that group holds.

The most important barrier to attitudinal change is that imposed by the existing attitude structure. As the functional theory of attitudes makes clear, people exercise a tremendous repertoire of psychological devices to deal with unfavorable sources of information in order to maintain their psychological stability and avoid cognitive dissonance. All of the techniques discussed in Chapter 3 are likely to be used to reduce the effectiveness of a campaign communication that directly challenges the set of beliefs and perceptions that the voter already has established. One particular attitude deserves to be noted separately as a barrier: party identification. In the United States party identification seems to be the most basic form of political belief and one that can be somewhat separate from opinions on particular issues, ideological position, and appraisals of current candidates. Even if some of the other attitudes relating to the electoral decision are changed, the person's established allegiance may cause him to vote as he originally would have.

Given these barriers, it is extremely hard for a campaign communication—particularly one through the mass media—to actually change attitudes and therefore votes. Since the possibility of conversion is so small, attempts are made to bypass the more serious barriers. Nimmo says that the purpose of this approach is "not to change the attitudes of the committed, but to shift the perceptions of voters with low involvement." [28] Thus, one would concentrate on those voters who have weak preferences or none and would try to change their perception of a candidate's image or, more likely, try to create one where none had existed before. Contemporary techniques make the mass media, particularly television, quite useful for this purpose. Through repeated broadcasts of messages that have little or no actual content, it is possible to make even an uninterested viewer aware of a candidate's existence and to associate some vague image with him. This is the same phenomenon as the learning of commercial jingles and slogans by small children who have no particular comprehension of the product itself. Advertising in politics can build familiarity with candidate names, just as it can with product brands. However, just as commercial advertisers lack a precise knowledge of the linkage between their efforts and sales, as opposed to brand familiarity alone, so we lack evidence of the usefulness of this creative effect in producing votes. Certainly, it would seem that having heard of a candidate and having some minimal impression of him would be required for someone to vote for him (though voters are quite capable of voting for minor offices on the basis of party without any knowledge of either candidate). But simple knowledge and vague image in themselves do not necessarily produce votes—and in the case of presidential elections, almost all voters will be aware of the contenders with or without any campaigning. By influencing the perception of candidates, campaigning through the mass media may be

[28] Nimmo, *The Political Persuaders*, p. 181.

able to have an influence on some voters. This influence, however, will be potentially significant for only a small minority of the population—those who lack both partisan loyalties and the interest to acquire other information. The perceptions established will also be weak in nature, capable of reversal by opposing messages or by non-media influences. In summary, our knowledge of the way people respond to communications and form their opinions suggests that the effect of campaigning, particularly through the mass media, is likely to be limited both in numbers of people who can be persuaded and in the effectiveness of that persuasion.

PERSUASION AND THE POLITICAL PROCESS

On the basis of the preceding discussion, we must conclude that it is highly unlikely that the American public is manipulated in any sense by political campaigning through the mass media or otherwise. There seems to be little or no evidence suggesting that such manipulation occurs, and both theory and existing empirical findings suggest that the possibility of its occurrence is quite small. This does not mean that no one is influenced in any way by what happens in a political campaign. Attempts to persuade by various means can be effective in certain contexts, both electoral and otherwise, and some of these will be discussed below. The point is that *manipulation* in the sense of insidious, self-serving influence wielded by anonymous technicians on the unsuspecting public (as some current criticisms of modern campaigning seem to imply) is impossible. This specter of media power is only that and, like all ghostly apparitions, vanishes in the light of fact.[29]

The Effective Use of Media Campaigning: Some Exceptions. If campaigning can change the minds of so few, why are so much money and effort devoted to it by presumably intelligent people? Aside from the not inconsequential fact that campaign funds are sometimes spent on contests in which they cannot possibly change the outcome, there are several possible answers. First of all, elections in America are often very close contests. Given that two candidates are relatively equal in the proportion of the public committed to each (as in the 1960 and 1968 presidential elections), then the relative division of the small percentage of voters who are still uncommitted will determine the outcome. In this sense, persuading a majority of 5 percent or less of the electorate who may be subject to having new perceptions easily created, can turn the tide. This will

[29] The metaphor must be credited to V. O. Key, Jr., *Public Opinion and American Democracy* (New York: Alfred A. Knopf, 1961), chap. 14.

not happen unless almost half of the total electorate already thinks a candidate worthy of their support. Campaign persuasion in this sense is an important factor, just as a candidate's physical appearance, his appeals to small minority groups, and last-minute happenings on the international scene are all important factors. None of these, however, constitute an important determinant of why one candidate wins and another loses.

Another reason why political campaigns attempt to communicate with the mass public is in order that stimuli that are consistent with previously held beliefs and do not challenge existing voting intentions are not screened out. It is in the interest of a political party to reinforce the attitudes of its committed partisans, to increase their enthusiasm for the current candidates, and to increase the probability that they will therefore actually go out and vote. This appears to be the main effect of personal contact at the precinct level, and it is likely that much of the consequence of campaigning is simply reinforcement. Reinforcement does bring dividends in electoral success, but this is hardly persuasion and certainly not manipulation.

If we shift our attention away from campaigns and elections to the broader topic of communication and opinion change, it is clear that many of the same psychological barriers to new information exist to hamper the effectiveness of all forms of "propaganda." Yet, under the right circumstances the public can be changed in its attitudes and perceptions toward various public questions. For instance, a carefully done study in two Wisconsin towns found that a public information campaign could increase the level of knowledge and produce attitudinal change on the topic of mental retardation.[30] A similar effect seems to have occurred on a national scale with respect to attitudes toward the problem of hunger and malnutrition in America, as the result of a mass media campaign in 1971. Both of these effects, however, came under certain relevant conditions: (a) there was no significant opposition to the ideas presented; (b) the arguments raised by the campaign were based on true and verifiable facts; (c) the previous knowledge of the public about the problems was limited; and (d) most importantly, deeply held values of the population were not challenged, but were activated in support of the desired attitudinal change. Thus, if a group has a good point to make with no organized opposition to it, a well-planned campaign can potentially be successful. If, on the other hand, the issue is sufficiently controversial to generate opposing arguments, if it challenges strongly held opinions, or if the campaign is based on dubious evidence, then even the most elaborate media usage is likely to have little success.

[30] Dorothy F. Douglas et al., "An Information Campaign That Changed Community Attitudes," *Journalism Quarterly*, 47 (1970), 479–87, 492.

Campaigns to increase public concern over the problems of sick and hungry children may be successful, while those designed to increase support for gun control legislation or to reduce racial prejudice face an infinitely harder task.

Implications for the Democratic Process.   Our conclusion that the public resists manipulation obviously has some positive implications for the possibility of popular control of government. It is reassuring to have some confidence that whatever public opinion may represent, it is something other than ideas subtly implanted in the public mind by those who have access to the mass media. It is worth noting here that even the most questionable attempts at persuasion are likely to be unsuccessful without at least some basis in fact. To the extent that the now famous (or infamous) commercials of 1964 that linked Barry Goldwater with nuclear destruction had any impact on the public (which is doubtful), they did so because there was serious public concern about his statements on foreign policy. Ideas expressed by candidates and parties can sometimes penetrate the perceptual screen erected by the mass public, but they are likely to have the desired effect only if they touch the existing concerns of those who hear them and if they offer at least a promise of some improvement.

The way in which the public deals with stimuli also has its negative side. As the public seals itself off from illegitimate attempts to manipulate, it also seals off logical arguments. Truth can be ignored as well as falsehood. As we have said, some of the ideas and appeals of candidates do get through the perceptual screen, but many, both good and bad, do not. Consequently, candidates who expect the rightness of their arguments and the validity of their positions to sweep them into office against an unfavorable distribution of party loyalty or the tides of events are likely to be disappointed.

A few concluding comments must be made. In our discussion of the possible effectiveness of media campaigning, we have implicitly assumed the existence of a political and social system that allows a degree of competition between opposing views. When Hitler spoke, the message was carried by loudspeakers to people in factories and on the streets. More importantly, overt criticism or disagreement was not allowed to be expressed. In such a context, communication can obviously have a tremendous effect. Happily, such a situation does not exist in this or most other societies. Even if one candidate for office has a tremendous advantage in resources to purchase media use, considerable offsetting competition is still provided by news coverage of his opponent, opinions expressed by editors and columnists, the efforts of party workers, and, above all, by interpersonal communication. And the relative advantage of the candidate who leads in media exposure is likely to have greatly diminished returns in actual impact on the public.[31]

Since we have drawn upon comparisons with commercial product advertising at several points, let us make one more such parallel to put the use of media in politics into proper perspective. If an advertising manager, through the spending of millions of dollars, is able to persuade 1 percent of all cigarette smokers to switch to his employer's brand, then he will be a success. A political consultant who does the same for his candidate will be likely to face future unemployment.[32] We must be careful of drawing too many conclusions about politics from the world of detergents, soft drinks, and patent medicines.

The mass media do play a significant role in modern society and in the political process. As an influence on individual opinion formation and political behavior, however, they are simply one of many social and psychological factors, and it is these other factors that determine media impact.

[31] It appears that the marginal effect of product advertising almost always decreases as the amount of advertising increases. See Julian L. Simon, *Issues in the Economics of Advertising* (Urbana: University of Illinois Press, 1970), chap. 1.

[32] This example is suggested by Raymond A. Bauer, "The Obstinate Audience," *American Psychologist,* 19 (1964), 319–28.

Individual Opinion Formation: A Summary Model

8

In the preceding five chapters we have discovered a considerable number of factors that go into the formation of the opinions held by an individual. Opinions are part of the system of mental functioning that aids people in keeping their psychological balance, and any given opinion is therefore tied to others. Opinions seem to flow in part from the values a person learns in childhood and are constantly subject to influence from the individuals with whom one communicates. A person's social and demographic attributes can sometimes offer a good prediction of his opinions, particularly when those tendencies are reinforced by conscious identification with a group. Opinions also seem to follow patterns of cultural variation along historical or geographic lines. Finally, opinions about public matters involve information that is derived, directly or indirectly, from various media of communication. For all of these factors we can find empirical evidence linking influence with opinions, and we can offer logical explanations for the linkages. Our purpose in this chapter is to sort out the various contributions to opinion formation and to offer a reasonably simple pattern of explanation as to how they interact to produce an opinion.

It is important to realize that the antecedents of opinions are not, in theory, distinct and separate influences. They are different manifestations of the same things. To put it another way, they represent different levels of explanation. Let us illustrate the point with an admittedly stereotyped example of a white southern male who opposes school integration. At the level of political culture, the individual in question has always lived in a society in which norms of white supremacy and racial separation have been dominant. At the level of socialization, such values were learned by him as they were by his peers. The man also has certain social attributes (race, sex, geographical residence, economic status, membership in a particular religious denomination) that exhibit a correlation with attitudes on racial questions. At a psychological level, this individual has internalized a set of attitudes toward race so that they are a part of his self-image, which must be defended by exhibiting a set of pro-segregation opinions. Finally, the man learns about proposed or actual school integration through the mass media (which may exhibit a bias along local cultural lines), and this information is interpreted in a way consistent with his existing beliefs. At the end of the process, an opinion emerges that is easily predicted, as most of the influences in this example would tend to have similar effects upon opinions. The point is that opinions are a product of all of these factors, both external and internal, but that the factors themselves are highly interrelated and that one (e.g., socialized values) is largely a more specific and contemporary manifestation of another (e.g., historically developed culture). But the factors are not so strongly associated as to form an undifferentiated mass nor are they always consistent in their impact on opinions. In the case of our hypothetical southerner, one could expect to find other individuals who grew up in much the same setting, yet had developed much more liberal opinions. Our task here is to attempt to specify the most important lines of association between these various factors and the way that they interact to produce specific opinions.

Our goal is to suggest a *model* of opinion formation that will demonstrate the role which each of the previously mentioned factors plays. By "model" we mean *a simplified, abstracted statement that represents the characteristic pattern of relationships involved in opinion formation.* Models of this type, being oversimplified, are not "true" statements in themselves, but rather are developed because they have "heuristic" value (i.e., they are useful in helping us to see relationships and gain a greater understanding of the total picture). A number of models have been applied to the problem of opinion formation. One that was mentioned earlier is the "stimulus-organism-response" model used by early voting studies (Chapter 3), which emphasizes a determination of opinions by external social forces. Another is the "funnel of causality," which emphasizes how political behavior is built up over time from past experiences and influences until a particular act, such as voting for a candidate, is produced.[1] Such models have been useful in guiding research and increasing comprehension of certain factors in the opinion formation process. Yet they tend to be somewhat overly general in nature and do not include all of the relevant factors that directly or indirectly go into the making of an opinion. We shall here attempt to construct a more comprehensive and specific model. To increase its usefulness, the

[1] This orientation is developed in Chapter 2 of Angus Campbell *et al.*, *The American Voter* (New York: John Wiley, 1960). For a graphic presentation, see Bernard C. Hennessy, *Public Opinion*, 2nd ed. (Belmont, Calif.: Wadsworth, 1970), pp. 186–92.

model should do several things. First, it should include the various factors that seem to be related to opinions and should specify the relationships between these factors. It should be based as much as possible on existing empirical findings. Finally, it should be such that the model as a whole could conceivably be subjected to empirical confirmation or rejection, given sufficient resources and appropriate means. We shall begin by examining a specific model based on empirical findings and then attempt to generalize that model to take into account a broader range of influences.

A CAUSAL MODEL OF VOTING BEHAVIOR

The existing piece of empirical analysis that comes closest to our need for a summary model of individual opinion formation is Arthur S. Goldberg's causal analysis of variables related to individual voting behavior.[2] The analysis is based upon data from the Survey Research Center's 1956 election study; what makes it unique is that the interrelationships between a number of independent variables are analyzed so as to demonstrate the causal linkages leading up to the voting decision. Since the idea of causal modeling is not intuitively obvious, yet has great value in increasing our understanding, we shall attempt to explain briefly what is involved.[3]

Suppose that we were to measure three different characteristics of some sort of sample of population and found that each was positively associated with the other two (i.e., that where X was high for an individual case, so were Y and Z). This pattern of association is depicted in diagram (1) of Figure 8-1. Perhaps we are interested in going beyond the simple fact that the different factors vary together and wish to speak in terms of one *causing* another. The single pattern in (1) could be a result of a number of causal patterns, some of which are represented by diagrams (2) through (5). Through the process of causal modeling, it is possible to test these various causal patterns and see which one best describes the data. Take pattern (4), for example. If this was indeed the true causal relationship, then the observed relationship between Y and Z would be *spurious* (i.e., the two would vary together only because both were caused by X, and if one were to control statistically for the effect of X, then Y and Z would show no significant correlation between them). An example of such a spurious relationship would be the observation that higher consumption of ice cream cones (Y) is associated with less juvenile delin-

---

[2] Arthur S. Goldberg, "Discerning a Causal Pattern Among Data on Voting Behavior," *American Political Science Review*, 60 (1966), 913–22.

[3] For a complete presentation of causal analysis, see Hubert M. Blalock, Jr., *Causal Inferences in Non-Experimental Research* (Chapel Hill: University of North Carolina Press, 1964).

Figure 8-1
Patterns of Association and Causation

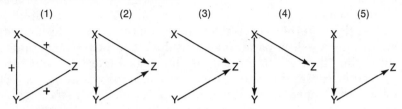

(1) = Observed pattern of association between three variables.
(2), (3), (4), (5) = Possible patterns of causation, assuming that Z is the dependent variable.

quency among children (Z); such a relationship would presumably not be causal, but would rather be a spurious one produced by some variable such as family income (X).[4] Application of the techniques of causal influence can therefore be of considerable use in identifying such spurious relationships, since they are not always so obvious in substance (e.g., if the Y variable were television viewing instead of ice cream eating.

In order to actually construct and test a causal model, certain assumptions must be made. One of these is the *direction* of the causality (i.e., which variable is the mover and which the moved).[5] In many cases, we can make the assumption fairly simply on the basis of the variables involved, particularly if there is a time dimension involved. Attributes of fathers may cause those of their children, but not the other way around. Or it may be that one variable is simply not capable of changing the other as society presently operates (e.g., having a college education may bring about certain political attitudes, but acquiring the attitudes will not bring about the award of a college career). "Cause," in the sense we are using it here, therefore means that we have observed a degree of association between variables that cannot be attributed to any other factors and that the direction of the causation is compatible with our knowledge of the real world.

With this background in mind, we can now look at Goldberg's analysis of individual voting behavior. Six variables were measured for each respondent: (a) father's social characteristics,[6] (b) respon-

[4] The example is suggested in Hubert M. Blalock, Jr., *Social Statistics* (New York: McGraw-Hill, 1960), pp. 337–38.

[5] Techniques have been developed to deal with reciprocal causation, but we will not deal with them here. See Hubert M. Blalock, Jr., *Theory Construction: From Verbal to Mathematical Formulations* (Englewood Cliffs, N.J.: Prentice-Hall, 1969).

[6] "Social characteristics" for both respondent and father were values on a combined index that included race, religion, region, class, and community size. See Goldberg, "Discerning a Causal Pattern," p. 922.

dent's social characteristics, (c) father's party identification, (d) respondent's party identification, (e) respondent's partisan attitudes,[7] and (f) respondent's vote for president in the 1956 election. Goldberg analyzes the patterns of association between these variables and then tests various possible patterns of causality. The pattern that appears to offer the "best fit" to the data is shown in Figure 8-2 and shows only those causal linkages that are statistically significant. The numbers that appear along the arrows are *beta weights* (standardized regression coefficients), which may be thought of as relative measures of the influence that one variable has upon another when the influence of other variables is removed.

The pattern presented by this model demonstrates important generalizations about the way in which individual preferences are formed. First, it shows the influence of the socialization process. The

Figure 8-2
A Causal Model of Individual Voting Behavior

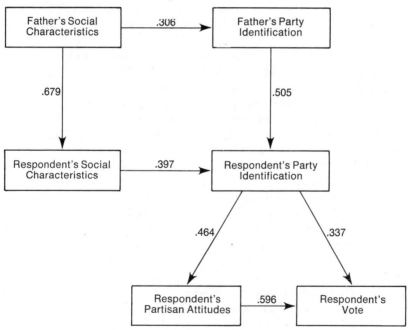

Source: Arthur S. Goldberg, "Discerning a Causal Pattern Among Data on Voting Behavior," *American Political Science Review*, 60 (1966), 919.

[7] "Partisan attitudes" is a single measure constructed from responses to questions dealing with six different dimensions of partisan evaluation (foreign affairs, Eisenhower, Stevenson, domestic issues, group-related attitudes, and attitudes toward parties as managers of government). This way of aggregating political attitudes is used in Campbell *et al.*, *The American Voter*, chaps. 3, 4, and 6.

most important influence on the voter's political party identification is the party loyalty he perceived in his father. Social characteristics also play a role in affecting the partisan preferences of both generations. Note, however, that there is no direct linkage between the social characteristics of the father and the party identification of the respondent. Such characteristics as class and religion of one's parents are important, but only indirectly, as they exercise a strong influence over the attributes that will be possessed by the child. Further, the effects of these parental and social factors on partisan attitudes and voting behavior are all indirect, being mediated through the respondent's party identification. Thus, according to this model, the various sociological regularities that we earlier observed to be related to the voting decision are so related because group membership affects party loyalties. Finally, we see that the vote is a function of both partisan attitudes and identification, the effect of the first being somewhat greater. However, attitudes themselves result in part from established party loyalties. This illustrates the principle that perceptions and opinions tend to be formed in consonance with previously held values. Since party identification is one such value that tends to be deeply rooted (having been acquired in early socialization), it is not surprising that Republicans tended to view Eisenhower as relatively better than Stevenson, while Democrats perceived Stevenson as better. All of these relationships can be independently verified and we have already discussed most of them. The important contributions of this causal analysis are to provide a way of viewing the whole set of variables simultaneously and of distinguishing between direct and indirect linkages. We might have been able to hypothesize the existence of a model of this type, but the causal technique provides an empirical basis and therefore should increase our confidence in the result.

The model is not an ideal and perfect one (as the real world is never as simple as our conceptualizations of it).[8] Above all, it is *probabilistic*. People *tend* to have the same party loyalty as their fathers did, but the relationship is quite imperfect. Overall, the degree of explanation of voting behavior is about one-half of the total variation. This constitutes a strong relationship in social science and would offer a good prediction for individual cases, but it indicates that we are only halfway along the road to a perfect explanation of individual political behavior. More precise and accurate measurement of these variables as well as inclusion of other factors would increase

---

[8] It should be noted that the same limitations extend to explanatory models in any field of inquiry, not just in the social sciences. Even the laws of physics are actually probabilistic, though with a higher predictive capacity than generalizations about human behavior.

the accuracy of the model, but we would not expect to completely explain political behavior. Goldberg does suggest some ways in which the model might be improved if data were available. One such improvement would be to measure an individual's perception of political events, which would certainly be related to his evaluations of parties and candidates. Another improvement would be to measure the variables at different points in time. An individual's attitudes in the past will have a great effect upon those in the future; his vote at one election may influence that at the next. We shall keep these ideas in mind as we proceed to the next step: attempting to outline a more general model of individual opinion formation.

TOWARD A MODEL OF OPINION FORMATION

The analysis presented by Goldberg dealt with voting behavior as the end product of the causal chain, and the other variables were cast in a partisan context. It is possible, however, to replace these variables with more generalized ones and to add some aspects not measured before, without straying too far from knowledge based upon empirical findings.

Rather than being limited to attitudes toward political parties, we can speak more broadly in terms of "values." By these we mean the very basic attitudes and orientations that characterize and shape our evaluations and expectations about elements of the political and social system. Values would include the kind of cultural assumptions we make about the role of the political system, attitudes toward other races and ethnic groups, and ideological views on both economic and noneconomic dimensions. Party identification is a peculiarly important example of a value in the United States, but it is only one of many. As we saw earlier, values are manifest at different levels of the opinion formation process. We should deal with them both as basic cultural values (i.e., the values transmitted by the family through childhood political socialization and by association with peers throughout one's life) and, most importantly, as values held by the individual (i.e., the values that have been internalized into his self-image). Internalized values result, directly or indirectly, from various external influences, and they also are affected by the individual's place in the social order. In this model the physical, economic, and social environment would be measured by the person's position on various relevant sociological variables—race, religion, economic status, and the like. If we were to attempt to operationalize such a model, it would be necessary to treat each of these factors separately, but we shall treat them all as one category for the sake of simplicity.

Goldberg's causal model had the voting decision as its final dependent variable; our goal is to predict and explain an opinion on a particular issue at a particular point in time. We can put the elements together in a causal ordering like that shown in Figure 8-3. This model conceptualizes the opinion as being a product of the interaction between an existing set of opinions and new information about the world. This new information, of course, will most often come through some form of mass media, but it must be perceived by the individual before it can affect him, and that perception, as the model suggests, will be greatly conditioned by previously held opinions. There is an inherent time dimension in this model, as its antecedents

Figure 8-3
A Model of Individual Opinion Formation

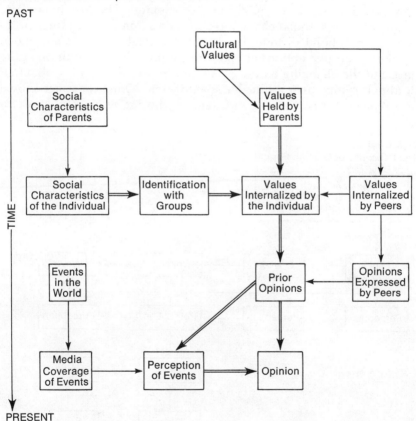

Arrows represent causal relationships. Double lines indicate relationships hypothesized to be of relatively greater magnitude.

go back to the previous generation and beyond. It is the particular way in which past and present combine that determines the nature of the opinion that emerges.

Thus, we have constructed a model that comes reasonably close to the criteria set forth at the start of this chapter. It is general in nature, yet empirically grounded, including what seem to be the major relevant factors, but it is still not so detailed as to be incomprehensible. There are, of course, refinements that might be suggested; other variables might be added and additional causal linkages could be present. One aspect that deserves note is the fact that the opinion formation process is a dynamic one. New information is constantly being received and opinions are always being revised, if ever so slightly. A complete paradigm of explanation should mention this dynamic, temporal character of opinion formation. Figure 8-4 suggests how this dynamic factor might be represented. The less immediate factors of values, social characteristics, and so on exercise their influence at each point in time, but theirs is a relatively constant effect. Opinions and perceptions at one time strongly influence those at the next, but the changing nature of the public world can bring about attitudinal change over a broader span of time. One aspect not shown in either model is the overt behavior of the individual. When opin-

Figure 8-4
The Dynamics of Opinion Formation

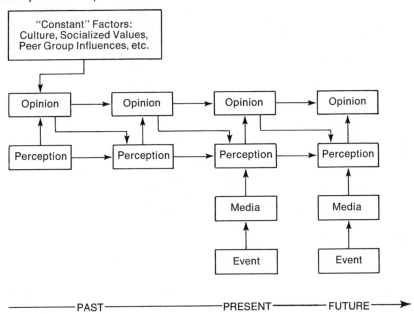

ions result in some physical act (such as voting, expressing an opinion publicly to others, contributing resources to one side in a controversy), then the effect of that decision on future opinions and perceptions is likely to be much greater.

As we suggested at the outset of Part II, opinion formation is a complex process, involving an interaction between the individual and the world. Constructing models as we have here makes the process somewhat more comprehensible, but no model can simplify it. If our goal is to be able to predict or explain with precision how any given individual will stand on even one issue, then this discussion has failed to provide an answer. (Though it is true that models such as these might offer a useful starting place for such a monumental effort.) The question of whether or not humans are so inherently unpredictable that accurate measurement of all relevant factors would still not allow complete determination of how they will behave is a metaphysical one that we shall not attempt to answer. As a practical matter, we are not likely to have such complete and error-free data anyway. We are not able therefore to perfectly predict or explain why a particular person holds an opinion on a particular subject. If, on the other hand, our goal is to increase our understanding of what opinions mean to people generally, how they tend to be stable, under what circumstances they might change, and why different aggregates of persons hold different views on issues, then we have reached at least some degree of success. Knowing something about this complex process of individual opinion formation will increase our ability to understand the role of public opinion in the political process.

Postscript to Part II

OPINION FORMATION AND THE POLITICAL SYSTEM

We come back again to the question of rationality: do individuals form their political beliefs and behavior so as to achieve their desired goals? In psychological terms, the answer has to be an affirmative one. Since people hold opinions that satisfy psychological needs and maintain a satisfying consistency, their patterns of opinions are designed to maximize their own utility. Outside observers may not see the logic of an individual's beliefs or may criticize the correctness of his perceptions, but the individual holds his opinions to satisfy his own needs, not those of an external critic. Thus, at a purely individual level, one would have to conclude that the typical pattern of opinion holding is "rational."

However, we are concerned with the political system. Do people behave rationally in the sense that they will choose actions that will influence the actions of government in accordance with their interests? Are the hopes of political philosophers about the qualities of citizens in a democracy at all justified? Here, the appraisal is more problematical. People do not react to the political world as philosophers or logicians, or even as politicians. Attitudes and perceptions about political objects become internalized and therefore are treated as a part of the self. Hence, the reaction to political stimuli will depend more on personal needs than on objective reality. On the other hand, those political objects that are not internalized are apt to be of so little salience that they are largely ignored by most individuals. In neither case are the criteria for the ideal democratic citizen likely to be met.

But if the public does not measure up to some hypothetical standard of political responsibility, neither is it completely irresponsible. The relationship of social characteristics to opinions indicates that reality does penetrate the perceptual screen with regularity and that on those issues that directly affect their lives, most individuals hold opinions consistent with their interests. Those who would seek to persuade and mobilize the public may despair at their stubbornness and apathy, yet these same attributes form a powerful barrier against attempts at illegitimate manipulation. For most of the public most of the time, most of the world of public affairs is of little importance. When the political does begin to touch the personal, people react strongly and often responsibly.

PART III

PUBLIC OPINION
IN CONTEMPORARY
AMERICA:
MACRO-POLITICS

Belief Systems of the American Public

9

Thus far, we have concentrated on the questions of who hold particular opinions and how they arrive at them, while giving only passing attention to the substance of the opinions themselves. We shall now shift our focus for several chapters to the patterns of opinion held by Americans today on several types of issues and examine the implications of public opinion in these areas for the political process. The logical starting point for this examination is that of the most basic attitudes held by the public toward political objects and the interrelationship between these attitudes.

THE PROBLEM OF IDEOLOGY

A simple way of organizing a large amount of information about the preferences of individuals on a number of issues would be to describe the *ideologies* held by the American public—how many "liberals," "conservatives," and so on there are. We have already used these terms as convenient ways for describing the policy positions favored by difficult groups. Yet this should not imply that we are safe in assuming that most Americans possess any sort of "ideology,"—liberal, conservative, or otherwise. The concept of a political ideology is one used in many different ways, but it usually implies some measure of a political philosophy (i.e., some consciously accepted set of beliefs that fit together into some sort of logical system and produce opinions on particular issues). When we think of ideologies in a strict sense, we think of the various "isms" that have arisen from time to time in the modern world—communism, capitalism, fascism, etc. Yet from what we know about the process of individual opinion formation, we would suspect that relatively few people have these conscious, well-developed, sets of beliefs that fall neatly into philosophical categories. As we shall see shortly, one must even be very careful in describing many Americans as "liberal" or "conservative." In short, ideology is a concept that is not very useful in analyzing the opinions of the mass public.

For reasons such as this, Converse suggests the alternative concept of a *belief system*, which he defines as "a configuration of ideas and attitudes in which the elements are bound together by some form of constraint or functional interdependence." [1] The fact that a person has a belief system does not imply that his ideas fit into any philosophical system. His beliefs are not completely unrelated, but they may be held together by the functioning of the psychological process and by the expectations of others in society, as well as by logic or philosophy. This concept is quite consistent with our understanding of the functional nature of opinions, for we have seen how an individual's opinions are often a reflection of his personal needs in combination with certain socialized values acquired from experiences in the larger society. Belief systems have a consistency, but it is internal and personal in nature, not necessarily resembling any existing philosophy. While we shall use ideological terms such as "liberal" in our examination of belief systems, we shall do so only for the purpose of simplicity in describing political positions, and not with the intent of implying any particular logical pattern of political philosophy.

Interrelationships Between Opinions. While trying to identify ideological or philosophical positions poses many problems in social research, it is not difficult to identify particular positions on issues of current public interest as being "liberal" or "conservative" positions. In the period since World War II, few would question the fact that political liberals have favored government spending for social welfare activities, increased protection for racial minorities, foreign aid, and the upholding of procedural rights of individuals over government. Conservatives are generally acknowledged to take the opposite point of view. Questions involving each of these issues have been widely debated and the arguments on both sides made abundantly clear. What has been the response of the public?

A simple way of ascertaining the extent to which individuals tend to think in consistently liberal or conservative terms is to compare the opinions of survey respondents on two separate issues. Several such comparisons are presented in Table 9-1. In each case, the consistently liberal position is represented by the upper left-hand corner (e.g., people favoring both medicare and school integration), while the lower right-hand corner represents the proportion of the total taking the opposite, conservative position on both issues. The other two corners show the proportion taking ideologically inconsistent posi-

[1] Philip E. Converse, "The Nature of Belief Systems in Mass Publics," in *Ideology and Discontent,* ed. David E. Apter (New York: Free Press of Glencoe, 1964), p. 207.

Table 9-1

Interrelationship Between Opinions on Pairs of Issues

(1) *School Integration Compared to Medicare*

		School Integration		
		Favor	Depends, No Opinion	Oppose
	Favor	24%	10%	16%
Medicare	Depends, no opinion	9	6	7
	Oppose	9	5	14

$\overline{100\%}$ N = 1,450

(2) *School Integration Compared to Foreign Aid*

		School Integration		
		Favor	Depends, No Opinion	Oppose
	Favor	26%	9%	17%
Foreign Aid	Depends, no opinion	10	7	12
	Oppose	5	4	9

$\overline{100\%}$ N = 1,450

(3) *Medicare Compared to Foreign Aid*

		Medicare		
		Favor	Depends, No Opinion	Oppose
	Favor	28%	10%	15%
Foreign Aid	Depends, no opinion	13	8	8
	Oppose	9	4	5

$\overline{100\%}$ N = 1,450

(4) *Domestic Economic Liberalism Scale Compared to Firing of Government Workers Accused of Being Communists*

		Liberalism		
		High	Medium, Unscaled	Low
	Disagree	18%	29%	10%
Fire Suspects	Depends, no opinion	6	14	2
	Agree	8	10	2

$\overline{100\%}$ N = 1,761

Sources: (1), (2), and (3) computed from the 1964 election study conducted by the Survey Research Center (University of Michigan). (4) is recomputed from V. O. Key, Jr., *Public Opinion and American Democracy* (New York: Alfred A. Knopf, 1961), p. 171.

tions.[2] As each of the pairs of issues shows, only a minority of the population demonstrates consistently liberal or conservative positions. In the tables dealing with school integration, medicare, and foreign aid, about 40 percent of the total sample are consistent in approving or disapproving of both policies, while about a quarter approve of one and disapprove of the other. In the last table, which compares opinions on the handling of suspected subversives during the 1950s with a domestic economic liberalism scale, consistency is even less frequent. True, in each of these cases, there is a statistical tendency for those who are liberal on one issue to be liberal on another, but it is a weak one, and it is clear that a majority of the respondents fail to demonstrate a consistent pattern of responses. Furthermore, this evidence compares only two issues at a time, and the proportion who demonstrate a consistency of response would be further diminished if they were subjected to an additional test.

This tendency for substantial parts of the American public simultaneously to hold a liberal position on one type of issue and a conservative view on another has been widely demonstrated.[3] However, many of these findings date from the late 1950s, an era not generally noted for its ideological emphasis. A number of more recent studies have investigated this question of the interrelationship between opinions on different issues.[4] In general, the findings have revealed an increased tendency of Americans to hold opinions that fall along consistent liberal or conservative lines. However, even this greater level of consistency is still far from perfect, particularly when one moves from one type of issue to another. Within a range of similar policy questions there is a substantial degree of relationship, though there will always be significant parts of the population that do not display the expected pattern. Domestic economic questions—such as government responsibility for insuring prosperity and full employment, spending for many social welfare purposes, and government regulation of business—form one such cluster of issues. Questions involving racial equality form another cluster, which shows a slight

[2] The cross-tabulation in Table 9-1 combines responses of "no response," "depends," etc., into "no opinion" category for reasons of simplicity. This manipulation does not affect the implications of the data.

[3] E.g., Converse, "Nature of Belief Systems," p. 228; V. O. Key, Jr., *Public Opinion and American Democracy* (New York: Alfred A. Knopf, 1961), chap. 7.

[4] Stephen Earl Bennett, "Consistency Among the Public's Social Welfare Policy Attitudes in the 1960's," *American Journal of Political Science*, 17 (1973), 544–70. See also Robert S. Erikson and Norman R. Luttbeg, *American Public Opinion: Its Origins, Content, and Impact* (New York: John Wiley, 1973), pp. 78–86. Interestingly, the level of relationship between attitudes on a number of issues appears to have *declined* between 1970 and 1972, according to Arthur H. Miller *et al.*, "A Majority Party in Disarray: Policy Polarization in the 1972 Elections," paper delivered at the American Political Science Association, New Orleans, September 4–8, 1973, p. 34.

relationship to the first. However, when we move to issues such as freedom of expression and criminal procedure, or foreign affairs, the tendency to be consistently liberal or conservative is rather weak. The more informed and politically active an individual is, the more likely he is to display ideologically regular opinions. Yet even political elites, such as congressmen, often display seemingly inconsistent patterns of opinion and behavior. And issues can arise that do not at all conform to the usual liberal-conservative patterns of alliance, the outstanding example being that of the Vietnam war, which split liberal northern Democrats into two warring camps in 1968. Thus, we must be very careful of assuming that the public will view the interrelationship of public issues according to any set pattern. If we set out to describe the mood of the electorate in terms of moving to the Left or Right (as we will attempt in Chapter 12), we must be specific as to the issues involved.

Conceptualization in the Mass Public.   If the public, for the most part, does not form its political opinions along consistent ideological lines, how does it conceptualize the political world? An answer to this question is suggested by a Survey Research Center analysis of data from its 1956 election study.[5] In this survey, respondents were asked open-ended questions about what they liked and disliked about the parties and candidates. Responses were then evaluated as a whole to ascertain the kinds of criteria the individuals seemed to be using in forming their political judgments. The results are presented in Table 9-2. Some respondents, constituting a tiny minority of the total, expressed some notion of the classic liberal-conservative continuum, though their comments were hardly examples of sophisticated political thought. A somewhat larger group was classified into a "near-ideology" category; these either used the terms "liberal" and "conservative" with little or no indication that they were aware of their content, or else mentioned some fundamental issue dividing the ideologies, usually the economic issue. Even by these generous criteria for ideological thinking, hardly more than 10 percent of the sample reflected a tendency to conceptualize in ideological terms. At the other end of the scale was a somewhat larger group of citizens who displayed virtually no awareness of particular issues in thinking about politics, but rather expressed at best only party loyalty or views on the personal attributes of candidates. The remaining two-thirds of the public fell between these two extremes, viewing politics in terms either of "group benefits" or "the nature of the times." The classic example of the group benefits level is the working man

[5] Presented in Chapter 10 of Angus Campbell *et al., The American Voter* (New York: John Wiley, 1960).

Table 9-2
Levels of Conceptualization in the Mass Public, 1956

Level	Proportion of Total Sample
Ideology	
Ideology	2½%
Near-ideology	9
Group Benefits	
Perception of conflict	14
Single-group interest	17
Shallow group-benefit responses	11
Nature of the Times	24
No Issue Content	
Party orientation	4
Candidate orientation	9
No content	5
Unclassified	4½

Source: Angus Campell *et al., The American Voter* (New York: John Wiley, 1960), p. 249.

who sees the Democrats as doing more for "people like me" and the Republicans as the "party of the rich." Slightly less sophisticated voters respond to their perception of whether the nation is prosperous or not, at peace or war, and the like. Both the "group benefits" and "nature of the times" types of conceptualization are likely to result in an emphasis on economic issues, though questions of race can also be dealt with in this manner. Clearly, most Americans have not been accustomed to thinking of political questions in an ideological framework.

As our discussion of the relationship between opinions on different issues has suggested, there seems to have been a trend in recent years toward a greater degree of ideological conceptualization. Surveys done in conjunction with the 1964 election reveal that the proportion of the public displaying an ideological or near-ideological level of conceptualization had risen to 27 percent, most of the increase coming at the expense of the "group benefits" category.[6] This may indicate an increasing trend toward ideology in the mass public, though at least part of the shift may have resulted simply from the public emphasis on liberalism versus conservatism that

[6] Erikson and Luttbeg, *American Public Opinion*, pp. 71–74. See also John C. Pierce, "Party Identification and the Changing Role of Ideology in American Politics," *Midwest Journal of Political Science*, 14 (1970), 25–42, and John Osgood Field and Ronald E. Anderson, "Ideology in the Public's Conceptualization of the 1964 Presidential Election," *Public Opinion Quarterly*, 33 (1969), 380–98.

characterized the 1964 campaign, rather than from any fundamental change in the way most people look at politics. In any event, it still is probably safe to say that the great majority of Americans are not "ideologues" in even the loosest sense of that term.

The Lack of Ideology: Some Possible Reasons.   Political issues are frequently expounded in ideological terms, not only by their advocates and opponents, but also in their coverage by the news media. Why is public opinion so deficient in ideological structure? One obvious possibility is that most people simply lack familiarity with ideological concepts or even the ideas of "liberal" and "conservative." Converse reports an exploration of this question in which respondents were asked the meaning of these terms and to match up the appropriate ideologies with the Republican and Democratic parties.[7] Only 60 percent of the sample was prepared to attempt a complete answer; of these over 80 percent gave at least a minimally acceptable definition of "liberal" and "conservative" and associated the Democratic and Republican parties, respectively, with those terms. At most, about half the population possessed the necessary knowledge to think along the usual ideological lines. This figure may even be a bit high, since it overlooks the possibility that some of the correct matches of ideology and party were based upon correct guessing, rather than actual understanding. Also, the criteria for acceptance of ideological definitions were quite low, and a large part of these definitions consisted only of the notion that liberals spend money more freely than conservatives. Thus, we find the same sort of result as in our comparison of opinions on different types of issues— that something less than half of the public displays any minimal evidence of thinking along ideological lines, that this consistency exists mainly for economic issues, and that probably only a very small minority are consistently and consciously liberal or conservative across a broad range of issues. Part of this pattern is due to a lack of familiarity with ideological concepts, but there are some indications that the public is even less ideological than its familiarity with concepts would indicate.

There are some other possible explanations of why most individuals fail to display consistently liberal or conservative opinions. One is that people lack either sufficient knowledge of particular issues or sufficient intensity to hold definite opinions on many issues. As the cross-tabulations presented in Table 9-1 suggest, 40 percent or more of the respondents on these pairs of issues were unable or unwilling to state preferences on one or both questions. When we realize that those issues were among the most widely debated of the day, it is not

[7] Converse, "Nature of Belief Systems," p. 221.

hard to see that there will be large parts of the population who will fail to express their preferences on most public questions. The point here is that if a person lacks opinions on many issues, for whatever reason, then it will be impossible for him to demonstrate any consistent ideological pattern of thinking.

The whole burden for a lack of ideological thinking cannot be placed upon the mass public. Certainly, the American political system hardly encourages adherence to a single liberal-conservative dimension. While political elites usually display somewhat more consistent patterns of preference than the public does, one can certainly point to many highly visible exceptions. Some leaders favor economic liberalism, but not racial equality; some self-proclaimed conservatives are also consistent civil-libertarians. Aside from economic policy questions (and not always there) it is hard to find any policy areas that consistently divide the two major political parties.[8] Hence, one should not be surprised to find that the average citizen is not particularly consistent along liberal or conservative lines.

There is no inherent reason to expect the mass public to think in ideological terms or to display certain patterns of preference. Notions of liberal or conservative philosophy represent only an external framework of belief systems derived rather haphazardly from the writings of past thinkers, current spokesmen, and certain historical occurrences. To expect to apply such schemes to the opinions of people who have no particular knowledge of or interest in the antecedents of these philosophies is foolish. If we know anything about opinion formation in the mass public, it is that opinions are intensely personal and internal, that they are a product of psychological needs, socialized beliefs, and personal experiences. To postulate any inherent relationship between how a man sees government responsibility in insuring economic stability and how he will view the international scene is to ignore the sources of both opinions. In short, there are no strong forces compelling Americans to form their opinions along consistently liberal or conservative lines across a range of issues; indeed, there are a number of inherent factors that work to discourage widespread regularity.

FUNDAMENTAL POLITICAL ATTITUDES IN THE UNITED STATES

Some patterns of political attitude in a society are so basic that they serve as a basis for the distribution of public opinion on many more

---

[8] See, for example, the data in Herbert F. Weisberg and Jerrold G. Rusk, "Dimensions of Candidate Evaluation," *American Political Science Review*, 64 (1970), 1167–85.

specific issues. Such patterns of belief, as we suggested in Chapter 6, constitute the political culture of a system. We shall not attempt in this book to completely characterize the political culture of the United States.[9] However, in the following sections, we shall outline the characteristic pattern of orientations for two aspects of the political process that determine the nature of any political culture and for a third—race—that is peculiarly relevant to the American experience.

Attitudes Toward Political Authority.   Perhaps the most basic element of a political culture comprises the affective attitudes of its population toward the government as an institution and toward other elements of the political and social system. How much support does the public give to government as a general object? What does it expect from government and are its expectations fulfilled? Does it see itself as having any influence over what government does? The answers to questions like these are necessary for an understanding of the distribution of opinion on specific questions of public policy.

At the most general level, we tend to overlook this basic element. It may seem obvious that, outside of a situation of repressive dictatorship, the citizens in a political system would have to be reasonably supportive of institutions and policies, for if they were not, there would at least be serious attempts to bring about change. Yet this is not necessarily the case. Banfield describes the culture of a remote and poverty-stricken village in southern Italy as being typified by "amoral familism." [10] In this society, there seems to be little support for, or confidence in, any group or institution outside the family group. People distrust not only local and national government, but also the church, political parties, businesses, and fellow citizens. Such a situation is not typical of political systems generally, nor of the Italian. Yet it serves to point out that it is possible to have a political system that is neither repressive nor revolutionary in which citizen orientations toward political authority are not positive.

It does not require reference to large amounts of survey data to see that most Americans hold far more positive views of their government, other social institutions, and each other than did the villagers studied by Banfield. Yet historians and others who have sought to generalize about how Americans feel toward their political world seem to come to contradictory conclusions. Some have emphasized a tradition of feelings of independence from government and a ten-

---

[9] For a comprehensive analysis, utilizing survey data to test the assumptions of historians and philosophers, see Donald J. Devine, *The Political Culture of the United States: The Influence of Member Values on Regime Maintenance* (Boston: Little, Brown, 1972).

[10] Edward C. Banfield, *The Moral Basis of a Backward Society* (Glencoe: Free Press, 1958).

dency to create private organizations to carry out tasks that government might normally be expected to perform. Others can point out long-standing traditions of fierce loyalty and support for the nation and its political institutions, particularly when these are perceived as being under attack. On one hand, the presidential office is seen to have great prestige and corresponding power; on the other, it seems as though its occupants are always under attack and lacking in the authority to accomplish what is expected of them. Perhaps it is difficult to reach consensus on the general level of support and affection Americans have for their political institutions because they hold an ambivalent view of politics, one containing elements of both love and hate. This is illustrated by the esteem accorded to persons in public office. Surveys of the prestige accorded to various job titles reveal that governmental officials (Supreme Court justices, senators, mayors, etc.) consistently rank at the top of the list, mixed with a few professional titles (physicians, lawyers, scientists).[11] Yet other surveys indicate that "politicians" are regarded with some disdain, that they are widely thought to be dishonest, and that most parents "wouldn't want my son to be one." [12] Any president of the United States can look forward to appearing prominently on the annual list of "Most Admired Men," with a similar honor accorded to his wife, but he must also look forward to as little as half of the population giving their approval to his performance in office. In short, Americans hold seemingly contradictory attitudes about their political system and its leaders, combining respect—and even awe—with criticism and occasional distrust.[13]

These seeming contradictions come about because people hold attitudes toward the political system on several different levels. Individuals may hold attitudes simultaneously toward an institution as a symbol or an ideal, toward appraisals of particular officeholders and their performance, and toward the general policies carried out by a series of officeholders of the institution. Thus, a man may hold the office of president in high respect, dislike its current occupant, and still support the basic kinds of policies that the incumbent and his predecessors have advocated. In this way, the American public often displays ambivalent patterns of support for the political system.

To generalize about these patterns is somewhat difficult, for de-

[11] Robert W. Hodge, Paul M. Siegel, and Peter H. Rossi, "Occupational Prestige in the United States: 1925–1963," in *Class, Status, and Power: Social Stratification in Comparative Perspective*, ed. Rheinhard Bendix and Seymour Martin Lipset, 2nd ed., (New York: Free Press, 1966), pp. 322–34.

[12] On this point, see William Mitchell, "The Ambivalent Social Status of the American Politician," *Western Political Quarterly*, 12 (1959), 683–98.

[13] For additional thoughts and evidence on this ambivalent pattern of public attitudes, see Robert E. Lane, "The Politics of Consensus in an Age of Affluence," *American Political Science Review*, 59 (1965), 874–95.

grees of support will vary with the times and with the particular in-dicator of support used as a reference point. To the extent that one can speak in general terms, it might be said that support tends to be greatest for political institutions and ideals at the symbolic level, with relatively strong support for many, but not all, of the most im-portant patterns of existing public policy, while appraisals of particu-lar individuals and their actions tend to draw more negative reac-tions. Certainly there is much evidence to justify the statement that the great majority of Americans do not question the legitimacy and desirability of the basic structural and functional arrangements that result in policy. When questions of possible change in constitutional or other structural arrangements enter into the arena of public de-bate, these are of a decidedly minor nature. A two-term limit of presi-dential tenure, a more specific and up-to-date system to deal with presidential disability and succession, possible reform or abolition of the electoral college, and the like, hardly suggest that there is deep dissatisfaction with basic institutional arrangements. And when asked the question of support in a simple form, Americans have tra-ditionally given their political system strong support. Such a mea-surement requires some sort of benchmark for interpretation; com-parison with responses from other nations offers an insight. As Almond and Verba's *Civic Culture* study showed, Americans tended to express greater support for their political system than did the in-habitants of four other Western nations.[14] Table 9-3 shows this phe-nomenon quite clearly; the U.S. respondents were much more likely to mention political institutions as a source of pride than respondents of any other nation, including Britain. This pattern of relatively high support by Americans for various aspects of their government and na-tion is confirmed by other measures used in the Almond and Verba study. That Americans do express highly positive orientations toward their political world is not surprising in view of what we know about the characteristic pattern of childhood political socialization. As we saw earlier (Chapter 4), children enter the political system with an idealized view of governmental institutions and their occupants. Ap-parently this view tends to persist into adult life, at least when politi-cal objects are considered at a very general and symbolic level.

Americans also tend to give substantial, though not overwhelming, support to most of the basic policies already being pursued by gov-ernment.[15] Opinion polls regularly reveal that definite majorities

[14] Gabriel A. Almond and Sidney Verba, *The Civic Culture: Political Attitudes in Five Nations* (Princeton, N.J.: Princeton University Press, published for the Center of International Studies, 1963).

[15] On this whole topic, see Key, *Public Opinion and American Democracy*, pp. 29–32, and the discussion of "supportive consensus" in Chapter 13 of this book.

Table 9-3
Pride in Different Aspects of National Life in Five Nations, 1959–60 *

	United States	Great Britain	West Germany	Italy	Mexico
Percentage Who Say They Are Proud Of:					
Governmental, political institutions	95%	46%	7%	3%	30%
Social legislation	13	18	6	1	2
Position in international affairs	5	11	5	2	3
Economic system	23	10	33	3	24
Characteristics of people	7	18	36	11	15
Spiritual values, religion	3	1	3	6	8
Contributions to the arts	1	6	11	16	9
Contributions to science	3	7	12	3	1
Physical attributes of country	5	10	17	25	22
Nothing, don't know	4	10	15	27	16
Other	9	11	3	21	14
N	970	963	955	995	1,007

Source: Gabriel A. Almond and Sidney Verba, *The Civic Culture: Political Attitudes in Five Nations* (Princeton, N.J.: Princeton University Press, published for the Center of International Studies, 1963), p. 102. Reprinted by permission of Princeton University Press.

* Percentages in each nation add to more than 100 percent because of multiple responses.

favor social security and other domestic economic and social welfare programs, including some that may seem to be matters of political controversy, past and present.[16] Much the same is true for most questions of U.S. foreign policy and for the general performance of public officials and agencies that are less visible to the public.[17] In general, those current activities of government in the United States that are less familiar to the public and that are not perceived as directly affecting their lives will tend to receive at least nominal support from most people. This is not to imply that there is wild enthusiasm for

[16] See the data presented in Lloyd A. Free and Hadley Cantril, *The Political Beliefs of Americans: A Study of Public Opinion* (New York: Simon and Schuster, 1968), pp. 9–22.

[17] At the urging of a client, the author once included an item on a statewide survey, asking whether or not the respondent approved of the job performance of the secretary of state of Illinois, the gentleman in question having been appointed to the post only a few weeks before on the death of his predecessor. Not surprisingly, the third of the sample who were willing to venture an answer gave him their overwhelming approval.

government or that there is no desire for modification or improvement. These patterns do, however, suggest that in the absence of any particular problems, public policies and performances are generally supported by most people in the United States.

This tendency to express support for the American political system seems to be of sufficiently long standing to be considered a basic part of the political culture. However, recent years have seen a distinct trend toward a loss of confidence in the performance of the political system. Since the late 1950s—and particularly since 1964—there has been a definite rise in the proportion of Americans who express cynicism about those who hold public office. Whereas less than one-fourth of the population in 1958 and 1964 said that the government could not be trusted all of the time, almost half expressed this distrust in 1970.[18] Similar increases in cynicism were found in responses to items dealing with the notions that political leaders are dishonest, stupid, and working only for the benefit of big interests. We shall deal with this loss of political trust more fully in Chapter 12 and attempt to offer some explanation for it at that point. But while this trend is both important and disturbing, it does not negate the existence of a long-term mass support for the political system as a general object, particularly at an abstract and symbolic level. In fact, the strength of that favorable belief in the system may possibly contribute to the growth of a cynical hostility when individual leaders fail and policies are not effective. The seeds for political distrust have always been present in the American culture. As previously noted, Americans seem to have always had an ambivalent orientation toward political leadership. Even quite alienated individuals typically hold positive attitudes toward the political system as a symbolic ideal, while seeing current leaders as destructive of that ideal. Critics on the political Right may see politicians as evil because they appear to be deviating from traditional policies; those on the Left may criticize presidents for usurping congressional prerogatives or failing to uphold constitutional guarantees of individual rights. Still others, less ideologically inclined, may be alienated by what they see as a failure of government to be responsive to their preferences and to protect their interests. But in each of these cases, the criticism is of the performance of the political leadership and not of the structure and ideals of the system as the individual perceives them.

Interestingly enough, the trend of the last decade toward distrust of politicians and political parties does not necessarily prevent the public from offering political support to politicians. Even though surveys prior to the 1972 election indicated a significant degree of ques-

[18] Richard E. Dawson, *Public Opinion and Contemporary Disarray* (New York: Harper and Row, 1973), p. 47.

tioning of the character and performance of Richard Nixon, he still (like the vast majority of incumbent congressmen) won reelection by a considerable margin. Indeed, although throughout much of 1973 and the early part of 1974 there was almost a popular consensus that the president had been guilty of some improprieties in connection with Watergate, only a minority expressed a desire to see him removed from office. There are many conflicting considerations affecting the public in their reaction to distrust of political leadership. Fear of rapid change in the political structure, uncertainty about alternatives, and a lack of sureness about exactly where the problem lies are some of them. At least through 1972, the usual political process seemed to offer no resolution for this ambivalent situation. To sum it up, it appears that Americans still have retained their *support* for the political system, while losing a good part of their confidence in its operation. The final outcome of this discontinuity remains to be seen.

Attitudes Toward Individual Rights. Political theorists have often argued that maintenance of a free and democratic society requires a high degree of popular support for the "democratic consensus" (i.e., fundamental beliefs in freedom, tolerance, and equality for all). One can certainly argue that the United States has, by and large, followed policies that have increasingly tended to insure these values. Yet every few years some journalist or scientific researcher rediscovers

Table 9-4
Support and Opposition Toward Guarantees in the Bill of Rights, 1970

(1) *Peaceful Assembly:* "As long as there appears to be no clear danger of violence, do you think that any group, no matter how extreme, should be allowed to organize protests against the government?"

Yes—21%   No—76%   Sometimes—0%   No response—3%

(2) *Free Press:* "Except in time of war, do you think newspapers, radio, and television should have the right to report any story, even if the government feels it's harmful to our national interest?"

Yes—42%   No—55%   Sometimes—1%   No response—2%

(3) *Free Speech:* "Do you think everyone should have the right to criticize the government, even if the criticism is damaging to our national interest?"

Yes—42%   No—54%   Sometimes—1%   No response—3%

(4) *Double Jeopardy:* "If a man is found innocent of a serious crime, but new evidence is uncovered later, do you think that he should be tried again for the same crime?"

Yes—58%   No—38%   Sometimes—1%   No response—3%

(5) *Preventive Detention:* "If a person is suspected of a serious crime, do you think the police should be allowed to hold him in jail, until they can get enough evidence to officially charge him?"

Yes—58%   No—38%   Sometimes—1%   No response—2%

(6) *Trial by Jury:* "In most criminal cases, the judge conducts the trial and a jury decides guilt or innocence. Instead of the jury, would it be better if the judge alone decided guilt or innocence?"

Yes—14%   No—82%   Sometimes—1%   No response—3%

(7) *Search and Seizure:* "If the police suspect that drugs, guns, or other criminal evidence is hidden in someone's house, should they be allowed to enter the house without first obtaining a search warrant?"

Yes—32%   No—66%   Sometimes—1%   No response—1%

(8) *Self-Incrimination:* "At their trials, do you think suspected criminals should have the right to refuse to answer questions if they feel their answers may be used against them?"

Yes—54%   No—42%   Sometimes—1%   No response—3%

(9) *Public Trial:* "In criminal cases, do you think the government should ever have the right to hold a secret trial?"

Yes—20%   No—75%   Sometimes—1%   No response—4%

(10) *Confronting Witnesses:* "During court trials, do you think the government should ever be allowed to keep the identity of witnesses secret from the defendant?"

Yes—40%   No—54%   Sometimes—2%   No response—4%

N = 1,136

Source: Robert Chandler, *Public Opinion: Changing Attitudes on Contemporary Political and Social Issues*, A CBS News Reference Book (New York: R. R. Bowker Co., 1972), pp. 6–13.

the fact that considerable proportions of Americans fail to give their support to some of the most basic of these. (Anyone who wishes to test this hypothesis might try drafting the Bill of Rights as a petition and take it door-to-door requesting signatures. If past experience holds true, he will probably find that only a small minority is willing to sign.) There is ample evidence that this phenomenon of lack of support for what are presumed to be fundamental rights of expression and procedure is indeed widespread.[19] Table 9-4 shows the results of just such a survey conducted on behalf of CBS News. As

[19] Two of the best-known studies on this point are James W. Prothro and C. W. Grigg, "Fundamental Principles of Democracy: Bases of Agreement and Disagreement," *Journal of Politics*, 22 (1960), 278–94, and Herbert McClosky, "Consensus and Ideology in American Politics," *American Political Science Review*, 58 (1964), 361–82.

the data clearly show, there is a significant degree of opposition to this body of guarantees. While some of the procedural rights do receive majority support, even there a substantial percentage of respondents express reservations. These questions, moreover, were posed in a relatively neutral setting; had respondents been asked about freedom of speech for communists or fair-trial guarantees for persons accused of murder, the percentage supporting these constitutional guarantees would undoubtedly have been smaller.

A few mitigating factors should be noted. Additional research in the CBS project revealed that many respondents were making assumptions about who was involved in these hypothetical cases. In particular, they often explained that they were viewing these cases in the light that the Mafia wanted to take the Fifth Amendment or matters of national security were involved. Clearly, there is a definite gap between attitudes toward individual rights at an abstract level and in particular instances. When asked about whether they agree with the general idea of freedom of speech or other constitutional guarantees, the vast majority of people will indicate their approval. However, when a situation is proposed, typically suggesting that some unpopular person or cause is involved, support for rights decreases markedly. It should be noted that there are important differences within the population in attitudes toward rights and liberties. In particular, it is clear that persons who are politically active give far greater support to protection of rights than does the general public. In part this is a consequence of higher levels of education and economic status among those who are active; it would also appear that they are more knowledgeable and sensitive to problems of civil liberties. It is this group of political influentials who will inevitably have a greater impact upon government policy than the members of the mass public. In this respect, the outlook for advocates of civil liberties may not be as bleak as would seem at first glance. The point still remains that a majority of the public is unwilling to extend some basic constitutional guarantees to all, or at least to unpopular or controversial groups.

A related, but less constitutionally involved topic is the question of insuring equality for all. Leaving aside the question of racial equality for later discussion, the question of equality for all generally comes down to the question of economic equality. Again, in the abstract, Americans express almost unanimous agreement with the ideal. However, when it comes down to specific policies that tend to promote greater equality in the distribution of wealth, there is considerable opposition. Proposals that would do this—whether they limit the fortunes of the very wealthy or give more to those in the lower part of the economic spectrum—simply do not gain popular support, as Senator George McGovern found during his 1972 presidential campaign when he made his ill-fated suggestions about limiting inheritances and granting one thousand dollars to everyone. It appears that popular belief in equality extends mainly to two aspects: to political and legal equality and, in the economic realm, to equality of opportunity. Americans will support programs and policies that they perceive will increase the chances that everyone will start from an equal point in the economic race—programs such as public education, "Headstart," etc.—and therefore programs are often titled appropriately (e.g., the "Office of Economic Opportunity").

Attitudes Toward Race. An area of opinion in the United States so basic as to require special attention is that of racial attitudes. As was pointed out in Chapter 6, the question of race accounts for a good part of the cultural differences among regions of the United States. Also, many current issues that seem nonracial in substance have definite racial overtones and implications in the public mind. Antagonism, conflict, and prejudice are not unique to the United States, for in many other nations there are long histories of differences among religious, language, and economic groups that still structure contemporary politics. But the nature and intensity of the racial issue are peculiarly American, and one cannot understand American politics without understanding the implications of this issue. The whole subject of racial prejudice is a very large one; we cannot begin to illuminate it here but can only attempt to briefly outline the subject. Since our concern is with what the American public characteristically believes, our discussion will deal with the attitude of the white majority toward the black minority.

The attitude of white America toward questions involving the black community appears ambivalent and contradictory. On one hand, a majority of whites agree with the idea that blacks are entitled to the rights and privileges of citizens and express approval of many policies designed to bring about their fulfillment. On the other, substantial proportions of the white population express some reservations or hostility toward blacks and opposition to some forms of personal contact with them. Table 9-5 illustrates white attitudes in recent years on a number of racial questions. And, certainly, there is substantial *behavioral* evidence (as opposed to preferences expressed in interviews) of racial prejudice on the part of large numbers of white Americans.

If one is to understand the structure of public opinion on race, the issue must be divided into several different levels of opinion. At an abstract level, whites agree fairly strongly that all races are entitled to equality under the law and equal access to employment, public fa-

Table 9-5
Attitudes of the White Population on Various Racial Issues

(1) "If your party nominated a generally well-qualified man for President and he happened to be a Negro, would you vote for him?" (1971)

Yes—68%   No—25%   No opinion—7%

(2) "When black babies and white babies are examined right after they are born, the white babies usually have more natural intelligence. . . . Would you agree or disagree with that statement?" (1968)

Agree—14%   Disagree—58%   No opinion—28%

(3) "Do you favor or oppose open housing laws?" (1968)

Favor—40%   Oppose—39%   No opinion—21%

(4) "What about black families of your own income and education level. . . . Would you be happy or unhappy to see them move into the neighborhood or area where you now live . . . ?" (1972)

Happy—11%   Unhappy—24%   Wouldn't make much difference—60%
Don't know—5%

(5) "The mayor of a large city has ordered the police to shoot on sight anyone found looting stores during race riots. . . . Do you think this is the best way to deal with this problem?" (1968)

Best way—58%   Better way—38%   No opinion—4%

(6) "Do you approve or disapprove of marriage between whites and nonwhites?" (1968)

Approve—17%   Disapprove—76%   No opinion—7%

(7) "In general, do you favor or oppose the busing of Negro and white school children from one school district to another?" (1971)

Favor—14%   Oppose—80%   No opinion—6%

Sources: (1) Gallup Opinion Index, no. 77 (November 1971), 14; (2) Robert Chandler, Public Opinion (New York: R. R. Bowker Co., 1972), p. 20; (3) Gallup Opinion Index, no. 40 (October 1968), 31; (4) William Watts and Lloyd A. Free, State of the Nation (New York: Potomac Associates, 1973), p. 285; (5) Gallup Opinion Index, no. 37 (July 1968), 17; (6) Gallup Opinion Index, no. 41 (November 1968), 12; (7) Gallup Opinion Index, no. 77 (November 1971), 24.

cilities, etc. Only a decreasing minority of whites is willing to verbalize a belief in any innate inferiority of blacks. Even white southerners have presently moved toward an abstract agreement with the ideal of racial equality, though less strongly than have those outside the South. The second level of opinion deals with attitudes on general policies, particularly existing federal laws, that do not necessarily pose any direct threat or will not have any immediate impact on the vast majority of respondents. Such questions tend to elicit generally pro-equality responses from interviewees, though there are a significant number of dissenters. At a third level and more likely to be opposed by whites are policies that could have a demonstrable impact upon them, such as busing to achieve racial integration, open housing laws, or requirements for racial integration in employment. Responses on issues such as these are likely to range from about evenly divided between pro- and anti-equality to decidedly negative, depending upon how many of the whites perceive it likely that their children will be bused, their neighborhoods integrated, and so on.

The fourth level of opinion on this issue encompasses a somewhat broader range of opinion distribution and includes questions that focus on the extent to which whites are willing to come into contact with blacks in a variety of situations, ranging from public facilities and employment (20 percent or less opposed) to interracial dating and marriage (nearly unanimous opposition). It is important to note that most of the questions of contact that are really likely to be matters of public policy (and that have already been enacted into law)—such as integration in employment, schools, and public accommodations—are not opposed by most whites, while those that excite the most opposition (e.g., intermarriage) would seem to be largely questions of private preference entering into the public arena only indirectly.

The last level of opinion is the one in which there is the most evidence of white antipathy; it deals with questions that link blacks with crime and violence. There is a tremendous reservoir of fear and hostility on the part of whites on questions of ghetto riots and "crime on the streets," which many whites perceive to be largely committed by blacks. To the extent that there has been a lack of liberalization in white attitudes in the last decade, a good part of it can be traced to the fact that questions of race have moved in the minds of many from an association with civil rights in the South to one with violence in northern cities. This "social issue" aspect of questions of race will be investigated more fully in Chapter 12. Let us simply point out here that the linking of blacks with crime and riots tends to reduce white support for integrationist policies by offering "practical" reasons that oppose such policies (e.g., integration of a neighborhood will increase crime).

This last observation perhaps sums up the characteristic pattern of white opinion on questions of race—"Yes . . . but. . . ." For many whites, racial questions pose psychological conflict and possible dissonance. Obviously, there is a distinct gap between the accepted values of the American political system into which most whites are socialized and which are largely reinforced by the influence of press and pulpit and, on the other hand, the objective reality of discrimination—something that many whites have also been socialized into accepting. Faced with this discontinuity, whites utilize a wide variety of cognitive techniques to both maintain agreement with the ideals (the "Yes") and avoid accepting the reality of black equality in all its implications (the "but"). Let us cite just a few of the more prominent ways of dealing with the problem. One timeworn technique is to argue that equal opportunity exists, if only blacks would take advantage of it, but that they lack initiative, are lazy, and so on (the more sophisticated may throw in a bit of social science about lack of male family leadership, lower-class values, etc.). A second technique is the equally venerable one of saying that "they" really don't want integration and equality anyway. This technique can range in form from the old southern belief that all of this integration business is the fault of the proverbial "outside agitator" to the more discrete and sophisticated belief of those who can cite evidence that some blacks favor separatism. Actually, fewer blacks (3 percent) than whites (23 percent) would favor creation of an all-black nation within the United States.[20] Finally, whites can reduce some of the obvious inconsistency in their position by citing "practical" considerations. Concern with property values, maintenance of the quality of the school one's children attend, and the like seem to be sufficient for many to justify opposition to policies that they should, in theory, support. All of this is not to say that these concerns and arguments have no empirical basis in reality or in personal experience. It is clear, however, that people use these ideas to reinforce their existing attitudes and to reduce dissonance in a less than objective manner. And questions of race, for most white Americans, are capable of creating more dissonance than any other type of issue.

If white America has not yet come to full acceptance of black equality by any means, one can point to very significant changes over several decades. Around the time of World War II, Gallup found that a majority of all respondents (including blacks) were in favor of segregation in streetcars and buses (51 percent), restaurants (69 percent), and the armed forces (51 percent), and that 84 percent believed there should be "separate sections in towns and cities for Negroes to live in." [21] On probably all of these items, whites today would express majority support for integration. Indeed, a substantial majority of the total population approved of enactment of the Civil

[20] Robert Chandler, *Public Opinion: Changing Attitudes on Contemporary Political and Social Issues*, A CBS News Reference Book (New York: R. R. Bowker Co., 1972), p. 25.
[21] Cited in Free and Cantril, *Political Beliefs of Americans*, p. 121.

Rights Act of 1964, which made most of such segregation illegal. Yet one cannot, on the basis of this attitudinal trend, predict the achievement of black goals of economic and social equality in the near future. Two barriers stand out. First, there is a gap between the kinds of policies and ideals that whites support and their actual behavior. That most whites will give approval to particular integrationist policies as a general notion does not mean that they will accept the actual implementation of those policies when it comes down to their own neighborhoods, jobs, and schools—as it ultimately must. A second barrier is that racial progress now requires something more than the largely symbolic acts of desegregation of public facilities, for what remains is a complex social and economic problem. Equality of opportunity may have been attained (at least in theory), but much more affirmative action will be needed and undoubtedly demanded by the black community. As was pointed out earlier, the belief of most Americans in equality does not extend beyond the notion of equal access to the means for individual success.

Thus, we are likely to have racial questions high on the list of public concerns for many years to come. The issue of race has ramifications far beyond controversies of integration and equality. For example, attitudes on the topic of crime and how to deal with it are greatly affected by white perceptions (correct or incorrect) of black involvement in crime. To take another current example, the question of welfare is to many whites a question of supporting lazy blacks, though in truth most of the recipients of various forms of public aid are white. Race has not lost its power as a political issue either. George Wallace did tap some nonracial concerns in his strong third-party candidacy in 1968, but when that same party nominated a conservative in 1972 who lacked appeal on racial grounds, it received only a tiny proportion of the vote. Clearly, the question of white attitudes toward blacks, which has dominated so much of American political history, continues to be a major determinant of public opinion in the United States.

THE BASIC BELIEFS OF AMERICANS: SOME CONCLUSIONS

This has been only a very brief description of the basic patterns of political attitudes held by the American public. Other areas of importance deserving of analysis are attitudes toward the economic system, religious values, and attitudes toward international affairs and other nations. From what has been examined, certain patterns tend to emerge. First, in each of the three areas outlined—attitudes toward political authority, individual rights, and race—there is a distinct dichotomy between attitudes expressed about these subjects in the abstract and attitudes expressed in terms of practical, often controversial, situations. Less support for ideals is found in the more specific instances. Perhaps this is because there are more competing influences in the particular situations. For example, when one is asked about rights of protesters against the government, he may inevitably weigh these against other ideals of order and practical considerations about the probability of violence, plus his own normative judgments about the goals and methods of protest. When asked about policies designed to end de facto segregation in schools, a respondent necessarily weighs ideals of integration against probabilities of those policies causing hardship within one's own family. When such questions as these are viewed in purely abstract terms, therefore, the main influence on opinions are the socialized cultural values of democracy, equality, and freedom—and the ideals will usually receive high support. But when other, more immediate, concerns compete, support for the ideals must inevitably be reduced.

While we can understand and explain this cleavage between the abstract and the particular, we must still recognize that it has the potential for posing a psychological conflict within the belief systems of many individuals. However, for most people the conflict is not a serious one because the subject matter is generally far removed from their experience and consciousness. Since most people never write letters to public officials, publish documents, or make speeches supporting the government—let alone in opposition to it—the guarantees of the First Amendment must necessarily remain at the abstract level, products of a learning process completed many years before. Thus, politics and public affairs are generally of low salience to most individuals, and questions of governmental support and individual rights are particularly so. Racial equality issues alone are likely to face most people in their daily lives, and it is here that the potential dissonance, and therefore the use of defense mechanisms, is the greatest. This is not to say that these basic attitudes have no effect upon public opinion and the political process. They may be thought of as setting limits, however vague, on the permissible activities of government. Public reaction to the crossing of those limits comes very seldom because, in the perception of the public, government simply does not overstep the fundamental boundaries.

As was made clear in the first part of this chapter, the mass public does not fit into conventional ideological categories; any attempt to summarize its basic patterns of political belief without overly general speculation is therefore extremely difficult. One successful attempt is that of Donald Devine,[22] who identifies what he calls a tradition of "Lockean Liberalism" (i.e., the philosophical tradition enunciated by John Locke, which had an important impact on Madison and others responsible for the construction of many basic American political institutions). There are eleven key values in this liberal belief system: popular rule and elections, legislative predominance, federalism, decentralized political parties, liberty, equality, property, emphasis on achievement, belief in God, religion, and altruism. Using survey data over several decades, Devine finds that all of these values receive support from heavy majorities of the population. Furthermore, almost all social groups within the population give at least majority support to almost all of them. Hence, there is a basic philosophical belief system adhered to by a popular consensus, even though few Americans may be conscious of it.

[22] Devine, *Political Culture of the United States,* chaps. 4 and 5.

Recent Presidential Elections and Their Implications

10

People who speak of "democratic" political systems invariably assume that the primary expression of popular sentiment and popular control is in the electoral process. It is through voting that the citizen is supposed to give guidance to government and to impose discipline when that direction is not heeded to his satisfaction. Whether or not elections in America do indeed perform this function is a complex question and will be considered later in Chapter 14. Our purpose in considering elections at this point is to see what, if anything, they reveal about the nature of public preferences in recent years. Certainly, periodic participation in elections is the sole mode of influencing government attempted by most individuals. And even those most skeptical about the validity of survey research must necessarily accept the verdict of election day as a measurement of public opinion. But to take the results of voting for parties and candidates and attempt to make statements about what the voters had in mind is a difficult task and one fraught with pitfalls. Yet politicians and pundits, amateur and professional, must draw such conclusions about the meaning of elections. In the following pages, we shall attempt to analyze the last four presidential elections in the hope of understanding what the major concerns of the voters were, how these concerns were translated into votes, and what the impact of decisions made in these elections was for the politics of future years.

A FRAMEWORK FOR ELECTORAL ANALYSIS

If one wants to evaluate the significance of any social phenomenon, it is advisable to have some sort of baseline or benchmark for comparison. This is certainly true of elections. The election of a Republican candidate by a landslide in certain parts of the rural Midwest would imply no particular change in partisan behavior or even any intensity of popular feeling if the same result had occurred in almost every election for the last century. On the other hand, even a narrow

Republican victory in some Democratic stronghold might suggest the importance of some current issue to the voters or even the beginning of long-term political realignment. As suggested in Chapter 6, the voting habits of individuals, and therefore of groups and geographic areas, tend to be quite stable over time. The student of elections who wishes to find significance in a particular outcome must for that reason be able to subtract the effects of long-term, stabilizing factors in election results and thereby see deviations and change.

The Normal Vote.[1]   A useful approach for separating these sources of stability, deviation, and change in election outcomes has been developed by researchers at the Survey Research Center, University of Michigan. This is the concept of the *normal vote,* which is based on the idea that most people tend to have an identification with a political party and that they will generally vote in accordance with that loyalty in the absence of any combination of forces favoring one party or the other. This situation, in which neither party benefits from short-term stimulation, is considered the "normal" one. The normal vote is therefore the division of the vote between the two major parties that would result if individuals voted according to their party identification, given usual rates of turnout and partisan defection. Thus, the normal, or *expected,* result of an election is based upon the distribution of party identification in the population and can be calculated from survey data on that distribution. The qualification about rates of turnout and defection is necessary for two reasons. First, not everyone will vote in any given election. Persons who express a "strong" party identification are more likely to turn out than are weaker partisans and independents. Partly because of their higher education and socioeconomic status, Republicans are more likely to vote than are Democrats. Secondly, in no election will there ever be perfect party-line voting. Even some strong identifiers will sometimes cast a vote for the other party. As it happens, Republicans appear to be slightly less likely to deviate than Democratic identifiers. Since there are fewer Republicans, an equal tendency of loyalists of the two parties to defect would lead to more net switches from Democrat to Republican than vice versa.

With these ideas in mind, we can see how the normal vote is calculated. Over the past two decades, there has been relatively little shift in the overall distribution of partisanship in the U.S. population, except for a slight increase in the number of independents. Roughly, about 45 percent of the adult population classify themselves as

[1] This concept is developed by Philip E. Converse, "The Concept of the Normal Vote," in Angus Campbell *et al., Elections and the Political Order* (New York: John Wiley, 1966), pp. 9–39.

strong or weak Democrats, about 25 percent as Republicans, with the remainder considering themselves as "independents," though most of these will admit to a leaning toward one of the two parties.[2] Given the differential rates of turnout and defections outlined above, the normal division of the vote is not as heavily Democratic as the partisanship of the population would indicate. Converse computes the normal vote for the nation as of 1960 to be about 54 percent Democratic and, since there has been little net shift in identification since that time, that is still presumably correct.[3] In other words, if all other things were equal (and they never are), a Democratic candidate for president could expect to receive about 54 percent of the vote and his Republican opponent only about 46. Our confidence in this analysis is increased by virtue of the fact that this is roughly the division of the popular vote cast nationally for congressional candidates in most recent elections.

Let us illustrate how this idea of the normal vote can be useful in explaining an election. In the aftermath of the congressional elections of 1970, there was a great deal of controversy over whether the results showed support of the public for the Nixon administration or whether the voters had, to some degree, repudiated it. While a great deal of ink was expended on the subject, the informed observer might have noted the overall distribution of the popular vote for congressional candidates: 54 percent Democratic, almost exactly the normal figure. Thus, the more reasonable interpretation would be that the election proved little. The division of the vote suggests that voters in 1970 largely voted the way they had for the past twenty years, and that positive or negative reactions to the president must have canceled each other out. It should be noted that the normal vote concept is not limited in its applicability to the national electorate as a whole, for it can be calculated for any group in the population for which the data on party identification is available. Applying this concept to subsets of the population—whether divided along lines of geography, religion, opinion, or other lines—can lead to important insights about voters, several examples of which will be seen later in this chapter.

Taking this concept of the expected vote and deviations from it, we

[2] The distribution of party identification from 1952 through 1968 is shown in Dan Nimmo, *The Political Persuaders: The Techniques of Modern Election Campaigns* (Englewood Cliffs, N.J.: Prentice-Hall, 1970), p. 23.

[3] Converse, "Concept of the Normal Vote," p. 27. By 1972, some of the parameters appear to have been altered, but the normal vote figure still has been calculated at 54 percent Democratic, according to Arthur H. Miller *et al.*, "A Majority Party in Disarray: Policy Polarization in the 1972 Election," paper delivered at the American Political Science Association, New Orleans, September 4–8, 1973, pp. 92–93.

can see that the outcome of any election can be explained as a combination of long-term and short-term forces. The long-term forces can be seen in the expected vote based upon party identification. The short-term forces can be thought of as the sum of all of the factors peculiar to one election—for example, candidates, current issues, events, and campaigns—that cause deviations from the normal vote. It appears to be the case that various groups of party identifiers within the electorate all seem to react to these short-term forces in the same way—all becoming relatively more Democratic, say, or all becoming less so in a given election, but to different degrees. The stronger a person's party identification, the less he will react to short-term forces. Figure 10-1 illustrates this. Here, in a situation of pro-Republican short-term forces, strong Republican identifiers become just a little more nearly unanimous in their party voting; strong Democrats deviate slightly for the Republican candidate; weak party identifiers deviate to a greater extent; and independents go disproportionately for the Republican candidate. Any election result is thus a combination of the past (long-term forces) and the present (short-term forces), and careful analysis can reveal which forces were the most significant for different segments of the electorate.

Figure 10-1
Election Results as a Product of Long-Term and Short-Term Forces

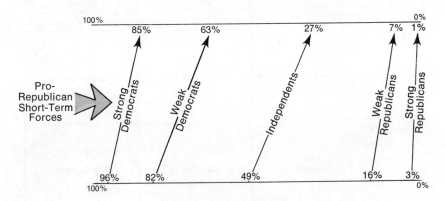

Actual Vote (% Democratic)

Expected Vote (% Democratic) on the Basis
of Party Identification (Long Term Forces)

Source: Adapted from Philip E. Converse, "The Concept of the Normal Vote," in Angus Campbell *et al., Elections and the Political Order* (New York: John Wiley, 1966), pp. 17, 27. "Actual Vote" figures are those for the 1956 election, as reported in Angus Campbell *et al., The American Voter: An Abridgement* (New York: John Wiley, 1964), p. 81.

This mode of analysis leads to a useful classification system for presidential elections.[4] First, we can divide elections into two categories depending upon whether or not the majority party (i.e., the party whose share of the normal vote is the greater) wins or loses. If this party's expected majority is attained, it might be called a *maintaining* election. Also, short-term forces sometimes are sufficiently great to bring victory to the minority, as in the Eisenhower victories of 1952 and 1956; these would be called *deviating* elections. But there is another possibility: that the long-term forces are undergoing a basic change. Should this be the case to the extent that the previous minority party is replacing its opposition as the majority, this would be a *realigning* election. Such sharp realignments occur rather rarely in American history; 1860 and 1932 appear as obvious examples in which, at a single election, there was a basic change in the pattern of party support among voters that persisted in future years. There is also the possibility that some basic change in party allegiance will occur in conjunction with an election, but that the old majority party will remain in control for at least the time being. This

Figure 10-2
A Classification of Presidential Elections

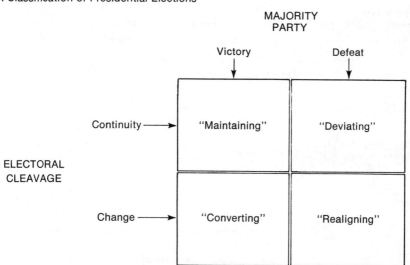

Source: Gerald M. Pomper, *Elections in America: Control and Influence in Democratic Politics* (New York: Dodd, Mead, 1968), p. 104.

[4] This election typology is developed in Angus Campbell *et al.*, "A Classification of Presidential Elections," *Elections and the Political Order*, pp. 63–77, and is further developed in Gerald M. Pomper, *Elections in America: Control and Influence in Democratic Politics* (New York: Dodd, Mead, 1968), chap. 5.

might be called a *converting* election. Figure 10-2 shows the relationship of the elements of this typology. Note that it is difficult to decide in all certainty whether an election was deviating or realigning, maintaining or converting, until we know what happens in the next election or two. In our examination of presidential elections in the last decade, we shall utilize the concept of the normal vote and the typology of elections in order to assess the reasons for the election results and their implications.

CONTEMPORARY PRESIDENTIAL ELECTIONS

We shall limit our examination of the implications of presidential voting to the elections of 1960, 1964, 1968, and 1972. To go much further back in time would be difficult, for we have almost no national survey data available before the 1940s. On the other hand, to concentrate on only the most recent election or two would be to lose the necessary historical perspective. And, as it will be argued here, the elections of 1964, 1968, and 1972 seem to have a number of common elements that differentiate them from the series ending with 1960.

Let us set the stage for the politics of the 1960s. In the late 1950s, the Democratic party coalition established during the administration of Franklin Roosevelt still flourished. This alliance combined strong support from organized labor and less affluent Americans generally, blacks, most self-conscious European ethnic groupings, Jews, Catholics, and southerners. Political issues still reflected many of the concerns dominant over the preceding decades: prosperity and recession, labor-management relations, and the question of international involvement versus isolation. While the first civil rights law in almost a century had been passed in 1957, questions of race were not major political concerns for most white Americans outside the South. There were some indications of political change as the South went partly for Eisenhower (but Stevenson still received all of his electoral votes in 1956 from the southern or border states) and as Eisenhower attracted about half of the Catholic voters (still far smaller a proportion than he attracted among Protestants). The Democrats had a clear majority of the expected vote on the basis of party identification, but short-term forces, particularly the relative attraction of the candidates, allowed Republican victories in 1952 and 1956—both prime examples of deviating elections. The Democratic majority, however, made itself clear in elections for Congress; Democrats have controlled both houses in every election since 1954.

1960: The Politics of Religion.   It is difficult to identify many substantive issues that divided the voters in 1960. To a great extent the election was fought over old issues along past alignments. The candidates made appeals less on the basis of what they hoped to accomplish or even the means they would use, than on their personal abilities to "get the country moving." Both Nixon and Kennedy presented themselves as being in the middle of the political mainstream and were largely perceived in that way. Disagreements came down to what from a distant perspective must be considered minor points, such as the relative strength of the United States and the Soviet Union in missiles and other weapons and the merits of defending some tiny islands between Taiwan and mainland China. In short, the choice seemed to be one only of party label and individual appeal and not one of policy preference. There is no particular evidence that many voters considered it otherwise.

The popular vote in 1960 produced an extremely close division: 49.7 percent for Kennedy to 49.5 percent for Nixon, the remainder going to various minor candidates.[5] Given this result, coupled with the lack of salient issues, one might be tempted to conclude that the electorate was simply returning to its normal behavior after the Eisenhower candidacies and to suppose that there was little deviation from established voting patterns. Such a conclusion would not be warranted, however, for it overlooks the presence of an issue that was largely unstated (at least by the candidates): religion. While Catholics had formed an important part of the Democratic coalition for many years, party leaders had been reluctant to nominate a presidential candidate of that faith out of fear of electoral reprisal from the Protestants, who made up an even larger part of the coalition. With Kennedy as the nominee, and one who made his religious affiliation clear,[6] the nation was presented with the question of whether or not anti-Catholic sentiment would play a major role.

Survey results reveal that religion did play a major role in voting. While three-fourths of the Catholics voted for Kennedy, over 60 percent of the Protestant vote went for Nixon. This considerable religious difference is only partly explainable by the fact of traditional Democratic loyalties among Catholics. When the expected "normal" vote is computed for both religious groups and compared to the way that each reports having actually voted, it is clear that the Catholic segment of the electorate was substantially more heavily Democratic

[5] Actually, Nixon may have actually had more popular votes than Kennedy, depending on how the votes for uncommitted Democratic electors in Alabama are allocated.

[6] Kennedy was advised on the basis of a computer simulation that the best approach to the religious issue would be a frank and direct one, though there is no proof that this is not the course he would have followed in any event. See Ithiel de Sola Pool *et al., Candidates, Issues, and Strategies: A Computer Simulation of the 1960 and 1964 Presidential Elections* (Cambridge: M.I.T. Press, 1965), p. 22.

than expected and the Protestant less so.[7] That this deviation was indeed due to the effect of the religious issue itself is further substantiated by the fact that deviations along religious lines were greatest for those Protestants and Catholics who attended church regularly and identified strongly with their religion, and least for those whose affiliation was only nominal.[8] Thus, the great bulk of changes in voting in 1960 from expected patterns can be attributed to religious polarization rather than to any other particular public issue.

In terms of election results, of course, much of the effect of religion was canceled out, as Kennedy gained votes from Catholics while losing them from Protestants. Overall, there was a slight net loss to the Democrats. Converse and his colleagues estimate that Kennedy registered "unexpected" gains from Catholics equal to about 4 percent of the total vote, while losing about 6 percent from Protestant Democrats and independents.[9] This net national loss (2.2 percent) accounts for most of the deviation of the Democratic vote from the normal figure. Thus, in popular votes, Kennedy was hurt by the religious issue, almost to the point of losing any popular vote margin. On the other hand, the effect of religious polarization probably resulted in a net gain in electoral votes.[10] The reasoning here is that most of the additional Catholic votes came in large, urban, industrial states of the North and East, states with large numbers of electoral votes at stake and states that were closely divided politically. Kennedy's major religious losses, on the other hand, came in the South where there were fewer electoral votes at stake and where the traditional Democratic base was much greater.

Analysis of the presidential election of 1960, perhaps more than that of any other year, suggests that elections sometimes reveal little about the policy preferences of the electorate. The main disruption of traditional patterns seemed to be due to the presence of a Catholic candidate and, aside from indicating that religious loyalties and hostilities were still present in American society, this analysis says little about opinions in the mass public. The religious effect, moreover, was definitely a short-term force, the impact of which probably did not reach beyond the years of the Kennedy administration.[11] In fact,

[7] Philip E. Converse, "Religion and Politics: The 1960 Election," *Elections and the Political Order*, pp. 97–98.

[8] *Ibid.*, pp. 106–19.

[9] Philip E. Converse *et al.*, "Stability and Change in 1960: A Reinstating Election," *American Political Science Review*, 55 (1961), 278.

[10] Pool *et al.*, pp. 117–18.

[11] As the Gallup poll figures cited earlier in Table 5-1 indicate, there has been a decline in voting along religious lines since 1960. Interestingly enough, each of the last three presidential elections has featured a Catholic candidate for vice-president, a

the dominance of religion in 1960 was probably responsible for obscuring some fundamental changes in electoral cleavage that were already under way. Shifts among several major groups, most importantly the white South, had to wait until the radically different context of 1964 to become manifest.

1964: Confidence and Ideology.[12]   It is hard to imagine a more disparate set of presidential elections than 1960 and 1964. One was close; the other was a victory of landslide proportions. One seemed to continue the alignments of the past, while the other disrupted traditional patterns with a vengeance. Whereas one seemed to minimize the differences in issue positions between the candidates, the other seemed to maximize the alternatives presented to the voters. In all elections it is difficult to separate the image from the reality, the short-term deviation from the enduring change. What were the real questions to which the voters responded in 1964?

It appears that three interrelated factors were crucial in 1964: ideology, confidence in the candidates, and the civil rights issue. All became important issues largely as a result of the candidacy of Barry Goldwater and the response of the electorate to his campaign. As was suggested at the start of Chapter 2, the Republican candidate and campaign, operating on an apparently false assumption about the preferences of the electorate, consciously projected a strong conservative philosophy, embodying a laissez-faire position in domestic economic and social policy, and advocacy of a strong military and foreign policy to counteract international communism. President Lyndon Johnson, on the other hand, supported the domestic social welfare policies of the Kennedy administration and a generally middle-of-the-road internationalist policy. It would not be far off to say that the Goldwater position challenged many of the basic policy positions taken by the administration, not only in the Kennedy-Johnson years, but in the Eisenhower, Truman, and Roosevelt years as well. Clearly, this attempt to sell a conservative candidate and philosophy to the electorate was unsuccessful, particularly when the issue came down to concrete programs such as social security, federal aid, and taxation. There is little doubt that the electorate disagreed with Goldwater on these issues, and their views were clearly expressed on election day in something approaching a mandate against a conservative alternative and for continuation of the long

---

fact that has occasioned no great comment nor had an observable impact on voting behavior.

[12] This section draws upon the data and analysis presented in Philip E. Converse *et al.,* "Electoral Myth and Reality: The 1964 Election," *American Political Science Review,* 59 (1965), 321–36.

trend of federal involvement in social welfare and economic stability.

The second factor in 1964 also had to do with the candidates themselves and, again, the issue was largely created by the Republican candidate. As a result of his general stance on foreign policy and some specific remarks with attendant publicity, Goldwater was perceived as insufficiently judicious to keep the peace in a nuclear age. Coupled with the reaction of many voters to his positions on domestic matters, he was simply viewed as "too wild" to be president. Johnson, if not universally beloved, had sufficient prestige and could inspire enough confidence to offer a more desirable alternative.

Both of these factors tended to have the same effect across almost all groups of the electorate, working to the benefit of the incumbent. The third factor—civil rights and the racial issue generally— produced a somewhat more complex pattern. As a part of the overall conservative philosophy, Goldwater opposed most of the civil rights programs enacted under Johnson. Since these policies were acceptable to most whites outside the South, this produced an additional negative reaction to him there. Among black voters, the response was, of course, uniformly negative. The black vote (about one-third of which had gone to Nixon in 1960) was almost unanimously for Johnson. The white South, however, reacted most strongly on this issue. The difference between Goldwater and Johnson on civil rights was clearly perceived by the electorate (and perhaps overperceived by some southerners). It is clearly this issue that accounts for the unprecedented Republican success in carrying five states in the deep South. Yet Goldwater failed to do as well in the South as a whole as the Republican candidates had done in 1952, 1956, and 1960, both in terms of electoral votes and popular votes. There are several reasons for this. First, southerners reacted to the nonracial issues just as northerners did, leading many to vote for Johnson. Secondly, Goldwater lost all support from the small, but increased, black electorate in the South. Most importantly, it must be remembered (as was suggested in Chapter 6) that the South is not one monolithic whole. The greatest shifts to Goldwater came in those areas of the deep South with the greatest (and least participating) black population, and therefore the greatest opposition by whites to racial integration: the proverbial "black belt." This was the area that had given support to the states' rights candidacy of Strom Thurmond in 1948 and that was to go most heavily for George Wallace in 1968, thus giving additional credence to the notion that Goldwater's southern support rested on the race issue. In the outer South—that is, the urbanizing states such as North Carolina and Florida, where other issues competed for attention and where blacks participated in meaningful numbers, areas where Republicans had been slowly making electoral gains for several decades—Goldwater lost, though not as badly as in the nation as a whole.

The result of the 1964 election was produced by both short-term and long-term forces. The effect of the relative confidence in the two candidates was obviously peculiar to the election only. While the repudiation by the electorate of the ideologically extreme domestic positions taken by Goldwater reflected an ongoing policy consensus, the effect of those extreme positions was limited to 1964, given that future Republican candidates would not be inclined to pursue the Goldwater strategy. The effect of the racial question, most responsible for the great upheaval of traditional geographic voting patterns, was more problematical. Whether this was only a temporary aberration or a permanent realignment could not be determined until later elections again posed a choice to the electorate.

1968: The Politics of Fear.   If the 1964 election represented a striking contrast to that of 1960, then the election of 1968 represented an even greater upheaval. It is estimated that a full third of the white electorate switched their party choice over the four-year period,[13] with the net result that the proportion of the vote for the Democratic candidate dropped from Lyndon Johnson's 61 percent to less than 43 percent for Hubert Humphrey. The most striking feature of 1968 was the third-party candidacy of George Wallace, the most successful in many decades. The tremendous vote turnover, coupled with controversy within the Democratic party, raised many questions about the mood of the electorate and the future of American politics.

Three issues emerged as dominating the concern of the electorate: Vietnam, race, and crime. That these reflected pressing questions facing American society cannot be denied, and the first of these, Vietnam, was certainly perceived by candidates and commentators as a key issue. Yet in order to see the effect of these issues, it is necessary to understand the way they were *perceived* by the voters. To overgeneralize only slightly, each of them tended to be cast in the greater context of the so-called Social Issue.[14] In each case, the particular issue was largely viewed not as a substantive question of issue-related problems and alternative policies, but rather as a question of a negative response to some highly visible and disturbing effects of these problems. The issue of Vietnam, thus, was seen not so much as one of foreign policy and military activity, but rather as one

[13] Philip E. Converse *et al.*, "Continuity and Change in American Politics: Parties and Issues in the 1968 Election," *American Political Science Review*, 63 (1969), 1084.

[14] This term was coined by Richard M. Scammon and Ben J. Wattenberg, *The Real Majority* (New York: Coward-McCann, 1970). The idea of the Social Issue will be explored in much greater depth in Chapter 12.

of protest over the war and the failure of incumbent officials to contain that dissent. Even among those individuals who held a generally "dovish" position on the war, a definite majority expressed hostility toward protesters and believed that there was not too much force used by police at the Democratic Convention in Chicago.[15] The racial issue brought much the same response. While in 1964 racial problems had been viewed by most white voters as a question of civil rights for southern blacks, the violent upheavals in urban ghettos during the mid-1960s, coupled with increased black militancy, brought about a reaction of fear. Along the same lines, crime and "law and order" emerged as an issue. Perception of skyrocketing crime rates, particularly in terms of violent acts, contributed to a general mood of fear on the part of much of the electorate as well as disapproval of alleged lenience on the part of public officials. There were other elements in this Social Issue, which we shall discuss in a later chapter, but these seemed to be the key concerns of the American voter in 1968.

Given that a considerable part of the public viewed the issues of Vietnam, race, and crime in these terms, it is not surprising that the vote for the Democratic candidate fell far below that which would have been otherwise expected. Humphrey was hurt in two ways by this discontent and fear. First, he was closely associated with the incumbent president and so was held partially responsible for the disquieting events of the previous four years and for the failure of the Johnson administration to deal with them satisfactorily. Secondly, he was the "liberal" candidate, and "liberal" in the minds of most people was associated with permissiveness—toward youthful dissenters, toward black militants, and toward criminals. Given this pattern of circumstances and these evaluations, Humphrey was bound to lose the support of a considerable part of the traditional Democratic coalition.

And what accounted for the surprising support received by Wallace, running as the candidate of the American Independent party? It seems clear that those who voted for him did so on the basis of *issues;* this is borne out by the fact that many more Wallace supporters cited his stands on current issues as the reason for their vote than happened with either Nixon or Humphrey supporters, as well as by the strikingly different patterns of opinion held by those voters.[16] Wallace voters were responding to the Social Issue concerns, as were other voters, but with greater intensity. Wallace voters tended to come from two groups: whites in the South (or from a southern background) and whites in skilled blue-collar occupations, particularly

---

[15] Converse, "Continuity and Change," pp. 1087–1088.
[16] *Ibid.*, p. 1097.

from households having union members.[17] While both Goldwater in 1964 and Wallace in 1968 gained votes from whites who were particularly resentful of demands for racial equality, there were considerable differences in the social character of their support. Goldwater got most of his votes (except for those in the deep South) from strong Republican identifiers, particularly those of upper economic and educational status who were inclined to agree with his emphasis on economic conservatism. On the other hand, aside from having a southern background, the typical Wallace voter was a young white male of limited education, having a blue-collar occupation.

The topic of who voted for Wallace raises the question of which party was hurt most by his candidacy. At first glance, the loss would appear to have been sustained by the Democrats. Across the nation, the percentage of the vote achieved by Wallace seemed to come from the total received by the Democrats in 1964, the Republicans remaining almost constant over the four years. Furthermore, Wallace was most successful in the South, traditional heartland of Democratic strength. But a conclusion that Humphrey would have won had Wallace not been a candidate is not warranted. It is true that the greater part of Wallace supporters were Democratic identifiers (just as it is true of the population as a whole). However, these were also voters whose second choice was predominantly Nixon, rather than Humphrey. Much of Wallace's support came from nominally Democratic areas in the deep South that had failed to support the Democratic ticket in 1964. Hence, Converse and his colleagues conclude that the absence of Wallace from the ballot would have probably increased Nixon's popular percentage slightly.[18] This conclusion also seems to have been borne out by the results of the 1972 election in which Nixon appears to have inherited Wallace's electoral strength.

The election of 1968, perhaps more than most others, illustrates certain basic characteristics of the public's electoral response to events and issues. The voters certainly showed that they are quite capable of moving away from ingrained party loyalty when displeased with the performance of incumbents. Regardless of any other factors, it is clear that the Johnson administration was being definitely repudiated by the electorate. But while the public used its ballot to speak strongly, its message was not a clear one. Although people expressed their dissatisfaction with what had been done, they gave little indication of exactly what they would prefer. A good part of the electoral change from past patterns came through defections by nominal southern Democrats to the Wallace movement, but, as in 1964, it was still not clear whether this was more than a transitory phenomenon.

[17] *Ibid.*, p. 1102.
[18] *Ibid.*, p. 1097.

1972: Confidence and Ideology Revisited.   There are so many parallels between the elections of 1964 and 1972 that one almost hesitates
to emphasize them. In quite a number of ways the circumstances surrounding the campaign of George McGovern seem to mirror that of
Barry Goldwater, and for much the same reasons. Let us outline the
most important similarities:

1. Both McGovern and Goldwater achieved their party's nomination only after a long and bitter process of primary elections in which
a number of challengers were eliminated. Neither was probably the
preferred choice of most of the rank-and-file party identifiers. Both
overcame this obstacle to nomination by the early establishment of
strong local activist groups that were able to dominate enough local
caucuses and conventions to secure a majority of the delegate votes
at the national convention. While these strategies were very appropriate for winning the nomination, they also brought about resentment and hostility within the party, which led to massive defections
in the general election.

2. Both McGovern and Goldwater were perceived by the electorate as being rather extreme in ideology. In part this reflected a conscious strategy by both candidates, who rejected the usual centrist
appeal of American politics. When it became clear that the perceived
ideology was a liability, there were attempts to moderate the expressed position, but this tended to result in an image of weakness
and lack of resolution.

3. In both 1964 and 1972, the losing candidates seemed to suffer
in terms of personal image as a potential leader. As a result of both
their perceived ideologies and some statements and events, both
Goldwater and McGovern were not viewed by the majority as capable of inspiring confidence. And each was running against an incumbent who, despite some weaknesses, possessed the customary level of
support granted to American presidents. The old political axiom that
incumbent presidents can expect to be reelected was verified again.
The preceding generalizations can be made from impressionistic observation of the events of 1972, but they also represent the fruits of
more systematic inquiry. Let us examine some of the findings on voting behavior in the 1972 election.

Above all, the outcome of the 1972 election was very clearly a
product of opinions on issues as perceived by the voters. As Miller
and his colleagues have shown, Nixon voters tended to hold conservative opinions on a wide range of issues, while McGovern voters
held liberal views.[19] Furthermore, this polarization holds true even
when the effects of established party identification are removed.

[19] Miller, "A Majority Party in Disarray," pp. 9–11.

When a normal vote analysis was performed on the 1972 election results, comparing the "expected" voting distribution with the actual results for different opinion groups,[20] the most important issues were found to be the Vietnam war and amnesty.[21] McGovern received a slightly greater share of the vote than would be predicted on the basis of party identification from those holding the most intense preferences for withdrawal and amnesty, but lost most of the votes from those who were opposed. The impact of various other issues—such as race, legalization of marijuana, and urban unrest—was lower in magnitude but of the same character. Consistently, it appeared that McGovern did well among the minority who held extremely liberal opinions, while Nixon carried those in the middle and on the Right—the latter by huge margins.

The effect of opinions on voting is always dependent upon the perceptions of the voters as to where candidates stand relative to the voters' own preferences. In 1972, these preferences were quite polarized, with McGovern seen by the electorate as being well to the Left as compared to a slightly conservative position occupied by Nixon. When these perceptions of the candidates and their proximity to individual voters are analyzed, the effect of the issues appears to be even greater than before. For example, those individuals who saw McGovern as being much closer to their own position on war-related issues voted for him at the rate of 93 percent, while 96 percent of those who felt Nixon much better represented their own views voted for him.[22] In terms of explaining the vote overall, issues clearly played a vital role. While party identification was, as always, important, it appears that issue perceptions were at least as important as party in the outcome of the 1972 election, if not more so.[23] In short, McGovern lost the 1972 election because voters believed that Nixon better represented their preferences on most major issues.

The other aspect of the election outcome is voter appraisal of the personal attractiveness of candidates. This factor cannot be fully separated from ideology and issues, for these considerations inevitably affect evaluations of the man—and that appears to have happened in 1972, just as it did in 1964. There is a popular line of argument which says that both presidential candidates in 1972 were personally unattractive to the electorate and that the choice was only between the "lesser of two evils." Such an explanation is only partially true. "McGovern was the least popular Democratic presidential candidate

---

[20] See Chapter 11 for another example of using a normal vote analysis to determine the importance of issues.

[21] Miller, "A Majority Party in Disarray," pp. 18–23.

[22] *Ibid.*, p. 30.

[23] *Ibid.*, p. 69.

of the last twenty years," according to comparable survey data.[24] In comparison to past elections, Nixon was at best moderately popular. However, in comparisons made among twelve leading political figures in 1972, Nixon was clearly the most popular alternative, whereas McGovern was ranked ninth by the respondents, slightly below George Wallace.[25] The conclusion could be drawn that it would have been difficult for any potential Democratic candidate to win in 1972, but that McGovern was hardly the most promising alternative. It has been argued that the "Eagleton affair" was responsible for part of McGovern's image weaknesses. The truth of this proposition has not been fully determined, but it seems safe to say that while the changing of vice-presidential candidates may have had a slight negative impact on McGovern's fortunes, it was certainly not a major factor. It is also difficult to make any generalization about the effects, if any, of the emerging Watergate scandal. Apparently, few voters thought the incident to be of any importance at that time, even though McGovern attempted to portray it as a major issue.[26]

Though issues were important in 1972, this does not mean that the election acted as a clear mandate for the policies of the victor and his party. The reason is that the issues became so heavily focused in terms of McGovern's perceived extremity, particularly on noneconomic issues such as amnesty, that the will of the electorate could be interpreted only as a rejection of the Left in favor of the center. This was a meaningful decision, but it did not offer a clear statement as to the preferences of the public on future policies. Given his problems of ideological position and lack of personal attractiveness, coupled with the inherent advantage of an incumbent president, it is not surprising that McGovern lost. Any success for his strategy would have required an ability on the part of the Democratic campaign to change some basic public attitudes and, as Goldwater had found eight years earlier, this does not seem to be possible in American politics.

What was somewhat surprising was the magnitude of the Nixon victory. Nixon carried all states, save Massachusetts and the District of Columbia, and his 61 percent of the popular vote was about the same as that achieved by Johnson in the 1964 landslide. The outcome was made even more striking than that of 1964 because of the fact that the Democrats still had a considerable edge in party identifiers.[27] In addition, the Nixon victory was perhaps the most wide-

[24] *Ibid.*, p. 55.
[25] *Ibid.*, pp. 56–59.
[26] *Gallup Opinion Index*, no. 88 (October 1972).
[27] Using the 54 percent Democratic figure of the normal vote as a baseline, we see that Johnson exceeded it by 7 percent in 1964, whereas Nixon's 1972 percentage was 15 percentage points over what would be expected for a Republican candidate.

spread ever recorded; the only major demographic segment of the population that did not give him a majority was the black population. This swing of short-term forces to the Republican candidate was so great that it tends to obscure differences within the electorate and makes it more difficult to ascertain the implications of 1968 for the future.

One generalization seems to be accepted by all observers: the overwhelming victory achieved by the Republican candidate in 1972 is no guarantee that the relative minority status of that party has changed. There is little indication of any swing toward the Republicans in terms of party loyalty by the voters, and the 1972 elections also produced the usual Democratic majority in both houses of the Congress. While the Watergate affair and Nixon resignation have not destroyed the Republican party, these events may have further weakened its already minority position. One change does seem particularly likely to remain permanent: the disappearance of the Democratic South. While in 1968 this change was obscured by the third-party candidacy of Wallace, it is not apparent that white southerners, particularly in the deep South, find the Republican party on the national level more congenial than the Democratic. Consequently, Nixon received larger majorities in that region than in any other. South Carolina, Georgia, Mississippi, and Louisiana have now failed to support the Democratic candidate for three successive elections and there seems to be little reason to think they will be likely to alter that pattern. Other shifts in electoral groupings are more problematical. Nixon made considerable gains among previously Democratic groups such as organized labor, Catholics, and European ethnic groups. Whether some of these shifts remain permanent will depend upon the course of events in succeeding years.

REALIGNMENT IN CONTEMPORARY
AMERICAN POLITICS

As we noted in the early part of this chapter, a major portion of the factors affecting the outcome of elections remains constant over time. Long-term forces, measured by the distribution of party identification, act as a base around which variations are produced by the product of short-term forces, such as events and candidates. But long-term partisan alignment does change on occasion as a result of the "converting" and "realigning" elections mentioned earlier in the typology of elections. An election that signals a basic shift in political loyalties of a significant part of the electorate has been labeled a "critical election." This concept was originated by V. O. Key, who demonstrated that a significant change occurred in political behavior in the 1928 election among Catholic workers in eastern cities.[28] It was this shift to the Democratic party that formed the basis for the New Deal Democratic coalition, though in 1928 the gain for the Democrats was obscured by the overwhelming defeat of Catholic Democratic presidential candidate Al Smith. The key to identifying such a critical change lies in the fact that, in normal circumstances, groups tend to shift in a parallel fashion. For example, in a pro-Democratic year, groups such as the poor, the black community, and the Catholic community may shift from a normally Democratic majority to an overwhelming one, while persons of middle and upper income, Protestants, and others may move from an expected Republican voting pattern to a slightly Democratic one. In a Republican year, the opposite would occur, but in both cases, the various groups would generally retain the same partisan positions relative to each other. However, in a period of critical change in which there is basic conversion and realignment taking place, some group or groups will move counter to the tide (or in the same direction as others, but to a much greater extent), thus indicating that they are not simply reacting to the same overall short-term forces in the same way as the rest of the voters. When this occurs, it appears that such shifts tend to be permanent, thus bringing about some lasting realignment.

We can use this principle of the relative change in voting habits of different segments of the population to ascertain whether or not particular elections were critical. One way of doing this is to look at election returns on a state-by-state basis. Shifts in these geographic patterns will indicate shifts in group support for the parties because different segments of the population (e.g., farmers, Catholics, union members, etc.) are concentrated in differing degrees in different states and because much of the political cleavage in the United States has historically been based upon sectional factors. There are several ways of going about this investigation, but perhaps the simplest is the device of correlating the partisan division of the vote for president in each state in one election with the division in the succeeding contest. A high positive correlation will indicate that the states maintained the same partisan preferences relative to each other over the four years, even if the overall level of support for the parties changed. A low (or negative) correlation indicates that the old pattern was not maintained and that some change has probably occurred.[29] If we use this (or some similar method) over the span of American history, we find that prior to the current era there seem to be particular elections in which critical change has taken

[28] V. O. Key, Jr., "A Theory of Critical Elections," *Journal of Politics*, 17 (1955), 3–18.
[29] This method is clearly explained in Pomper, *Elections in America*, pp. 101–11.

place—1836, 1864, 1896, and 1928—and these represent eras in which our knowledge of history suggests that there were some basic realignments in the political system.[30]

Each of these previous critical elections occurred after a lapse of roughly thirty years, and the obvious question therefore arises whether there has been such a realignment in the past two decades. One writer who thinks so is Kevin Phillips, whose thesis is summed up in the title of his book *The Emerging Republican Majority*.[31] As pointed out earlier in Chapter 6, Phillips argues that a basic pattern of partisan change has been building up over the years, in which the areas of the nation that previously were the most Republican—the Northeast and other Yankee-settled parts of the country—have been becoming more Democratic. At the same time, the old strongholds of the Democracy—the South, the border states, and the southern-settled areas elsewhere—are swinging to the Republican party. This trend, he says, was brought to a head by the election of 1964, though its effects were obscured by Goldwater's massive loss, just as the changes of 1928 were hidden by the Hoover landslide. The net result, however, according to Phillips, is that once the presence of a third-party southern candidate such as Wallace in 1968 is removed, there should be an electoral majority expected for Republican presidential candidates.

What do the results of the last several elections tell us about this hypothesis? Table 10-1 reports correlations between state-by-state percentages for Democratic presidential candidates for succeeding elections since 1948. They are relatively high until the comparison between 1960 and 1964 is reached. The latter year brought about a pattern that was strikingly different from that previously experi-

Table 10-1
Correlations Between Partisan Division of the Vote by States in Successive Presidential Elections, 1948–72

Election Pair	Correlation *	Election Pair	Correlation *
1948–1952	+.74	1960–1964	−.11
1952–1956	+.60	1964–1968	+.86
1956–1960	+.54	1968–1972	+.88

Source: The figure for 1968–1972 computed by the author; all other figures are as given in Walter Dean Burnham, *Critical Elections and the Mainsprings of American Politics* (New York: W. W. Norton, 1969), p. 167.
* Correlations are Pearson product-moment correlations between the proportion Democratic of the total vote in each state from one election to the next.

[30] *Ibid.*
[31] Kevin Phillips, *The Emerging Republican Majority* (New Rochelle, N.Y.: Arlington House, 1969).

enced. It was a year which saw states such as Maine (one of two which did not vote for Roosevelt in 1936) give almost 70 percent of its vote to Johnson, while Mississippi (once the solidest in the "solid South") gave 87 percent to his Republican opponent. And this pattern, the data show, was not a onetime fluke, for the correlations return again to moderately high levels in 1968 and 1972, thus indicating that the pattern of 1964 has been retained for eight years.[32]

There are some indications therefore that conversion, if not net partisan realignment, has taken place, and the Phillips thesis would seem to explain its geographic patterns. This is not to say that all of Phillips' conclusions must be accepted, for there are some obvious qualifications that must be noted. Chief among these is the fact that survey data indicates as yet that there is no great increase in the proportion of the electorate identifying themselves as Republicans. Along with this, there are not yet many signs that these shifts are extending themselves to voting for any offices below the presidential level. Yet it is undeniable that some very basic changes have occurred in the American political map and that these are indications of shifts in opinion in the mass public.

Why do critical elections occur at intervals and what do they mean? These periodic restructurings of the political landscape do not come about without strong cause. At its root, this seems to be a buildup of tensions within the political system. Parties become wedded to an issue and the cleavages around it. As time goes on, the old issues, which form the basis of distinction between the parties, become outdated and irrelevant to the contemporary concerns of the public because new issues, which cut across the old cleavages, have emerged. When the tensions generated by this inconsistency reach a sufficiently high level, and the catalyst in the form of a candidate presents itself, critical change occurs.[33] Perhaps the clearest example of this is in the years leading up to the Civil War era. The old Whig versus Democrat system, based on an East versus West sectionalism and related economic and philosophical questions, became increasingly irrelevant to a nation concerned over the question of the expansion of slavery versus abolition. At length, that party system collapsed; the old Democratic party split; and the Whigs were replaced by the Republicans. Thus, stability and realignment in partisan politics are intimately related to the concerns and preferences of the mass public. As long as the differences between parties reflect the

[32] This method of using the Democratic percentage of the total vote in effect lumps the Wallace vote in 1968 together with the Republican—an assumption that the 1972 experience suggests is not invalid.

[33] This explanation of the causes of critical elections is partially suggested by Walter Dean Burnham, *Critical Elections and the Mainsprings of American Politics* (New York: W. W. Norton, 1970), pp. 1–10.

concerns of the public, the party system will remain. When partisan cleavages become irrelevant to the changing course of public opinion, they are ripe for change.

We seem now to be in such a period of realignment. Burnham suggests that several phenomena are associated with periods of critical change, such as increase in ideological polarization, controversy over the nominating process itself within parties, and the rise of strong third-party movements.[34] Each of these has occurred in one or more of the last three presidential elections, giving additional weight to the conclusion that realignment has occurred. Exactly what the political future will look like and what basic policy decisions the voters have made in this critical period are not yet entirely clear. If one can speculate, the conclusion might be drawn that politics in America will be divided less along the lines of economic status, for the old unity of liberalism in economic matters and in social issues has been greatly weakened. Once again, we see evidence that the public has spoken in a voice that is loud in emphasis, but vague in meaning.

[34] *Ibid.* See also James L. Sundquist, *Dynamics of the Party System: Alignment and Realignment of Political Parties in the United States* (Washington: The Brookings Institution, 1973), chap. 13.

Public Opinion and Vietnam

11

Perhaps the most significant controversy in American politics over the past two decades has revolved around the war in Vietnam. Some argue that this issue has wrought permanent changes in the political and social fabric of the nation. It is clear that for a number of years the war was viewed by the public as constituting the most significant problem facing the country, and this at a time when a host of domestic crises (racial violence, economic problems, crime, drug abuse, etc.) competed for attention.[1] It is often doubted whether the preferences of the mass public have much impact on the making of foreign policy, primarily because most individuals have relatively little knowledge about or interest in international affairs.[2] However, the question of Vietnam involvement seems to be different from other contemporary issues of foreign policy because of its obvious visibility, its duration, its apparent impact on domestic matters, and the intense controversy surrounding it. If there was ever an international question that produced a strong input of preference from the mass public, Vietnam was to be that issue.

This question of what the average American thought about the war certainly entered the controversy over it. Political campaigns at all levels of government, both successful and unsuccessful, were staked

[1] Inspection of Gallup poll results from 1965 through 1972 on questions that asked what the "most important problem" facing the nation was, showed that Vietnam was always the choice of the most people, except in 1971, when it ran second to "economic problems," which included inflation and unemployment. Due to differences in question wording and categorization of responses, no precise comparisons of the importance of issues in different surveys can be made. It was also the author's experience with a number of surveys in the early 1970s that Vietnam was consistently the most widely cited national problem.

[2] See, for example, Warren Miller and Donald E. Stokes, "Constituency Influence in Congress," American Political Science Review, 57 (1963), 45–56; V. O. Key, Jr., Public Opinion and American Democracy (New York: Alfred A. Knopf, 1961), pp. 212–15; Lloyd A. Free and Hadley Cantril, The Political Beliefs of Americans (New York: Simon and Schuster, 1968), pp. 59–61; and Bernard C. Cohen, The Public's Impact on Foreign Policy (Boston: Little, Brown, 1973), pp. 193–200.

upon assumptions that the voters were hawks or doves. Opponents of the war cited mass protests as evidence of popular agreement with their criticism, while a president argued that a "silent majority" existed that agreed with him. A whole panoply of stereotypes emerged: radical students, hawkish hard-hats, warmongering upper classes, and repressed opponents. The total volume of controversy over what the American people thought about the war may have exceeded commentary on the war itself. Many of these estimates of public sentiment on both sides lacked any empirical substantiation. Even when the customary survey procedures were invoked, the situation remained less than clear. For example, in 1966, the Gallup poll found that 70 percent of their respondents favored the "hawkish" policy of bombing certain targets in North Vietnam, while barely two months later, over half favored the "dovish" move of submitting the whole problem to the United Nations.[3] To a great extent, it appeared that the status of public opinion on the war depended on the form of the question asked.

Among substantive topics in public opinion demanding careful empirical analysis, the Vietnam issue therefore is outstanding. In this chapter, we shall attempt to summarize what is known about the issue, ascertain the actual preferences of the public, and evaluate the validity of the popular stereotypes about who held what opinion. We shall also consider whether the pattern of public opinion on Vietnam is really different from that for past American involvement in war and explore the implications of this issue for the political process.

THE SHAPE OF OPINION:
DISTRIBUTION AND CONTENT

Regardless of debate about when American involvement in Vietnam really began, it appears that the public really did not become widely aware of that involvement until the 1964 election and that many were largely unaware until the increase of troop buildups in late 1965.[4] With increased awareness in this early period came a substantial degree of popular support for American actions there. As noted earlier, it is difficult to evaluate the nature of popular sentiment on this issue over time because of the variation in responses caused by questionnaire wording. One item that was consistently used by the Gallup organization for a number of years was ". . . do you think the

---

[3] This and other examples of the difficulty in measuring public opinion on the issue are cited in Philip E. Converse and Howard Schuman, " 'Silent Majorities' and the Vietnam War," *Scientific American*, 222 (June 1970), 17–22.

[4] John E. Mueller, "Trends in Popular Support for the Wars in Korea and Vietnam," *American Political Science Review*, 65 (1971), 363–64.

U.S. made a mistake in sending troops to fight in Vietnam?" Results of that question are depicted in Figure 11-1. As the figure indicates, there was a relatively steady drop over the years in the proportion believing that American entry had been a good idea and a corresponding increase in those opposed. The favorable proportion dropped from a high of about 60 percent in 1965 to between 30 and 40 percent by 1968 where it leveled off. The proportion regretting involvement became the greater in late 1967 and eventually reached almost 60 percent. Excluding minor variations (which are to be expected due to sampling error), the trends are quite regular and give relatively little indication of responsiveness to particular events.

The question of whether Americans should ever have been in Vietnam, while offering a general opinion measure over time, really tells us little about public policy preferences on the issue. It is quite possible for an individual to say that it was a mistake to have begun, but for him still to support current policy. Conversely, someone else might well believe initial involvement was advisable, but that it was

Figure 11-1
Support and Opposition to American Involvement in Vietnam, 1965–73

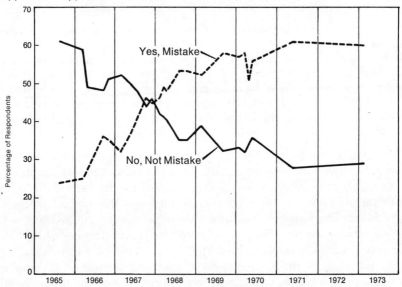

"In view of the developments since we entered Vietnam, do you think the U.S. made a mistake in sending troops to fight in Vietnam?"

Source: Gallup poll, as reported in John E. Mueller, "Trends in Popular Support for the Wars in Korea and Vietnam," *American Political Science Review,* 65 (1971), 363–64; and *Gallup Opinion Index,* no. 69 (March 1971), 12, and no. 92 (February 1973), 8.

now time to pull out. What did the American public actually think should be done?

The most basic generalization that can be made about public preference on our policy in Vietnam is that it was neither consistently hawkish nor dovish. The Gallup poll found that about one-fifth of its respondents were "superhawks" (who favored all-out military escalation) while the same proportion were "superdoves" (favoring immediate withdrawal) and that these proportions remained almost constant over a period of years.[5] The rest of the population preferred alternatives somewhat between these two extremes. This finding is borne out by the analysis of Verba and his colleagues of attitudes toward escalation and de-escalation.[6] In their research, two scales of nine items each were constructed and administered to a national sample, one scale measuring approval of various steps toward military escalation and the other, of steps toward de-escalation. In both cases, the respondents were rather widely dispersed over the range of the scales with some tendency toward concentration in the middle ranges. The correlation between attitudes on the two dimensions was relatively low (r = −.37), indicating that significant numbers of respondents were either favorable to both escalation and de-escalation or else opposed to either. The authors concluded:

. . . few respondents took consistent "dove" or "hawk" positions. The opinions of most tended to be moderate. Our findings showed a relatively permissive majority behind the president, suggesting that the public would support him in some escalation of the war, but would oppose extreme escalation. There would seem to be more willingness to see a reduction of the war but, symmetrical with the opposition to major escalation, was an opposition to precipitous withdrawal. We did not find . . . a populace which wanted some quick and precipitous resolution of the situation.[7]

The American public tended to follow a centrist position with regard to actions in Southeast Asia. This should not be interpreted to mean that there was necessarily firm support for the then-current administration policy at most points throughout the period. Indeed, there is ample evidence that most Americans were dissatisfied with the way things were going, as indicated by increasing belief that the war was a mistake, doubts about the "credibility" of the information communicated by the government, decreasing presidential popularity during the Johnson years, and continuing pessimism about the ul-

[5] George Gallup, "Public Opinion and the Vietnam War: 1964–1969," *Gallup Opinion Index*, no. 52 (October 1969), 2–3.

[6] Sidney Verba *et al.*, "Public Opinion and the War in Vietnam," *American Political Science Review*, 61 (1967), 317–33.

[7] *Ibid.*, p. 321.

timate probabilities for the success of the South Vietnamese govern-ment.[8] Thus, the status quo became, for most Americans, an "unhappy medium." Frustrated with the situation, majorities of the public willingly gave approval to a number of different alternatives that seemingly offered some prospect for settlement, including such measures as increased bombing, bombing halts, negotiations, United Nations involvement, "Vietnamization," coalition government, and some troop increases. Obviously, many of these potential policies were mutually exclusive, but an interpretation inferring that the atti-tudes of the mass public were therefore irrational or illogical would not be quite correct. The point is that people were unhappy with the situation; they wanted out; and they were not very particular about what means were used to achieve that goal. Presidents could usually gain support (and increase their own popularity) simply by taking some sort of new action that might offer a means to an ultimate reso-lution. As time went on, demands for a solution increased and so did support for de-escalatory measures, but this overall pattern of frus-trated centrism and grasping for solutions correctly describes public opinion on the war through to the cease-fire agreements in 1973. When the peace settlement was announced, 80 percent of the Gallup respondents said that they were satisfied with the agreement, even though a plurality thought that it would not last.[9]

THE DEMOGRAPHY OF OPINION: SOCIAL CORRELATES

A great deal of misinformation entered the public dialogue about the kinds of people who opposed and supported the war. Opinion cleav-ages were quickly assumed to follow sociological cleavages, particu-larly on the variables of age and education. Were these stereotypes true? Was opposition to the war concentrated among the young and the well educated?

The first observation which must be made is simply that various social groups differed little in their attitudes toward the war. Table 11-1 reports the results of one of the last Gallup polls (conducted during January 1971) to ask whether or not the war was a mistake. As the data clearly indicate, there is almost no difference among various segments of society in their opinions. Where minor differences do emerge (as in income groups and persons from different sizes of com-munities), there is no regular relationship. This unusual lack of social

---

[8] Several of these trends are summarized in Gallup, "Public Opinion and the Viet-nam War," pp. 1–10.

[9] *Gallup Opinion Index*, no. 92 (February 1973), 5–7.

Table 11-1
Proportions of Social Groups Believing Vietnam Involvement to Be a Mistake, 1971 *

National	59%		
Sex		*Politics*	
Male	60	Republican	61%
Female	59	Democrat	59
		Independent	60
Race			
White	59	*Region*	
Nonwhite	61	East	62
		Midwest	61
Education		South	54
College	58	West	60
High school	58		
Grade school	64	*Income*	
		$15,000 & over	64
Occupation		$10,000–$14,999	53
Prof. & business	54	$7,000–$9,999	58
White-collar	59	$5,000–$6,999	60
Farmers	61	$3,000–$4,999	62
Manual	56	Under $3,000	65
Age		*Community Size*	
21–29 years	52	1 Million & over	61
30–49 years	55	500,000–999,999	66
50 and over	67	50,000–499,999	58
		2,500–49,999	59
Religion		Under 2,500, rural	57
Protestant	58		
Catholic	57		

Source: Gallup Opinion Index, no. 69 (March 1971), 12.
* Percentage answering "Yes" to the question, "In view of the developments since we entered the fighting in Vietnam, do you think the U.S. made a mistake sending troops to fight in Vietnam?"

correlates of opinion appears to have been the case throughout the history of the issue.[10]

While the differences between groups are small, some occurred regularly enough to permit generalizations. The most interesting of these concerns the alleged generation gap. In most surveys of opinion on Vietnam, differences did appear between old and young—but it was the older voters (over fifty) who expressed the most opposition to the war and the younger (under thirty) who expressed the most support.[11] The relative gap between the two groups narrowed somewhat over time, but the older individuals always remained the most

[10] This nonrelevancy of most social characteristics appears in data from early 1966. See Verba *et al.,* "Public Opinion and the War in Vietnam," pp. 322–23.

[11] Hazel Erskine, "The Polls: Is War a Mistake?," *Public Opinion Quarterly,* 34 (1970), 134. It should be noted that until the adoption of the eighteen-year-old voting age most public opinion surveys limited their samples to persons twenty-one and over.

opposed to the war. Somewhat related to this finding is the one for education. In the years 1966 and 1967, support for the war tended to come from the most educated segment of society and the greatest opposition from those with no more than a grade school education. Not until 1970 had the relationship reversed, with the more educated expressing slightly greater dissatisfaction than the less educated.[12] Thus, there is a great difference between the findings of survey research and the perceptions most people had of the opponents of the war.

How can we account for these surprising findings? On the question of education, one must realize that the "college" group in most national surveys includes anyone who has attended any college at any time. Such a person is more likely to be a graduate of a small college some years ago, or someone who attended a college briefly at some time, than a member of the contemporary college population. As Converse and Schuman found, the relationship between education and opposition to the war was curvilinear: it was relatively high among the least educated and decreased as the level of education rose until the very highest level of education was attained (i.e., postgraduate work), where it shot up to the highest level of all. The same authors also found that opposition to the war was the greatest among those who had attended the more prestigious institutions.[13] Thus, opposition to the war came from two very different groups: the highly educated—who constituted a very small portion of the population, but accounted for much of the vocal dissent—and the least educated.

We can account similarly for the findings relating age and opinion. Most of the people in the "21–29" category are not college students, never were, or if they did attend college, did so in a time unlike the present. As such, there should be no particular reason to expect them to reflect the views vocally expressed on campuses. Even among the student population, dissent on Vietnam was not as widespread as it sometimes appeared. In a Gallup survey of college students conducted in late 1969, it appeared that exactly half of the respondents gave their approval to Nixon's handling of the Vietnam situation.[14] This approval rate was somewhat less than that of the general public, and a much greater majority of students expressed dovish views than was true of the nation as a whole. Still, this sort of data suggests that stereotypes of dissenting youth, even on college campuses, gave a rather distorted image of reality. The tendency for opponents of involvement in Vietnam to be disproportionately concentrated among

[12] *Ibid.*, p. 135. However, in some later polls, such as the one shown in Table 11-1, the less educated were again more opposed.

[13] Converse and Schuman, " 'Silent Majorities,' " pp. 24–25.

[14] *Gallup Opinion Index*, no. 55 (January 1970), 15–19.

the old and uneducated (who tend to represent the same group) had important implications for the role of public opinion in policy making on Vietnam.

Two other social relationships appear often enough in surveys on Vietnam opinion to deserve mention. Both women and blacks appeared somewhat more dovish than the population as a whole.[15] These attitudinal differences do not show up so much in terms of overall disaffection (as measured by the tendency to say it was a mistake), but rather in a tendency to be more in favor of peace moves and less supportive of escalation measures. The relationships were regular, but still did not account for much of the distribution of opinions. And the kinds of variables that usually differentiate the public, such as economic status and party identification, turned out to be unrelated to the issue of Vietnam. This lack of similarity between cleavages of opinion on the war and those of established political decisions may have contributed to the inability of the political process to structure alternatives in a more meaningful way.

THE PSYCHOLOGY OF OPINION: REASONS FOR SUPPORT AND OPPOSITION

In order to understand the complex of opinions that developed around the Vietnam issue, it is necessary to ask what motivated some people to support American involvement and others to oppose it. Questions of motivation are always difficult to answer, but in the case of the Vietnam war, some generalizations can be made. Once more, easy stereotypes fail to hold up under close scrutiny.

One might suppose that Americans supported their nation's actions in Vietnam because of a clear and intense belief in the importance of maintaining a pro-U.S. regime and in the efficacy of our actions there. Such a set of beliefs may have been held by a portion of the minority of the public who can be clearly identified as committed "hawks," but certainly were not held by most who expressed some degree of support for the war. Most Americans who supported the war did so for less precise and less directly related reasons. To a great extent, the psychological source of support might be summed up as "patriotism" (i.e., many people viewed support for American policy as a natural correlate of their established support for the political system).[16] This is not to say that patriots must be hawks nor that doves are unpatriotic. However, strong voices sought to establish a linkage between support for the political system and support for ex-

[15] Verba et al., "Public Opinion and the War in Vietnam," pp. 325–26, and Converse and Schuman, " 'Silent Majorities,' " p. 22.

[16] Milton J. Rosenberg et al., Vietnam and the Silent Majority: The Dove's Guide (New York: Harper and Row, 1970), pp. 42–43.

isting Vietnam policy. Such arguments came not only from administration spokesmen who, not surprisingly, sought to generate patriotic support for their actions, but also, in a rather perverse way, from some opponents of the war who linked support for the existing political and social system with support for the war. Questions of war and peace tend to be viewed in highly abstract and symbolic terms by many, and supporters of the war could justify their support by reference to "We never lost a war," preservation of national honor and reputation, maintenance of international commitments, opposition to communism, and the like. Most people are accustomed to registering their general approval of existing federal policy, particularly in areas such as foreign affairs in which they have little direct interest. Vietnam offered a number of culturally based symbols which could be used as reference points for that support. As was pointed out earlier, relatively few Americans really displayed consistently hawkish attitudes in favor of escalation as a hypothetical alternative. Most who supported the war simply gave their support to the president and his current policies, whether those policies involved escalation or de-escalation. Thus, much of the support for the war was neither intense nor related to actual preferences for increased military activity.

As a psychological object, Vietnam was rather diffuse. But there was a more sharply outlined issue that was closely interrelated in the minds of many: what we referred to in Chapter 10 as the Social Issue.[17] As a result of widespread protest demonstrations, particularly on college campuses, a generalized "law and order" reaction became linked with the Vietnam issue. Indeed, for several years in the late 1960s protest over Vietnam nearly became a more salient issue for much of the population than the Vietnam war itself. The war was far away, while the protesters were at home; no one seemed to know how to win the war, but many people could easily draw the conclusion that more law enforcement would defeat the enemy on the nearest college campus. Hence, attention was focused on domestic dissent, to which the reaction was overwhelmingly negative. Disruption on college campuses was cited by significant proportions of the public as a major problem, and substantial majorities expressed their distaste for war protest activities. This negative reaction was even expressed by people in nominal agreement with those who were more active in expressing their dissent. The Survey Research Center study of the 1968 election found that over half of those respondents who themselves favored complete withdrawal from Vietnam also viewed war protesters negatively.[18] Even in cases such

---

[17] This term, coined by Richard M. Scammon and Ben J. Wattenberg, *The Real Majority* (New York: Coward-McCann, 1970), is more fully discussed in Chapter 12.
[18] *Ibid.*, p. 45.

as the 1968 Democratic convention in Chicago and the Kent State episode, popular sympathy rested with the police and soldiers, and hostility was expressed toward demonstrators and students.

The reasons for this reaction lie not so much with the Vietnam question itself, for increasing proportions of the population were having their own doubts on the subject. Rather, fear and opposition toward dissent arose from a dislike of the means of expression used and because of the interrelationship of protest with changing life-styles and advocacy of change in other policy areas. The tendency of many protesters to demand not only withdrawal from Southeast Asia, but also rejection of capitalism, materialism, and established social norms, could lead only to the loss of possible allies on the war issue. It can probably not be proved, but there is certainly reason to suspect that the net effect of several years of active protest against the war was probably to retard the development of opposition to it in public opinion. In short, the occurrence of vocal and sometimes violent dissent on the war presented a clear and present reference point for many people for whom the issue would have otherwise remained a vague one, and reactions to that reference point were so negative as to offer an additional psychological basis for supporting the war.

As we saw earlier, an increasing number of Americans came to oppose the war, and this group eventually outnumbered the supporters. Persons who expressed some degree of opposition may be roughly divided into two categories: those who were opposed for moral reasons and those who might be best called the "war weary." The first group generally fits the usual stereotype of the Vietnam dissenter: well-educated, usually young, possessed of a generalized liberal or even radical ideology, and believing that American intervention in Southeast Asia, regardless of its success or failure, was inherently wrong. This group represented only a tiny fraction of the American public at any time and was perhaps a tenth as large as the remaining group of nonsupporters.[19] The "war weary" opposed the war, not on the basis of any sweeping moral judgments, but rather out of a sense of frustration at its lack of resolution, resentment of the costs it imposed on the nation, and a feeling that there was no valid reason for it in the first place. When we understand that it is reasons such as these which account for most of the opposition to the war, the finding that opposition tended to be concentrated among the older and less well-educated becomes more comprehensible. We see that much of the opposition came from those who in many ways reflected a tradition of "isolationism" (i.e., a lack of concern with international matters). Such opposition, therefore, was not concerned with the par-

[19] Converse and Schuman, " 'Silent Majorities,' " p. 24.

ticular means for disengagement. The great bulk of the opponents of the war, like those who gave it general support, were usually willing to approve any sort of new policy announced by the president that would seem to lead to peace. Thus, there seems to have been relatively little difference between the policy preferences of most of those who opposed the war and most of those who supported it. Both groups were weary and frustrated with the situation and both eagerly grasped for potential solutions, while rejecting the arguments raised by the small minority of articulate dissenters on moral grounds. The major difference between opponent and supporter lay in how much each believed that some useful goal might be accomplished by continuing the war. As on so many issues, American public opinion on Vietnam accumulated in the center of the range of alternatives and differed slightly on means, while maintaining a consensus on ends.

One final stereotype about opponents and supporters of the war might as well be disposed of at this point. Opponents sometimes suggested that it was a problem of knowledge: if people knew more about the situation, then they could not approve of it. To the extent that we can test this proposition objectively, the reverse seems to be true. Verba and his colleagues found that respondents who scored high on a simple set of questions about the facts of the situation were slightly more disposed toward escalation than those who did not know the right answers.[20] A 1968 survey showed that those who reported paying greater attention to news about the war were somewhat more likely to believe that intervention was a correct policy.[21] The differences between the better and less-informed are relatively minor and can be explained, in part, by the lower education of opponents of the war. But it would be a mistake to assume that a greater level of public knowledge about the Vietnam situation would have led to greater opposition.

PATTERNS OF OPINION ON PAST WARS

Was the Vietnam situation a unique one in American history, as far as public opinion is concerned? The United States has been involved in two other wars—World War II and Korea—since the advent of modern survey research. Comparison of the course of opinion on the Vietnam war with that surrounding these other conflicts reveals several parallels.

The changing pattern of support and opposition toward Vietnam involvement is rather similar to that displayed during the Korean

[20] Verba *et al.*, "Public Opinion and the War in Vietnam," pp. 327–28.
[21] Converse and Schuman, " 'Silent Majorities,' " pp. 22–24.

conflict. In both cases, support (as measured by the proportion of those saying that entry was not a mistake) started at higher than 60 percent and eventually declined to about half that figure. In the case of Korea, however, the decrease in support was quite sharp, following the entry of the Chinese, while opinions on Vietnam changed at a more slow and steady pace.[22] Aside from those generated by Chinese intervention in Korea, opinions toward neither war seemed to show much reaction to events. In both cases, Americans reacted to mounting casualties with lessened approval of the war, but only as casualties reached very high figures.[23] While the reaction to events was only marginal in terms of overall attitudes toward the two wars, opinions did change markedly on policy alternatives in reaction to presidential action. In a number of instances the public was not favorably disposed toward a potential policy (e.g., bombing Hanoi) before it was taken, but did give it majority support after that action had been taken.[24] We see again the characteristic pattern of support by the public for any sort of action that might bring about an end to a frustrating situation.

How do the overall levels of support and opposition on Vietnam compare with those for previous wars? Contrary to many impressions, Vietnam has not been the least popular war in American history. The proportion of the public saying that Vietnam involvement was a mistake never topped the 62 percent figure saying that about Korea.[25] Public opinion polling was not systematically done during World War I, but a retrospective question in 1937 showed that 64 percent thought it had been a mistake for the United States to enter World War I.[26] World War II did enjoy much greater popular support, of course, though even here a significant amount of doubt was expressed at all times. Why, then, does it seem that Vietnam was so much more unpopular than Korea? The answer rests with the much greater amount of highly visible and vocal dissent produced in response to Vietnam. Korea simply did not bring forth morally based criticism from the liberal and academic segments of society. Nevertheless, it must be remembered that this vocal opposition amounted to only a tiny fraction of the total sentiment on Vietnam, however much publicity it may have received.

[22] Mueller, "Trends in Popular Support," pp. 361–65.

[23] Ibid., p. 367. A statistical analysis by Mueller shows that support for both wars dropped by 15 percentage points as American casualties increased by a factor of ten (e.g., from 100 to 1,000 or from 1,000 to 10,000).

[24] Ibid., p. 369.

[25] Erskine, "The Polls," p. 136. A Gallup survey in January 1973, just on the eve of the peace settlement, found that 60 percent of the public felt the involvement in Vietnam had been a mistake and 29 percent felt that it had not. Gallup Opinion Index, no. 92 (February 1973), 8.

[26] Erskine, op. cit.

One additional historical parallel might be drawn. The experience of Korea reveals that wars may sometimes become more popular in memory as they become more distant in time. While belief that the United States should have been involved in Korea was below 50 percent at the conclusion of hostilities, a survey taken in 1965 found that two-thirds of the public felt that our action in Korea had been correct.[27] Ironic as it may seem as of this writing, it may turn out that U.S. involvement in Vietnam will be remembered in later decades as much less unpopular than it actually was at the time.

VIETNAM AND THE POLITICAL PROCESS: SOME IMPLICATIONS

As an issue that dominated the concerns of Americans for several years, Vietnam had an inevitable impact on the political process. In this section, we shall investigate its implications in national elections and also see what it can tell us about the nature of public opinion and the policy-making process in general.

Vietnam and Presidential Voting. While American involvement in Vietnam had begun by the time of the 1964 election campaign, it does not appear to have been an issue at that time. Goldwater's comments on the use of tactical nuclear weapons and defoliation were of some importance, but only as part of a larger issue involving his approach to national security and international politics, and the context of Vietnam was not particularly noticed by the public. It was only in the 1968 and 1972 elections that Vietnam involvement became an important question.

Those who had hoped that the 1968 election would be a national referendum on the question of the Vietnam war were disappointed. In part because of the nature of the presidential nominating system, in part because of the assassination of Robert Kennedy, it seemed that no clear alternatives were actually presented to the voters. Such a conclusion is empirically demonstrable, for the voters perceived little difference between the major party candidates on the issue. The Survey Research Center's study of the 1968 election asked interviewees to place their own preferences, and those they attributed to the candidates, on a seven-point scale ranging from immediate withdrawal to complete military victory. The medians of the responses were 4.05 for Humphrey and 4.39 for Nixon, with the respondents classifying themselves at 4.15.[28] Page and Brody argue that the pub-

[27] Mueller, "Trends in Popular Support," p. 371.
[28] Benjamin I. Page and Richard A. Brody, "Policy Voting and the Electoral Process: The Vietnam War Issue," *American Political Science Review*, 66 (1972), 983. The median position of Wallace was 6.51, almost completely to the "complete military victory" end of the scale.

lic was probably quite correct in this assessment, since analysis of
the public statements of Nixon and Humphrey suggests that both
agreed on "war as usual, with a gradual de-escalation of American effort if and when certain conditions were met." [29]

As a result of this centrist position adopted by both major candidates and its generally correct perception by the voters, severe limitations were placed upon the ability of Vietnam preferences to play
a major role in the voting decision. Still, public feelings on the issue
did bear some relationship to the vote. This is most clearly seen in
Boyd's normal vote analysis, which compared the division of the vote
expected on the basis of party identification with the actual vote for
various opinion groups.[30] The results of this analysis are illustrated
in Figure 11-2. Humphrey received less than the normal vote from
all opinion groups, but his greatest deviation came among those who
favored taking a stronger stand. The best Democratic showing came
among those who favored roughly the status quo position, but, as was
pointed out earlier, even those who rejected other alternatives were
not particularly pleased by the existing situation. The greatest gains
for Nixon—and particularly for Wallace—came from hawks, rather
than disaffected doves. The Vietnam issue did not explain the outcome of the election, however, for its magnitude as a short-term force
ranked behind a number of domestic issues.[31]

Vietnam, for all of the political sound and fury it generated, proved
therefore to be of limited relevance to the election outcome in 1968.
While a part of this lack of impact can be blamed on the undifferentiated positions taken by the major candidates, it is hard to conceive
that the choice could have been otherwise. If, indeed, voters' choices
are consistent with the degree to which they perceive a candidate's
position to be close to their own—and there is reason to believe this
is the case—then a candidate who advocated a strong "dove" position would probably not have been successful.[32] The distribution of
public opinion on Vietnam almost guaranteed that the "real alternative" some hoped for would not be offered.

While the 1968 election had failed to offer real alternatives on
Vietnam to the voters, 1972 may have offered more choice than was

[29] Ibid., p. 985.
[30] Richard W. Boyd, "Popular Control of Public Policy: A Normal Vote Analysis of
the 1968 Election," American Political Science Review, 66 (1972), 429–49.
[31] Ibid., p. 448.
[32] For discussion of this assertion that voters do choose their perceived best alternative, see Chapter 14. The conclusion that a candidate expressing a position of complete and immediate withdrawal would not have been successful assumes that (a) he
would not have won on the basis of other issues and (b) a change in the content of
campaign debate would not have greatly affected public attitudes on Vietnam.

Figure 11-2
The Normal Vote and Opinions on Vietnam, 1968 *

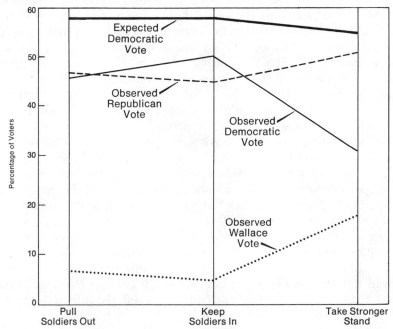

Source: Richard W. Boyd, "Popular Control of Public Policy; A Normal Vote Analysis of the 1968 Election," *American Political Science Review*, 66 (1972), 433.

* The "expected vote" is the normal vote division expected from each group of opinion holders on the basis of their party identification; the "observed vote" is the way that each group actually did vote. The question and alternatives on which the groups are divided are:

"Which of the following do you think we should do now in Vietnam?
1. Pull out of Vietnam entirely.
2. Keep our soldiers in Vietnam, but try to end the fighting.
3. Take a stronger stand, even if it means invading North Vietnam."

desired by most. As noted in Chapter 10, the Vietnam war and the related question of amnesty were the most important issues in causing short-term deviations from established voting behavior. Though overall sentiment had moved somewhat to the dovish side of the issue by 1972, the public was still not ready to vote for a candidate who favored complete withdrawal. This is illustrated by the analysis of the Center for Political Studies survey research on how voters evaluated the candidates on the issues. On their seven-point scale ranging from "withdrawal" (1) to "victory" (7), the mean position attributed to McGovern was 1.7, while President Nixon was placed at 4.6. Since the average voter saw himself as being at 3.6, Nixon was clearly more in line with the preferences of the electorate.[33] As a result McGovern gained some votes from the third of the population who were on the Left on the issue, though these tended to be Democrats anyway, but lost most of the votes from those who took a moderate or a hawkish position. This is quite understandable, in light of the reasons for popular disapproval of the war. Most of that opposition can be attributed to war weariness and dislike for the costs imposed by the war. Hence, the Nixon strategy of gradual withdrawal of U.S. troops, while maintaining a constant policy of bombing, was sufficient to accord with the preferences of the majority of opponents of the war, though not with those who opposed it for moral reasons. The premature announcement of a peace agreement a few days before the election certainly did not hurt Nixon, but he had already attained an overwhelming lead over McGovern. In short, Nixon was successful in dealing with the Vietnam issue as far as the preferences of the public were concerned. Converse and Schuman suggest that during his first term, Nixon was able to align himself with popular majorities believing that the war was a mistake in the first place, that American troops should be withdrawn, and that this withdrawal should not be complete and immediate.[34] This presidential agreement with public opinion apparently served the incumbent well when it came to his re-election in 1972.

Implications for the Study of Public Opinion. The whole history of the Vietnam issue in the mind of the public illustrates several basic attributes of public opinion that are true of a great many other issues. Most of these have been discussed earlier, so a brief listing should suffice at this point:

1. The distribution of preferences is not static over time, but changes slowly, and not necessarily in response to particular events.

2. The public is mainly concerned with ends, rather than means, and almost any realistic policy that might achieve the desired goal can receive popular approval.

3. The prestige of the presidential office should not be minimized; the public is inclined to accept the occupant's choice of means.

4. The public tends to be centrist; even where status quo policies are not popular, they still tend to be more acceptable than deviations to any extreme.

5. The reasons behind public preferences are usually a combina-

[33] Arthur H. Miller *et al.*, "A Majority Party in Disarray: Policy Polarization in the 1972 Election," paper delivered at the American Political Science Association, New Orleans, September 4–8, 1973, p. 14.

[34] Converse and Schuman, " 'Silent Majorities,' " p. 20.

tion of practical considerations and socialized attitudes toward the political system, rather than sophisticated ideology.

In addition to these conclusions about the dynamics of public opinion, the Vietnam issue also substantiates the functional nature of opinions.[35] Consider the sort of psychological bases with which the average American confronted the subject. He already believed that the United States is generally right in what it does, that communism is an evil to be opposed, and that his country never loses a war. As time went on, it became obvious that the United States was not winning in Vietnam, that the domestic costs of the war were increasing, and that a significant number of his fellow citizens felt the war was wrong. Certainly, there was a very strong basis for cognitive dissonance and corresponding attitude change. But, while attitudes toward the war as a general object did gradually become negative, there were still a number of psychological options for continuing support of many administration policies, whether they called for escalation or de-escalation. Perhaps the most important was a strong negative reaction to dissenters, encouraged by their perceived challenges to established social and political values. In this way, hostility and frustration could be projected onto a convenient target to the point of believing that it was war protests that prolonged the war. The tendency of much of the antiwar rhetoric to tie opposition to the war with calls for radical change in other areas of social life was much more likely to foster increased support for the war than it was to move the electorate to the Left. The nature of the Vietnam situation, with its conflicting information about the success of U.S. military policy and competing arguments over its moral rightness from all sides offered a wide variety of psychological supports for those who wished to adjust their perceptions of reality to fit their opinions. Through this maze of subjective reality, the public did eventually develop its preferences in opposition to continuation of the war. But this was a long and slow process and at all times left a considerable amount of latitude in policy decisions in the hands of those who held political power.

If Vietnam proves nothing else, it shows that the objective and systematic study of public opinion is essential to those who wish to understand the political process and affect the outcome of policy decisions. At the elementary level of appraising public opinion, it is clear that most of the popular stereotypes about opinions on the war were simply not correct. The presidential assertion of the existence of a

[35] An extensive analysis of attitudes toward the war in terms of functional and dissonance theory appears in Rosenberg *et al.*, *Vietnam and the Silent Majority*, pp. 80–116 and 133–55. See also Ralph K. White, *Nobody Wanted War: Misperception in Vietnam and Other Wars* (Garden City, N.Y.: Doubleday, 1970).

"silent majority" that always gave its support to administration policy was undoubtedly an overstatement with political motivations, but it did give a more accurate view of the situation than would reliance on casual observation of vocal dissent. The history of popular reaction to the antiwar movement and its activities suggests that an objective understanding of what people are thinking and why is a vital prerequisite to changing their opinions. To blindly and indiscriminately attack an individual's most deeply held values for the purpose of changing one of his opinions is likely to be quite counterproductive.

Ideology and the Social Issue

12

If different observers of the mass public offer conflicting and confusing generalizations as to current trends in public opinion, it is far from surprising. As we have already seen, popular preferences on single issues such as the Vietnam war are often complex and easily misinterpreted. When we move to conclusions about whether the public mood is moving to the political Right or Left or is polarizing, then we tread on treacherous ground indeed. Yet, such macro-political statements are the kind that we would expect a scientific examination of public opinion to enable us to make.

If one wishes to begin by cataloging the various conclusions that have been made about the general trend of public opinion over the last few years, he would have no trouble in assembling a bewildering collection. There are fervent arguments that the nation and its leaders are rapidly moving toward semifascist repression, while there are equally strong ones that the future will fulfill a radical vision. Some see an increased consensus, while others see a widening gap between ideologically opposed groups. Many of the more extreme assessments can be readily dismissed by anyone who knows anything about public opinion, but the question still remains: Is public opinion changing and in what direction?

This chapter, while not presuming to provide precise and unchallengeable answers, will attempt to assess the trends and their implications. We shall look at opinion change both in terms of ideological self-perceptions and issue groupings. The most important of these issue groupings is one that was touched on earlier: the Social Issue. We will also suggest what the future of public opinion holds in light of the recent past and consider the implications of that future for the political process.

THE SOCIAL ISSUE

In their controversial analysis of contemporary politics, *The Real Majority*, Scammon and Wattenberg point to the emergence of a new type of public concern during the latter part of the 1960s, which they termed the "Social Issue." This is defined as "a set of public attitudes concerning the more personally frightening aspects of disruptive social change." [1] This notion deserves two points of emphasis. First, the Social Issue represents a number of different substantive elements that are linked together by the perceptions of the public, rather than by any inherent similarity. Second, people tend to perceive these elements as threatening and, therefore, to react to them with hostility. The one substantive thread that seems to link the elements is that all seem to represent sudden changes from the status quo and to challenge traditional values and practices. It is not surprising that people react quite negatively to these elements of social change, given what we know about the tendency of most people to resist challenges to their existing values and perceptions. And since these elements are such that they are easily perceived as personal threat in a physical as well as an attitudinal sense, the reaction to them has particularly strong effects upon other attitudes and political behavior. Scammon and Wattenberg distinguish several major elements in the Social Issue, and we shall deal with each of these.

Crime. The preeminent element of the Social Issue is fear of crime. Statements of concern over crime, a lack of law and order, and other similar expressions have made their way into surveys as major problems in the past several years as they never did in previous decades. While the volume of mentions of crime-related issues has never exceeded that for economic and international problems, the intensity of concern seems to be relatively greater. When Watts and Free questioned respondents in 1972 as to how much they were concerned about various problems, "the amount of violence in American life," "the problem of drug addicts and narcotic drugs," and "crime in this country" all ranked with inflation and Vietnam at the top of the list.[2] This intense concern probably resulted from the fact that falling victim to criminal activity is a very real possibility to a considerable segment of the population. A Gallup survey in late 1972 found that over 20 percent of all respondents (or other members of their households) had personally suffered from one or more of five types of assault and theft in the preceding year.[3] Hence, much of the public has either been victimized or has close contact with others who have been, par-

---

[1] Richard M. Scammon and Ben J. Wattenberg, *The Real Majority* (New York: Coward-McCann, 1970), p. 43.

[2] William Watts and Lloyd A. Free, *State of the Nation* (New York: Universe Books, 1973), pp. 34–35.

[3] *Gallup Opinion Index*, no. 91 (January 1973), 11. Survey data of this type are more revealing than are the usual statistics compiled from police records, as a substantial proportion of crimes are not reported to the authorities.

ticularly in large cities where the proportion of victims rises to one-
third. Debates over the accuracy of crime statistics notwithstanding,
many people believe crime in their locales to be on the rise; 35 percent of the Gallup respondents believed that there was more crime
than a year earlier and only 11 percent said there was less.[4] As a
result, about 40 percent of the population in 1972 stated that there
were areas within a mile of home in which they would be afraid to
walk alone at night, an increase of 10 percent over a similar question
four years before.[5] Findings such as these clearly substantiate the
generalization that crime, particularly in its violent forms, has come
to represent a major concern of the American public.

This concern over crime has an inevitable impact on preferences
as to what ought to be done about it. The public increasingly displays approval for a number of "get tough" measures. Support for the
death penalty rose to 57 percent at the end of 1972, the highest figure since the 1950s.[6] Three-fourths of the population have been reported as believing that the courts do not deal harshly enough with
criminals, and similar majorities agree with various proposals for
"preventive detention," denial of parole for habitual offenders, and
the like.[7] At the same time, Watts and Free report the greatest support for "cleaning up social and economic conditions in our slums
and ghettos" in order to reduce the causes of crime and less support
for "really cracking down" than for any other reform proposal.[8] In
some ways, these seemingly contradictory preferences parallel opinions on Vietnam policies: people are concerned about the problem
and will accept any move that promises a solution. This tendency
further substantiates the degree of intensity and apprehension that
the issue of crime produces.

Race.   We have already discussed the central place the racial issue
holds in the concerns of many Americans (Chapter 9), and it is not
surprising to find that this subject is intertwined with other elements
of the Social Issue. Among the fears that beset many white Americans is that of violence and militancy on the part of blacks. To a great
extent, this fear is a reflection of concern over crime, as many whites
view with alarm the incidence of violent crime in black areas. The
fact that most of the victims of such crime are other blacks hardly
removes the apprehension felt by whites. A related source of this
fear is the occurrence of civil disorders in the urban ghettos of Har-
lem, Watts, Detroit, and countless other communities during the

[4] *Ibid.*, p. 12.
[5] *Gallup Opinion Index*, no. 82 (April 1972), 13.
[6] *Ibid.*, p. 14, and *Gallup Opinion Index*, no. 9 (December 1972), 27.
[7] *Gallup Opinion Index*, no. 45 (March 1969), 12–14.
[8] Watts and Free, *State of the Nation*, pp. 118–20.

mid-1960s. Race riots are not new to this country, but those of previous decades often involved whites attacking blacks. The
emergence of more militant black leaders during the 1960s, even
when these leaders had no connection with violence, served to keep
white fear alive. Thus, in part, this aspect of the Social Issue reflects
real occurrences of violence and destruction, though they are often
magnified by a mirror of subjective perception. Also in part, the racial fear reflects the existing racial prejudices of the white community, apprehensive of demands for racial equality, and using the
crime and violence aspect as a justification for their concern.

This reaction of fear toward blacks has had predictable effects on
public preferences. Considerable proportions of the white population endorse various hard-line measures toward persons involved in
riots, including the order of the mayor of Chicago to shoot on sight
anyone involved in looting.[9] Not all whites feel this way; a significant minority does not see escalation of force as an answer, and some
blacks would like strong measures taken to curb disorders. But, in
general, the patterns of response to such disorders are predictably
polarized.

The fact that the Social Issue is likely to come down to one of
racial fear for many whites might lead some to say that it is nothing
but a contemporary manifestation of American racism. Yet such an
interpretation would reflect a failure to understand some of the underlying reasons for fear. On the various measures of crime and fear
of crime cited earlier in this chapter, blacks exhibit a greater concern
than do whites. Whites flee racially changing neighborhoods, citing
increased crime as the reason; those blacks who can leave the ghetto
do so for similar reasons. A more substantive issue than simply fear is
that of busing to achieve racial balance in schools, but it too seems to
involve the Social Issue. A vast majority of all whites voice opposition to busing measures; and many would cite the inferiority of
schools in black areas, the possibility of racial disorders in the
schools, and the overall possibility of subjecting their children to
possible crime as reasons for this opposition. It is quite probable that
a good part of this resistance is really a reflection of unstated prejudice—but the objections are not totally unrealistic. As a matter of
fact, the black community is split on the advisability of busing for
this purpose, particularly if it is "forced," rather than voluntary.[10] A
negative reaction to such integration measures may thus reflect
something more than simply white prejudice toward blacks.

[9] *Gallup Opinion Index,* no. 37 (July 1968), 17. See also Robert Chandler, *Public
Opinion: Changing Attitudes on Contemporary Political and Social Issues* (New
York: R. R. Bowker Co., 1972), pp. 27–31.

[10] A 1972 survey showed that 7 percent of the whites and 24 percent of the blacks
favored a mandatory racial balance in schools. Watts and Free, *State of the Nation,* pp.
98–100.

Dissent.   One very obvious change in the politics of the 1960s from that of previous years was the emergence of various forms of protest demonstrations. First appearing as civil rights demonstrations in the South, these later became particularly associated with protests against the Vietnam war and other governmental policies by college students. Such modes of dissent—and even dissent in general—were not well received by the public; and, for a time, disorders on college campuses threatened to become a major national issue. As we saw in Chapter 9, while paying homage to the abstract ideal of freedom of speech, most Americans would not necessarily extend the right to vocal disagreement with existing policy very far. When campus protests occasionally went beyond the bounds of propriety, therefore, public reaction was extremely negative. Virtual unanimity was found for "taking a stronger stand on student disorders" in 1969, and strong majorities backed various proposals for expulsion of demonstrators, denial of financial assistance, and the like.[11] Such reaction seemed to be as negative as that of the white population to civil disorders in black ghettos, though the alternatives posed by surveys were less extreme. The degree of hostility often expressed toward campus demonstrators is particularly striking in view of the facts that demonstrators were white and middle class (and therefore not prior targets of prejudice), their demands (such as withdrawal from Vietnam) were not always so repugnant to a considerable part of the public, and hostile reactions were produced in situations in which there was no particular violence committed by the demonstrators. It would seem that while there was some linkage between the reaction to dissent and the elements of the Social Issue described earlier, the hostility did not grow directly out of personal fear in most instances.

Rather, the key to understanding this part of the Social Issue seems to be the public's evaluation of what they perceived to be the changing values and life-styles of the young. The identification of certain patterns of personal appearance, speech, and entertainment among "student types" with radical political beliefs made it possible for many to greatly overestimate the leftward trend of ideology among college students and to react accordingly. As we have seen earlier, while college students tend to have more liberal political beliefs than the population as a whole, it is certainly not the case that anything near a majority would qualify as even passive political radicals.[12] But this assessment of student opinion is based upon survey research—not upon the characteristic perceptions of the mass public,

[11] *Gallup Opinion Index,* no. 46 (April 1969), 10–11; no. 49 (July 1969), 26; and no. 61 (July 1970), 22.

[12] To cite one more example, the annual Gallup survey of college students found that over one-half favored the expulsion of demonstrators who broke the law. *Gallup Opinion Index,* no. 48 (June 1969), 11.

reacting to new and disconcerting patterns of personal behavior and
seeing the college campus as the source of these unwanted innovations. Public concern over campus dissent has waned with the decline of such protest. The changing values that accounted for much
of the hostility still make up a significant portion of the Social Issue,
however, and it is to that topic that we now turn.

Changing Values.   Along with fear of crime, the basic changes that
seem to be occurring in the norms and values of society are perhaps
the deepest source of the Social Issue complex. Old standards of conduct seem to be being discarded, and behaviors once thought taboo
are accepted in some segments of the population. Perception of these
changes causes a natural reaction of hostility by those who believe in
the validity of the lost standards, for a dissonance situation is created.
And, while the subject matter of these changing values may lie outside the normal sphere of public policy, the reaction to them may
well have an indirect effect on political attitudes and preferences.
Since much of this concern over the loss of old standards does not directly involve governmental action, it has been largely unexplored
by the usual practitioners of national survey research. We shall concentrate on some aspects that fall within the public sector and at
least speculate about some other aspects.

One area in which there has been a particularly marked change in
behavior is that of sexual mores. Among other manifestations of this
change are increased public acceptance and governmental permission of printed and visual media depiction of sexual subjects in a
more explicit manner. Anyone who compares the content of literary
works that were prosecuted just a few years ago because of a few of-
fending words, with the nature of material readily available today
must be struck by the extraordinary magnitude of change. The public
has become considerably more tolerant, but this liberalization has
not been as great as the change in what is legally allowed. Twelve
percent of the population report having received some "objectionable sex literature" through the mail, 25 percent complain of such material in magazines and movies and 38 percent have seen something
objectionable on television.[13] If one could add in the unmeasured
number who are aware of the existence of "adult" bookstores and X-
rated movies, and concerned about them, but have not had occasion
to patronize them, the proportions might well be higher. Eighty-five
percent would support stricter laws on the sending of obscene materials through the mails, and 75 percent, on that sold locally.[14] Thus,
there is a sizable proportion of the public that is at least somewhat

[13] *Gallup Opinion Index*, no. 49 (July 1969), 16–17.
[14] *Ibid.*, pp. 18–19.

concerned about the liberalization of expression in this area. That policy changes have come almost entirely as a result of federal court decisions, frequently over the objections of elected officials, may have served to increase the degree of public frustration on this issue.

Another issue that, like the issue of sexual mores, illustrates the linkage between overt fears and a more diffuse concern over social change is that of drugs. Concern over the prevalence of drug usage in contemporary society has resulted in its being cited as a major social problem by the public, even apart from the general category of crime. Not surprisingly, very great majorities of the public are opposed to liberalization of penalties for use and sale of narcotics, and two-thirds approved of the proposal made by former Governor Rockefeller in 1973 that all convicted sellers of narcotics be given life sentences without possibility of parole.[15] The same degree of hostility extends to more controversial drug categories, such as marijuana. Eighty percent of Gallup respondents in 1972 opposed lessening penalties for marijuana sellers, and the same proportion opposed its legalization.[16] In short, all of the arguments as to the merits of liberalizing policies on "soft" drugs seem to have had little effect on the mass public and may have conceivably strengthened its opposition.

The areas of pornography and drugs represent situations in which a diffuse concern over changing social patterns and values become questions of public policy. But because this concern is so ill-defined, even by those who share it, its prevalence has probably been grossly underestimated by most observers. One occasionally finds reports in surveys of small percentages of the population citing "moral decay" or "loss of religious values" as major problems. Two surveys conducted by the Gallup organization found that "national disunity and political instability" had become major components of popular "fears and worries" for the nation during the late 1960s, being expressed by as much as one-fourth of the public in 1971; and this appears to be an unprecedented development in the history of American public opinion.[17] Instances of this diffuse concern over changing values sometimes appear, therefore, but for the most part, they are either left untapped or else relegated to the inevitable "other responses" category, when answers to open-ended questions are coded.[18] But

[15] *Gallup Opinion Index*, no. 92 (February 1973), 20. This proposal has now become law in New York.

[16] *Gallup Opinion Index*, no. 82 (April 1972), 18–20. See also Chandler, *Public Opinion*, pp. 114–25.

[17] Albert H. Cantril and Charles W. Roll, Jr., *Hopes and Fears of the American People* (New York: Universe Books, 1971), pp. 22–25, and Watts and Free, *State of the Nation*, pp. 256–58.

[18] This was the author's experience in analyzing a number of surveys taken for political purposes in the early 1970s. Since such expressions of uneasiness, dismay, and

while this diffuse concern may be left unstated or unrecorded, this does not mean that it has no impact upon public attitudes. Rather, it may represent a force that cements together a set of prevalent fears and corresponding preferences on a range of more precise public issues, some of which we have discussed earlier. The fact that an individual's dismay at such things as changes in church liturgy or marriage by Catholic clergy may affect his attitudes on public issues may not seem very logical to an external observer. Psychologically, it is a real possibility.

The Social Issue: Some Conclusions.   It should now be clear that while the Social Issue idea is a difficult one to measure, it is a very real thing. Its diffuse and often hidden nature makes generalization difficult. Yet a few conclusions and observations can be confidently advanced. First, it seems clear that while its elements may be objectively separate and distinct, they are psychologically interrelated. For significant numbers of people, the rise in crime, outbreaks of dissent, racial threats, and disrespect for established social norms all become a part of the same problem in society. Secondly, many specific aspects of the Social Issue produce a pattern of consensus among respondents. This does not always extend to proposed remedies for the problems, but it frequently does. And this consensus of concern frequently appears in almost all social groupings.[19] The Social Issue is really not a new one. There is no reason to doubt that Americans have always been opposed to crime, narcotics, pornography, and dissent or that whites have always resisted black demands. In fact, public opinion on most of these phenomena has probably liberalized in the last decade. The thing that makes them a current topic is that contemporary events have increasingly thrust them into the consciousness of the average American and made them topics of public debate. The reaction to this change has been fear, and because people are afraid, the Social Issue has assumed an increasingly great importance in public opinion.

THE OTHER ISSUES

Broad as the Social Issue may be, it does not encompass all areas of public concern. The other areas are not particularly tied up with social fears and opinions, and bear little resemblance to those discussed in the previous section. These other issues, moreover, in-

---

alienation do not fit easily into the usual policy categories such as Vietnam, taxes, and unemployment, they tend to be ignored by both politician and pollster.

[19] If the reader would care to consult the various survey results cited earlier in this chapter, he will find that there is little variation in this concern among social groups, whether black or white, rich or poor, young or old.

clude some of the most important substantive questions of public policy. Scammon and Wattenberg emphasize the central place of traditional domestic economic issues as an alternative set of public concerns. Also prominently displayed in the universe of non-Social Issue concerns would be many questions of international affairs and environmental regulation. We shall briefly investigate some of these other issues and note the difference in their trends from those of the Social Issue.

We might take as a baseline for looking at contemporary trends the period from 1960 to 1964, for it was not until after this time that the Social Issue really started to develop. It is clear that then there was still widespread public acceptance of continuation of most New Deal principles of strong federal involvement in the insurance and expansion of social welfare activities—education, medical care, remedies for unemployment, poverty, and urban decay.[20] Indeed, it seems clear that Americans have not changed their essentially liberal position on these substantive domestic questions in the last decade. About one-third of the public was willing in 1972 to keep spending to provide public jobs for the unemployed at the present level and almost half wanted to increase the amount.[21] About as many (62 percent) favored some sort of compulsory private or government-financed health care program for everyone as had favored medicare for the elderly alone eight years earlier.[22] The imposition of wage and price controls under the Nixon administration—the strongest move since World War II toward government intervention in the economy—received widespread popular approval. While significant parts of the population expressed doubts as to the efficacy or fairness of these controls, they were much more in favor of more, rather than less, strict enforcement.[23] Even on the question of welfare per se, with its Social Issue overtones, there was a strong consensus for maintaining or increasing levels of support.[24] On the question of a guaranteed income, the median level of support for a family of four that was suggested by respondents in one survey was $5,200 per year, far more than most legislative proposals called for.[25]

This willingness to accept an enlarged federal role in social wel-

[20] This is substantiated by Lloyd A. Free and Hadley Cantril, *The Political Beliefs of Americans: A Study of Public Opinion* (New York: Simon and Schuster, 1968), chap. 2. We have already presented much of this data in Chapter 5 under the heading of "operational liberalism."
[21] Watts and Free, *State of the Nation*, p. 170.
[22] *Ibid.*, pp. 130–32.
[23] *Gallup Opinion Index*, no. 70 (April 1971), 18, and no. 82 (April 1972), 25.
[24] Watts and Free, *State of the Union*, p. 172.
[25] *Ibid.*, pp. 174–76. It should be noted that there was also a strong consensus for implementing this guarantee through some sort of work program, even if that proved to be more costly than simply distributing the money.

fare activities is particularly striking if we compare it to opinions on other spheres of federal expenditures. While Americans approve of programs that would require maintaining or increasing expenditures for these domestic purposes, they take an almost exactly opposite position on military activities. Forty percent advocate the current level of military and defense spending and almost that many would like to reduce it, while 10 percent or less would favor an increase.[26] Table 12-1 shows the relative priorities that Americans today assign for government spending. Without exception, domestic programs

Table 12-1
Support for Governmental Spending on Major National Issues, 1972

Issue	Composite Score *
Combating crime	88
Helping the elderly	87
Coping with narcotic drugs and drug addicts	86
Cleaning up our waterways and reducing water pollution	81
Reducing air pollution	80
Improving the education of low-income children	80
Improving medical and health care for Americans generally	80
Helping low-income families pay their medical bill through medicaid	74
Making a college education possible for young people who could not otherwise afford it	72
Rebuilding run-down sections of our cities	69
Meeting the overall problems of our cities generally	68
Providing government-paid jobs for the unemployed	67
Providing better and faster mass transportation systems	66
Establishing more parks and recreation areas in our cities and countrysides	66
Providing better housing for people generally	64
Building better and safer roads, highways, and thruways	63
Helping to build low-rent public housing	62
Improving the situation of black Americans	57
Helping low-income families through welfare programs	53
Contributing to the work of the United Nations	36
Spending on our defense forces	32
Maintaining U.S. forces in Europe	29
Maintaining U.S. military bases throughout the world	28
Spending on the space program	25
Providing economic and development loans to foreign countries	24
Providing military aid to foreign countries	21

Source: Table 7 of *State of the Nation,* edited by William Watts and Lloyd A. Free, © 1973 by Potomac Associates, Washington, D.C.
 * Composite scores are based on values of 100 for increased federal spending, 50 for maintenance of present level, and 0 for reducing or ending spending.

[26] *Gallup Opinion Index,* no. 71 (May 1971), 23, and no. 88 (October 1972), 22.

rank higher than those for military, international, and space exploration purposes. A few of the domestic items (crime and drug addiction) represent positive responses to Social Issue concerns; the others, almost without exception, refer to the amelioration of substantive social problems, particularly those faced by the poor. Similar findings on the preference for social welfare activities have been reported by other surveys.[27]

The implications of all of this are unmistakable. While the whole pattern of fear and response on the Social Issue would seem to suggest a rightward trend, the mood of the population on these substantive policy questions is anything but conservative. The same liberal trend would seem to be true, though less dramatically, outside the economic area. If we can separate out the foreign policy dimension from the question of U.S. involvement in Vietnam, then the trend is not to the political Right, but rather away from it. To take one enduring issue, that of Communist China and the United Nations, there was a slow, but steady, change in American public opinion toward approving the seating of the mainland government prior to the time that it actually happened.[28] Even on those issues that by their nature seem to be involved with Social Issue fears, one can point to at least some evidence of liberalization. As was noted in Chapter 9, white Americans have come to voice greater acceptance of black equality in many areas of life and to support policies to accomplish that goal, even while expressing fear and hostility toward some blacks. Even on a highly controversial question such as abortion, which certainly represents a challenge to social mores, the public displays at least as much support for change as do its elected leaders.[29]

Once again, we see the necessity for distinguishing different types of issues in assessing public opinion. The Social Issue is a very real one to many people, and their reactions of fear can cause them to support quite severe and even repressive policies toward those persons and behaviors that appear threatening. At the same time, there is probably an increasing degree of support for positive solutions for obvious social problems. Thus, while the response to the Social Issue suggests a rejection of contemporary liberalism, other types of

[27] E.g., Scammon and Wattenberg, The Real Majority, pp. 75–76.

[28] Hazel Erskine, "The Polls: Red China and the U.N.," Public Opinion Quarterly, 35 (1971), 125–30, and Gallup Opinion Index, no. 72 (June 1971), 16.

[29] A Gallup poll taken just prior to the U.S. Supreme Court decision on abortion found that the population was evenly divided on the subject and that this represented a trend toward acceptance of abortion. Gallup Opinion Index, no. 92 (February 1973), 21–23. However, a survey a few months earlier found that 64 percent of respondents agreed with the statement that "the decision to have an abortion should be made solely by a woman and her physician." Gallup Opinion Index, no. 87 (September 1972), 14.

issues indicate that the public is becoming more liberal. Both phenomena are quite real and to ignore either is to profoundly misinterpret contemporary opinion.

RIGHT OR LEFT: SELF-CLASSIFICATIONS

The suspicion that the public may have moved both to the political Right and the Left at the same time makes it difficult to offer any overall statement about the trend in the public mood. One approach that gives a single measure, one that allows us to let individuals themselves select the dimension to which they are responding, is that of looking at how people describe themselves in terms of liberal and conservative ideology. From time to time, surveys have asked respondents to classify themselves as "liberal" or "conservative," sometimes allowing for more precise categories. There are some severe limitations to the usefulness of this sort of data, for as we have already seen, a considerable part of the population has little or no conceptualization as to the meaning of these terms. Furthermore, most Americans, even though they may be aware of the concepts, do not formulate their political opinions in an ideological framework. Still, their self-classifications are not without meaning. Most are able to correctly classify political candidates on an ideological spectrum, and there appears to be a definite tendency to vote for the presidential candidate who is perceived as being closest in ideology to the individual voter.[30]

Figure 12-1 shows the tendency of Americans to describe themselves as "liberal" or "conservative" over the past three decades.[31] As the figure clearly shows, there were roughly equal numbers of liberals and conservatives up into the early 1960s, with the liberals actually taking a small lead in 1963. However, paralleling the events that led to the emergence of the Social Issue in the second half of the decade, there was a significant trend toward conservatism. In all of the surveys since 1968, conservative identifiers outnumbered liberals by a ratio of at least three to two. The shift is hardly of dramatic proportions, but it does indicate that there has been a definite preponderance of conservatives over the last several years, a situation that had not existed for the previous thirty. All of this is not to imply that most Americans are to be found on the far Right. As of 1972, only

[30] This point will be more fully developed in Chapter 14.

[31] There is a severe problem in comparability of survey items here. The data in Figure 12-1 are based upon combining all categories of liberal and conservative and excluding "middle of the road," as well as "no opinion" groupings. Most items are based upon some version of a "Do you consider yourself to be . . ." sort of question; however, the data for 1960 to 1962 are based upon a choice between hypothetical "liberal" or "conservative" political parties.

Figure 12-1

Self-Classification as Liberal and Conservative, 1939–72

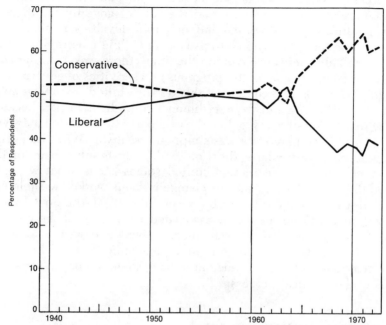

Sources: Computed from survey data reported by Hazel Erskine, "The Polls: Some Gauges of Conservatism," *Public Opinion Quarterly,* 28 (1964), 155–57; Lloyd A. Free and Hadley Cantril, *The Political Beliefs of Americans: A Study of Public Opinion* (New York: Simon and Schuster, 1968), p. 204; Richard M. Scammon and Ben J. Wattenberg, *The Real Majority* (New York: Coward-McCann, 1970), p. 72; and *Gallup Opinion Index,* no. 50 (August 1969), 9; no. 59 (May 1970), 8; and no. 83 (May 1972), 10.

14 percent of the Gallup sample placed themselves in the "Very Conservative" category; 23 percent thought of themselves as "Fairly Conservative"; while a third of the respondents took "Middle of the Road." [32] Hence, the majority might be best described as ideologically moderate, though with something of a conservative bias. This bias can have a definite impact upon certain policy preferences, as indicated by the fact that almost twice as many people in 1970 were in favor of conservative judges being appointed to the Supreme Court as wanted liberal appointments.[33]

The limited cognitive content of ideological positions for so many Americans makes substantive explanation of this apparent conservative trend difficult. However, the following sort of explanation seems

[32] *Gallup Opinion Index,* no. 83 (May 1972), 10.
[33] *Gallup Opinion Index,* no. 59 (May 1970), 10.

reasonable. For most of the time since the advent of the New Deal, the liberal-conservative debate centered on substantive issues of economies and social welfare and the role of government therein. This produced a relative standoff in public loyalties in that there was, on one hand, a basic consensus against "big government" in a theoretical, abstract sense, yet, on the other, there was a similar consensus in favor of many of the programs and activities of government. During the 1960s, the content of this debate shifted somewhat away from this economic and welfare dimension, perhaps in part because of the realization of many political participants that a Goldwater-type assault on the welfare state was simply not realistic. With the events of the 1960s—particularly the riots and protests—the focus of the liberal-conservative distinction shifted somewhat to what we have called the Social Issue. And this change in focus worked to the detriment of liberal popularity, for the term "liberal" in the Social Issue context seems to be inevitably associated with some of the goals of disorder (opposition to the war, black power) and with a leniency toward its means. The change from an economic to social focus was only marginal, but it was sufficient to have some important repercussions in the political process.

IDEOLOGICAL CHANGE AND THE FUTURE OF AMERICAN POLITICS

The emergence of the Social Issue, has had an obvious impact on American politics. It is this complex of fears that can be given credit for the presidential resurgence of the Republican party and the surprising show of strength by George Wallace. Just as issues of domestic economic policy have worked to the advantage of Democratic (and liberal) candidates for the past forty years, the Social Issue offers an inherent boost for Republicans (and conservatives). Scammon and Wattenberg point out that this juxtaposition of issue, ideology, and party suggests some strategies that candidates might profitably follow.[34] Democrats, they say, should attempt to neutralize the Social Issue by making it clear that they are against crime, drugs, and the like, while exploiting their inherent advantage on substantive economic and social legislation matters. Republicans should logically do the reverse: hit their liberal opponents with social fears, while neutralizing the economic aspect by coming up with some meaningful programs. This advice, it appears, was well placed and was probably followed by a number of candidates in both parties in the 1970 elections. Those who did pursue the indicated strategy

[34] These recommendations are made in Chapter 20 of *The Real Majority*.

seemed to win; those tho ignored it did not fare so well.[35] The 1972 presidential contest fits this model almost perfectly. The choice was between McGovern, who was perceived very heavily in Social Issue terms, and the incumbent Nixon, who could point to a moderate record on substantive programs—and the outcome was as expected. Once again, the importance of understanding the complexities of public opinion was demonstrated.

If we look beyond current questions of partisan advantage, the existence of the Social Issue has additional implications. The fact that a substantial proportion of the public suffers from a deep uneasiness about the course of public affairs must have an effect upon its behavior. This degree of uncertainty is sharply documented by Cantril and Roll's 1971 study. Using the "self-anchoring ladder rating," which allows respondents to rate the past, present, and future in terms of a continuum from the worst possible state of affairs to the ideal, they found a definite increase in pessimism among the American people. This instrument has been administered to samples in a number of nations over the years and, with only one previous exception, the respondents saw the present as being an improvement over the past. However, in this U.S. survey, respondents gave the present a *lower* rating than they did the past. As the authors conclude,

. . . Americans sense that their country has lost, rather than gained ground over the past five years . . . people expect the United States in 1976 . . . to be merely where it was a full decade earlier, having barely recovered the reverses of the previous half decade.[36]

This unprecedented dissatisfaction was perhaps temporary, for replication of the study one year later revealed that Americans in 1972 rated the present as almost exactly equal with the past and the future as likely to be better.[37] However, this degree of optimism seems to be a cautious and limited one. Later, in 1973, Gallup reported a continuing decline in people's satisfaction with the future they saw before them.[38]

The source of this dissatisfaction seems to lie with public affairs and the nation as a whole, rather than with the personal problems of

[35] This is a difficult generalization to substantiate, but a number of 1970 senatorial contests serve to illustrate the point. Those liberal candidates who could be successfully associated with antiwar militancy by their opponents (such as Gore in Tennessee and Goodell in New York) lost; those who could symbolically neutralize the Social Issue (such as Stevenson in Illinois, who took to wearing an American flag on his lapel) won. Hartke of Indiana was particularly vulnerable to attacks on his record of antiwar dissent, but heavy campaigning on the basis of traditional economic questions brought him the narrowest of victories.

[36] Cantril and Roll, *Hopes and Fears*, pp. 25–26.

[37] Watts and Free, *State of the Nation*, pp. 26–27.

[38] *Gallup Opinion Index*, no. 101 (November 1973), 1–3.

individuals. In terms of their own personal lives, Americans have consistently perceived that things were getting better. But perceptions of the political system have been radically different. As was noted in Chapter 9, there has been a marked drop in public confidence in the honesty and effectiveness of various political institutions and in the ability of government as a whole to respond to the needs of the people. Comparison of findings over the last fifteen years reveals that:

This trend toward pervasive discontent had actually begun about 1964; it intensified between 1968 and 1970 when confidence in government reached a low point which remained unchanged into 1972. In 1964 and 1968, 22 and 35 percent of the population, respectively, said they could trust the government to do what is right only some of the time; by 1972 that figure had increased to 44 percent. . . . Parallel changes in responses to questions about the honesty and competence of the people running the federal government also indicate a significant decrease in respect for government officials.[39]

Easy explanations for this loss of political trust may be misleading. Its genesis cannot be laid to the revelations of wrongdoing in connection with Watergate and related scandals in 1972, for the trend was well established before this time. These charges of corruption, however, have undoubtedly contributed to the increase and possible acceleration in the loss of confidence. Somewhat more valid an explanation would be that groups on the political Left, including blacks and young people, reacted to the Vietnam war and other policies in the Johnson and Nixon years with alienation. This might account for a part of the trend. The shift, however, is much greater than this explanation could account for. The loss of trust is common to almost all demographic and political groups, though to varying degrees. Indeed, one analysis suggests that political cynicism is the highest among those who hold the most conservative political views on different types of issues.[40] Since this decline in the confidence people place in government is true of the old as well as the young, white as well as black, conservative as well as liberal, its causes must be broad and deep. At the root, it would seem that people are reacting to their perception that government has simply not been successful

[39] Arthur H. Miller et al., "A Majority Party in Disarray: Policy Polarization in the 1972 Election," paper delivered at the American Political Science Association, New Orleans, September 4–8, 1973, pp. 45–46. For a complete analysis of this data on political trust, see A. H. Miller, T. A. Brown, and A. S. Raine, "Social Conflict and Political Estrangement: 1958–1972," paper delivered at the Midwest Political Science Association, Chicago, May 3–5, 1973.

[40] Teresa E. Levitan and Warren E. Miller, "The New Politics and Partisan Realignment," paper delivered at the American Political Science Association, Washington, September 5–9, 1972, pp. 13–15.

in formulating and administering policies in recent years.[41] While politicians have promised more in the last decade, they have been able to deliver less. This gap between expectation and reality may be a matter of concern for a variety of different policy areas, but the most important is probably the Social Issue. As we have noted earlier, the Social Issue reactions of fear—which have intensified since 1964—are capable of having a particularly great impact on other public attitudes. When other failures of public policy—such as inflation, unemployment, and an emerging energy crisis—are added to this complex of social apprehensions, the public's appraisal of government effectiveness can hardly fail to drop. To anticipate a point that will be made in the next chapter, people evaluate government on the basis of what it has accomplished. To the average citizen of the early 1970s, the performance of the political system must leave much to be desired. The level of public trust in the future will depend, above all, on the perceived effectiveness of government in dealing with public concerns.

To put the situation into perspective, let us note that the loss of popular confidence in government is not limited to the United States. Suggesting that the leadership of other major Western nations faces a general decline in public faith, columnist Joseph Kraft concludes:

The basic fact is that governments are not up to the responsibilities that have been thrust upon them. . . . This incapacity becomes manifest as soon as any problem emerges. Whether the difficulty be Watergate or energy or inflation, the result is to make manifest the weakness of government. Disappointment sets in, and builds to the crisis of confidence now everywhere apparent.[42]

Whether governments here or abroad will be able to satisfy public needs in the future or whether the political process will offer some mechanism for the public to effectively express their lack of satisfaction remains to be seen.

---

[41] For an analysis of the last decade that brings home this point very well, see David S. Broder, *The Party's Over: The Failure of Politics in America* (New York: Harper and Row, 1972).

[42] *Daily Pantagraph* (Bloomington, Ill.), December 28, 1973.

The Dynamics of Public Opinion

13

In the preceding four chapters, we have emphasized the way the public as a whole has tended to view a number of important topics. We shall now complete that discussion by focusing on public opinion at an entirely aggregate level and attempting to deal with it abstractly. Our concern here will be with the characteristic pattern of division of opinion and its degree of changeability. These dynamics of public opinion have received too little attention from researchers in the past. The principal author who analyzed public opinion in this way was the late V. O. Key, and he must be credited with many of the concepts examined here.[1] The goals of this chapter are to suggest several different dimensions of opinion at an aggregate level, how different types of issues will tend to be arrayed on those dimensions, and the implications of these patterns for the political system.

THE DISTRIBUTION OF OPINION

Our first concern must be with the way in which public preferences are numerically distributed. Certainly, the effect of public opinion upon public policy and upon the social system will be much different if there is a sharp conflict in preference between two halves of the population rather than if a great majority were to stand firmly for one side of the issue with only a few dissenting. We shall therefore examine the relative frequency of these patterns of conflict and consensus.[2]

Conflict. The distribution of opinion can be easily represented by means of a frequency graph, the height of the curve corresponding to

[1] V. O. Key, Jr., *Public Opinion and American Democracy* (New York: Alfred A. Knopf, 1961), chaps. 2, 3, 4, 10, and 11.

[2] In addition to being discussed by Key, the patterns of opinion distribution are discussed by Robert A. Dahl, *A Preface to Democratic Theory* (Chicago: University of Chicago Press, 1956), pp. 90–105, and Robert E. Lane and David O. Sears, *Public Opinion* (Englewood Cliffs, N.J.: Prentice-Hall, 1964), pp. 94–113.

the relative occurrence of a particular point of view. The sketches in Figure 13–1 are examples of such graphs. The convention is that the scale across the baseline of the distribution represents a continuum of all possible alternatives of an issue, the middle of the scale representing a position of neutrality on the issue. In practice, one often does not have any measurement of opinion that permits a precise gradation of preference. It is therefore necessary to be quite careful in making statements about conflict and consensus. For instance, if the only question posed is a dichotomous one that makes no provision for any preference other than complete agreement or disagreement on an issue, then a picture of conflict may emerge, even though the population is not very divided. Or a pattern of consensus may emerge when there is real division, simply because one of the two alternatives presented was much more extreme than the other. We shall use examples in this chapter that permit at least some differentiation of degrees of agreement and disagreement, but the student of public opinion must often work with questionnaire items that are not so discriminating.

A hypothetical case of complete conflict is presented in graph (1) of Figure 13–1. In this situation, there would be an almost complete polarization of opinion, with half the population holding one position and half the other, and with no one taking the middle ground. Such a distribution almost never happens in the real world. About as close as reality ever comes to this is the case depicted in (2), which represents public opinion on the issue of federal involvement in insuring equal job opportunities to blacks. On that issue, most of the population was fairly evenly divided between support and opposition to such a policy. Note, however, that this distribution only includes those who held an opinion on the issue; if those who answered "don't know" or reported that they had no interest in the issue were added to the neutral "depends" category, then this middle proportion would rise to over 20 percent of the whole. Even in a fairly clear case of conflict such as this, the interpretation is at least partly a matter of perspective. If we considered opinions on an issue of racial equality in terms of a spectrum from complete white domination (as before the Civil War) to some hypothetical state of complete black control, then we would probably find most of the population expressing opinions near the center of that scale and conclude that there exists a consensus for racial equality. Hence, conflict is muted in practice by two factors: the tendency of most people to avoid the logical extremes of an issue and the inevitable presence of a significant group of people who will take some sort of middle position, whether through even-handed reason or a lack of preference. Therefore, when patterns of conflict are found, they tend to resemble the graph

Figure 13-1
Patterns of Conflict: Real and Hypothetical

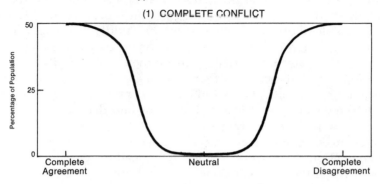

(1) COMPLETE CONFLICT

Percentage of Population

50

25

0

Complete
Agreement

Neutral

Complete
Disagreement

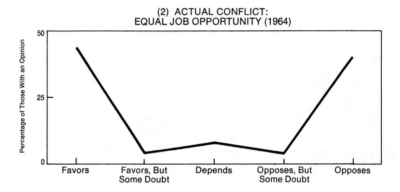

(2) ACTUAL CONFLICT:
EQUAL JOB OPPORTUNITY (1964)

Percentage of Those With an Opinion

50

25

0

Favors

Favors, But
Some Doubt

Depends

Opposes, But
Some Doubt

Opposes

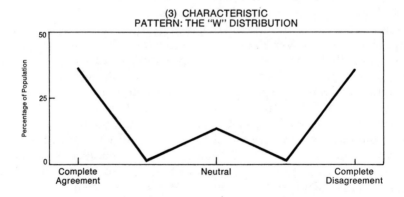

(3) CHARACTERISTIC
PATTERN: THE "W" DISTRIBUTION

Percentage of Population

50

25

0

Complete
Agreement

Neutral

Complete
Disagreement

Source: Data in (2) is from Survey Research Center (University of Michigan) 1964 election survey.

in (3), which resembles the letter W. While there is a definite difference expressed, there will always be a number of people at the center point.

Given the problems in measurement and interpretation of conflict, it is not possible to specify precisely the extent to which different issues will produce conflict distribution. To the extent that one can generalize, it would seem that issues of the type that we have labeled "social"—issues involving race, morality, and the like—will most often produce conflict. To the extent that there is no consensus on questions in these areas, conflict here will tend to be most distinct. The reason for this is that many of these issues seem to be seen in *symbolic* terms. In this respect, they differ from other issues, such as economic ones, concerning which questions tend to be those of marginal advantage and practicality. These symbolic issues are often expressed in what might be labeled "emotional" terms (i.e., they are viewed as absolute questions of right and wrong, rather than as preferences for one policy over another on the grounds of relative utility).[3] They are likely to be closely allied with one's self-image, and debate over them therefore raises ego-defense mechanisms. At any rate, they are likely to be perceived as having little or no middle ground. Whereas there would probably be a wide range of opinions on an economic question—such as the appropriate tax rate—symbolic issues will tend to divide the population more sharply. This is not to say that such issues can contain no middle ground, for even the most controversial—such as abortion, busing to achieve integration, and the limits of dissent—can always be subdivided and compromise positions reached. But the tendency of the public is to see them in dichotomous terms.

Another factor that affects the degree of conflict over an issue is the degree of interest and intensity displayed by the public in it. If a great many people have little or no knowledge or interest in the question, then the proportion falling in the middle, if only by default, may outnumber those holding contrary opinions. Thus, many issues that might be seen in symbolic terms display only moderate conflict. A hypothetical example might be possible U.S. reaction to a communist takeover of some far-off corner of the world. The issue of communism has been sufficient at some points in U.S. history to excite and polarize portions of the public. But the remoteness of the subject to the life and interests of most Americans would probably be sufficient to cause most of them to register no strong feelings either way on the matter. On the other hand, some symbolic issues do

[3] This distinction between types of issues closely parallels the difference between "realistic" and "nonrealistic" conflict developed by Lewis Coser, *The Functions of Social Conflict* (Glencoe, Ill.: Free Press, 1956).

strike close to everyday life. Race is the most important among these, and the whole range of the Social Issue complex discussed in Chapter 12 seems to qualify also. On issues of this sort, there will be few who are neutral, and conflict may be very clear.

Consensus. The other side of the coin is the idea of consensus—that is, a situation in which most people are in agreement. The first graph (1) in Figure 13-2 illustrates a hypothetical situation in which agreement exists in an almost complete form, while (2) depicts an actual consensus on giving foreign aid to other countries. Although (2) does show a definite majority in favor of aid, there are a few who are opposed and a large number who are neutral. Most consensus situations reflect the pattern in (2) more than (1), because complete unanimity is rarely achieved. The characteristic pattern of consensus is represented by (3), which can be called a "J" distribution or by (4). The latter is really an exaggerated version of the "W" distribution presented earlier (Figure 13-1), as the consensus is really a middle one—most people falling between the extremes.

Patterns of consensus are found on a variety of issues. Questions involving basic social norms or political values may produce almost complete agreement or disagreement. Many current issues of the type discussed throughout this book reflect a moderate degree of consensus. If one asks about most of the existing programs undertaken by government, there will be a consensus favoring their retention, though there may be less agreement on their expansion. As was pointed out earlier, an apparent consensus may develop (of the "double J" variety) when a majority of the population lacks interest in a subject, or when a number of alternatives are presented and the majority is concentrated around the moderate responses. This is particularly true for many questions of domestic economic policy, where few people would favor moving far to the Left or Right, but most would rather choose among incremental modifications of the status quo. Hence, moderate consensus is a more common pattern in American public opinion than is polarized conflict.

STABILITY AND CHANGE

Assertions sometimes appear in print—usually by people who know little about the scientific study of politics—that public opinion is highly volatile, that it changes erratically from week to week. In actuality, however, a much better case could be made that the preferences of the public on most issues of any importance tend to be rather stable. This question of the extent to which the distribution of opinions changes and under what conditions is obviously an impor-

Figure 13-2
Patterns of Consensus: Actual and Hypothetical

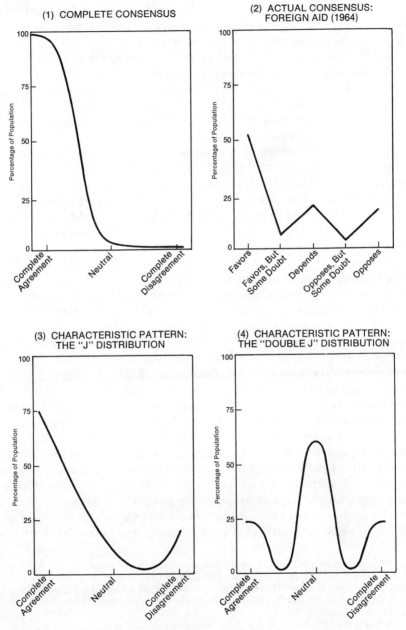

(1) COMPLETE CONSENSUS

(2) ACTUAL CONSENSUS: FOREIGN AID (1964)

(3) CHARACTERISTIC PATTERN: THE "J" DISTRIBUTION

(4) CHARACTERISTIC PATTERN: THE "DOUBLE J" DISTRIBUTION

Source: Data in (2) is from Survey Research Center (University of Michigan) 1964 election survey.

239

tant one. Unfortunately, there has been relatively little investigation into the area. In part this is due to the lack of availability of comparable survey data over time. While the establishment of several "data banks" makes survey data from a number of sources quite accessible to researchers, the problem still remains that very few issues are regularly surveyed at different points in time using the same questionnaire items.[4] With these difficulties in mind, we shall attempt to offer some generalizations about the pattern of movement in public opinion, basing these generalizations in part on the few available analyses of change over time and in part on less systematic observation of a number of issues.

While the distribution of opinion in America is certainly not one of complete stability, change tends to occur quite slowly. Key offers the metaphor of "viscosity" (i.e., public opinion does "flow," but in a slow and sluggish manner).[5] This is particularly true for those issues that have a long history and a fairly high degree of public awareness. Questions such as the role of government in the economy tend to show only marginal changes over time. As might be expected, somewhat greater changes occur when the objects of opinion are much less familiar or more ephemeral. For instance, most people were not concerned about environmental problems and particular solutions until the subject was publicized and debated in the late 1960s. To take a very extreme example, one might say that the effect of the famous radio dramatization "Invasion from Mars" in 1938, which temporarily convinced many unsuspecting listeners that the earth was under alien attack, is an illustration of how a completely new subject can generate opinions.[6] A more common source of new objects of opinion is political personalities. At every election, the voters are presented with a new set of candidates, many of whom were not previously known to most. Hence, new perceptions and evaluations are made, though often on the basis of existing political loyalties. As the results of polls throughout presidential campaigns suggest, these evaluations seem to change relatively little from the time they are first established.[7] If one looks at the available data on changes in public opinion on most substantive issues, there will be little evidence of rapid or erratic change. Perhaps a few issues, either trivial

[4] Observation of comparable items that do exist will be greatly facilitated by the publication of George H. Gallup, ed., The Gallup Poll: Public Opinion, 1935–1971, 3 vols. (New York: Random House, 1972). Articles on "The Polls" by Hazel Erskine appear regularly in the Public Opinion Quarterly and present available survey results over time on specific topics.

[5] Key, Public Opinion and American Democracy, p. 235.

[6] The effects of this incident on the public are investigated in Hadley Cantril, The Invasion from Mars (Princeton: Princeton University Press, 1947).

[7] See, for example, the data presented earlier in Figure 7-1.

or unknown to most people, might exhibit less regularity, but visible and important questions almost always present only slow trends over periods of years.

There are a number of obvious reasons for this relative stability of public opinion. Of prime importance is the functional nature of opinion holding. As we have seen repeatedly, people resist changing their minds. Other influences tend to reinforce this tendency. To some extent, opinions are a reflection of social factors (such as economic status, race, and religion), and these inputs will generally be constant, therefore stabilizing, influences. Much the same is true for the reinforcing effects of personal contact in everyday life. People tend to talk to others who hold the same views. The political system also works against change. Political parties and political leaders tend to take the same sorts of positions over the years, thus leading loyal partisans to emulate them. Finally, it must be remembered that we are here concerned with the overall distribution of preferences. Individual changes in opinion may largely cancel each other out. In sum, our knowledge of the individual basis of public opinion suggests that its aggregate stability is to be expected.

But opinions do change, at least in the long run, on some major issues. Under what conditions does this occur? First of all, opinions may be significantly altered by some cataclysmic event, such as mobilization for all-out war or a major depression. The occurrence of the latter in the 1930s certainly had an effect on the political attitudes and policy preferences of the public, for it greatly altered the actual social and economic environment of many individuals. Such events, though, have occurred very infrequently (at least in the United States), perhaps less often than once in every generation. Leaving aside this sort of influence, what causes the slow trends over periods of five or ten or twenty years? An inevitable source of change is the continual turnover in the population as some people die and are replaced by those reaching adulthood. However, the effects of this turnover are somewhat negated by the transfer of opinions to the young in the process of political socialization.

There is some systematic research that bears upon the conditions under which opinion changes. Mueller has taken the one question asked by the Gallup poll in almost every survey over the past thirty years—presidential approval or disapproval—and attempted to explain the varying degrees of support given to the chief executive at different times.[8] His findings showed results that differed according to four factors: first, presidents inevitably tend to become less popular as time progresses; second, international crises generally produce

[8] John E. Mueller, *War, Presidents and Public Opinion* (New York: John Wiley, 1973). Some of his findings on attitudes toward war were discussed in Chapter 11.

a temporary increase in support; and third, a decline in prosperity causes a decrease in approval. The fourth factor, the existence of wars, had a different effect, depending on the president in question. This question of presidential approval differs somewhat from most questions of public preference in that reactions are somewhat affected by personal style and party loyalty. Still, these findings suggest some generalizations about public opinion change in a more general context. The most important of these is that the public reacts to events and conditions in the world. The reaction will be greatest and most enduring for those events that most clearly touch the individual's own life, and economic conditions offer the clearest case of this. Reactions to specific events that attract great coverage in the mass media, but have little effect on everyday life, may produce temporary spurts of concern and corresponding shifts in preference that disappear with the immediate crisis. Finally—and this conclusion is highly tentative—there seems to be a tendency for public opinion on a major issue to move continually in the same direction. Short-term fluctuations may appear, but the trend over a number of years will usually be consistent.[9]

IMPLICATIONS FOR POLICY MAKERS

The behavior of the mass public as it forms and reforms its attitudes and preferences might be expected to have some effect upon the political process. If one believes the American political system to be at least somewhat democratic, then he would expect the nature of public opinion as an aggregate quantity to have some important implications for those in a position to determine public policy. The phenomena we have discussed in this chapter do have an effect upon the political process, though perhaps not the one that might be expected.

Let us begin with the situation of consensus. If policy is to respond to opinion, then we would expect it to follow best on those issues on which there is a clear majority holding one preference. Yet, because there is another dimension to opinions, the mere existence of a numerical majority does not seem to be sufficient. Not only does it matter how many people favor a particular action, the extent to which they are likely to get upset about the lack of such action is also significant. Key suggests that this second consideration delineates three types of consensus situations: *permissive, supportive,* and *decisive.*[10] The first seems to be the most prevalent and occurs when the public

[9] Examples of this were seen in the move toward believing that Vietnam involvement was a mistake (Chapter 11) and in the attitudes of the population on economic issues discussed in Chapter 12.

[10] Key, *Public Opinion and American Democracy*, pp. 32–37.

generally favors a proposed policy, but lacks much intensity on the subject. Therefore, the people are, in effect, permitting government to take an action if it so desires. Such a situation will come about on those issues that have little clear and direct relationship to the individual, for example, policies designed to benefit people far removed, whether by distance or social status. There are many instances in which some proposal seems like a good idea to the majority, which voices its approval but is not prepared to take any political action to back up its declared preference. A clear example is the question of gun control legislation, which has received majority support as long as it has been surveyed. In this instance, a less concerned popular majority has been repeatedly bested in the legislative process by a more intense minority.

The supportive consensus differs from the permissive consensus in that it deals with existing policies and actions. In general, people forming this type of consensus will tend to support the general range of policies and activities undertaken by government, as well as the occupants of official positions, and the political system as a whole.[11] This type of consensus does give some direction to policy makers, presumably making them aware that existing policies ought to be continued and that there are some cultural boundaries, however ill-defined, that should not be transgressed. The supportive consensus, however, gives little direction as to the course of future policies, and to the extent that it does affect attempts at innovation, its implication must be to support the status quo.

The third consensus situation, the decisive, involves not merely majority support for some new action, but also a high degree of concern that it be taken. Essentially, this is a situation in which the public demands some action by government, with the implication that incumbents will be displaced if they do not comply. This consensus of decision is a rare phenomenon indeed. Key suggests that public demand for support of the Allies prior to American involvement in World War II may have constituted such a situation. It is difficult to think of another such issue in the years since.[12] It is only once in a very great while that the public will speak with one voice and do so forcefully enough that government must listen.

The implication, then, is that even the existence of a numerical

[11] This may be, in part, a result of the fundamental nature of American political culture, as discussed in the section on "Attitudes Toward Political Authority," in Chapter 9.

[12] Some might suggest that such a consensus developed demanding American withdrawal from Vietnam, but, even here, there continued to be support for leaders and policies that did not bring withdrawal. An example might be the public reaction to President Nixon's initial refusal to release subpoenaed tape recordings in October 1973, though this hardly represents a basic decision on public policy.

consensus is probably not sufficient, in and of itself, to exercise a necessary effect upon government. The problem here is one of *salience*. For public opinion to have a direct effect upon policy, it is necessary for individuals to have an opinion, to attach some intensity of feeling to it, and to have some knowledge of what government is or is not doing.[13] For most issues, one or more of these prerequisites are lacking. Some issues are too far removed from common experience to achieve intense concern. Others, such as domestic economic policies, do touch upon daily life, but produce only support, not demands for future action; for the consideration of alternatives requires more knowledge and interest than the public is usually willing to give. To repeat a point made elsewhere in this book, the public emphasizes the achievement of results, rather than the means used to achieve those results. Therefore, it characteristically offers little direction as to what new policies ought to be adopted.

If consensus is characterized by a lack of intensity, what of these issues that produce both strong feelings and a lack of agreement? Even the most dedicated advocate of democratic theory ever elected to public office would be placed in a quandary when asked to respond to a public that firmly states that its preferences are 45 percent for, 45 percent against, and 10 percent neutral. The political system has a way of dealing with these situations of clear and intense conflict: it avoids them. It can be argued that any sort of representative government will tend to try to ignore those symbolic issues that are most often involved in conflict, or at least pass them on to some branch or agency of government that does not have to stand for reelection.[14] In the United States, issues involving race, dissent, and civil liberties have generally been resolved by the federal courts, not Congress. This is the great paradox of public opinion. On those issues where there is the greatest unanimity, there is often apathy; on those where there is intensity, there is a lack of consensus. And the responsiveness of government to the public suffers for it. Given that the public has such inherent weaknesses in its ability to directly communicate its wishes to government, we cannot rely on the mere existence of public preferences to produce democracy. This does not preclude the system responding to the public as a result of other mechanisms. Succeeding chapters will investigate some of these means.

[13] Angus Campbell *et al.*, *The American Voter: An Abridgement* (New York: John Wiley, 1964), p. 98.

[14] This line of argument is pursued by T. Alexander Smith, "Toward a Comparative Theory of the Policy Process," *Comparative Politics*, 1 (1969), 498–515.

Postscript to Part III

THE FUTURE OF AMERICAN PUBLIC OPINION

It is always difficult to predict the future behavior of the public, even if one has a good grasp of the past. At the risk of being proved wrong by the turn of events, we shall try to extrapolate from the present and suggest what some trends might be.

The safest statement is that opinions in future years are likely to be similar to those today. Public opinion on most issues changes slowly, even under the pressure of events. And most of the individuals in the public will still be here ten and twenty years from now. New adults are always replacing old, but the gap in preferences between young and old is not enormous. Thus, the changes wrought by a changing population will be only marginal, even if the youthful members of the population keep their current liberalism as they grow older.

The trend of opinions on domestic policies in the area of economic and social welfare legislation seems to be to the liberal side, and there is no reason to doubt that it will continue. Americans seem increasingly supportive of government action to provide aid for medical care and other social needs. At the same time, this does not necessarily mean there will be support for extension of the pattern of proliferation of agencies and programs in the federal bureaucracy that characterized the 1960s. People are concerned also about economic burdens of taxation, and inflation and bureaucracies —including the military—are apt to be popular targets. Perhaps the greatest support in domestic affairs will come for those programs that appear to accomplish their goals directly (such as regulation to curb environmental abuses) rather than through a complex system of agencies and grants.

While economic issues will always be of considerable concern to the public, the Social Issue fears will still be significant. The apparent decline in some of the most obvious symptoms, such as campus protests and racial militancy, has reduced attention to these fears somewhat, but the substantive problems of crime and racial tension will continue. One change that has probably occurred already is that it is no longer possible for political candidates to make easy electoral hay purely by a rhetoric of fear and hostility. The public will probably no longer settle for slogans on these matters. With the absence of the Vietnam war issue as a polarizing force on the Social Issue, the concern of the public may have shifted more toward substantive solutions to the underlying problems. As the changes that have occurred so rapidly in public mores and behavior remain, furthermore, they may not seem quite so threatening. Thus, an admittedly optimistic conclusion would be that the Social Issue as a complex of fears may be gradually and quietly transformed to a set of preferences about policies on social issues. The difference may be only one of style, but style can be important.

PART IV

PUBLIC OPINION AND PUBLIC POLICY: LINKAGE POLITICS

Elections: Are They Meaningful?

14

In the concluding chapters of this book, we shall deal with the most important and most problematic question of all: Does public opinion influence public policy? This is the question of democratic theory raised in Chapter 1, and its resolution had to await our inquiry into the nature of public opinion itself. Having established the nature and characteristic behavior of public preferences in contemporary America, we can now examine the relevance of those preferences for the actions taken by government. As noted in Chapter 13, one can hardly expect public opinion in and of itself to automatically determine the course of public action. Indeed, almost no one ever suggests that such responsiveness regularly occurs. We must therefore examine several possible sources of linkage between people and government. The most obvious possibility is the electoral process, to which we now turn.

THE PROBLEM OF ELECTIONS

It is usually assumed that in any political system which pretends to be at all "democratic," the main input from the public will come in the form of its votes. Except for occasional questions put up for direct referendum balloting, voting entails the selection of parties and individuals to exercise the powers of government. The question we are concerned with is whether or not this selection process causes public policy to be in line with public opinion. Certainly, many authors, both classical and contemporary, have doubted that voters determine policy.[1] Whether it is the philosopher who doubts that people have the wisdom to direct government, the social scientist who

---

[1] Gerald M. Pomper, *Elections in America: Control and Influence in Democratic Politics* (New York: Dodd, Mead, 1968), pp. 38–39, argues that those who criticize voters for not making policy are implicitly accepting criteria established by those who really were opposed to the notion of democracy; hence, we should not really expect elections to perform a policy-making function.

claims that they lack the interest, or the social critic who argues that those who are elected forget those who put them there, attacks on the meaningfulness of elections abound. We shall attempt to use all available evidence to evaluate the electoral process in America, both in terms of individual voters and the aggregate behavior of the system. Our concentration will be on elections as a linkage between opinion and policy. There may be other advantages to be gained from elections, such as increasing the perceived legitimacy of the political system, but we shall not inquire into those here.[2] Our main concern will be with whether the electoral process substantially increases the responsiveness of government to public opinion.

WHO VOTES?

The first question that must be considered is the correspondence between the public as a whole and those who participate in elections, for the latter is a significantly smaller group. Voting turnout in the United States is highest for presidential elections, but even here, no more than 64 percent of those of voting age have ever turned out in an election in the last fifty years.[3] And the proportion has not been increasing very much at all. Figure 14-1 shows the turnout rate in presidential elections over the last century. While turnout has increased since the 1920s, it has declined again over the last three elections, reaching a low of 56 percent in 1972. If one excludes from the base those who were legally unable to vote in the past (such as women in most states before 1920), the rate of electoral participation is apparently lower today than it was before 1900. This decline in turnout in the past few years is particularly striking because participation in southern states, traditionally far lower than in the rest of the nation, has increased markedly, largely as a result of federal action to prohibit racial discrimination.[4]

If we get only a slight majority of the public to participate in presidential choice, the record is far worse in other elections. The turnout for congressional elections in presidential years runs four to five percentage points lower than in presidential contests and runs roughly 40 to 50 percent in the alternate years. With occasional exceptions, turnout in state elections held at other times, local contests, primaries, and referenda is even lower still, sometimes abysmally so. It is clear that most choices made through the electoral process are made by only a minority of the population.

[2] Some of these other advantages are discussed in *ibid.*, chaps. 2 and 9.

[3] This 64 percent turnout was achieved in 1960. All turnout figures given here are in terms of those of voting age, *not* of those registered to vote.

[4] For a discussion of turnout in the states, see Lester Milbrath, "Individuals and Government," in *Politics in the American States*, eds. Herbert Jacob and Kenneth N. Vines, 2nd ed. (Boston: Little, Brown, 1971), pp. 27–81.

Figure 14-1
Turnout in Presidential Elections, 1880–1972

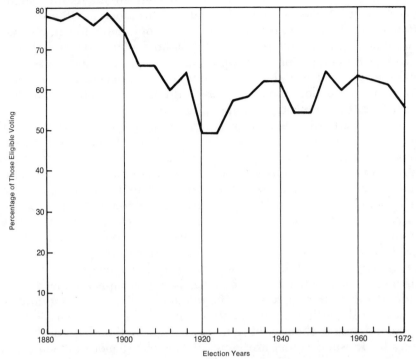

Sources: 1880–1916: Robert E. Lane, *Political Life: Why and How People Get Involved in Politics* (New York: Free Press, 1959), p. 21; 1920–64: *Statistical Abstract of
the United States, 1969,* p. 369; 1968–72: *The 1973 World Almanac and Book of Facts,*
pp. 40, 147. Figures prior to 1920 include men and women (in those states where they
were eligible to vote) twenty-one and over.

It would be a definite exaggeration to attribute this lack of participation entirely to public apathy or disgust. Though some people do
not vote simply because they do not choose to, there are a number of
other reasons why turnout is not higher. Many of these are an outgrowth of the characteristic set of legalities that surround the act of
voting in America. In almost all states and localities, it is necessary to
be registered prior to election day, and this may involve a degree of
inconvenience to some people. Furthermore, varying periods of residence within a state, county, township, and precinct are customarily
imposed, thus disenfranchising a significant part of an increasingly
mobile population.[5] Kelley and his colleagues found significant relationships between several types of legal requirements and the degree to which the population was registered to vote in American

[5] Recent judicial decisions have greatly reduced or eliminated many of these resi-
dency requirements.

cities.[6] There are also a host of minor legal and practical reasons for nonvoting that are difficult to calculate and are therefore usually overlooked. Andrews suggests that groups such as the institutionalized population, convicted felons, people who are ill, etc., account for a significant part of the potential electorate and that as many as 85 percent of those who really can participate in presidential elections actually do.[7] At any rate, there are some valid excuses for nonparticipation, though these would hardly account for the low turnout rates produced by nonpresidential elections.

The key question here is whether the actual electorate is really much different from the population as a whole. If nonvoting were a random phenomenon, then imperfect turnout would not affect the ability of election results to reflect public opinion. This, however, is not the case, for there are obvious differences between voters and nonvoters. Not surprisingly, electoral participation is strongly related to economic status and education.[8] Nonvoters are disproportionately found among those with the lowest levels of income and education. Less obviously, younger voters—those under thirty—are less likely to participate. Traditionally, women have been less likely to vote than men, though the discrepancy has largely disappeared today outside of the poorest part of the population and some ethnic groups. Blacks still participate in elections at a lower rate than whites, though dramatic changes have been wrought in the South in the last decade. In sum, voters are generally an older, more affluent, and more educated group than are nonvoters.

The effect of these social correlates of participation must necessarily be to introduce at least some distortion of public opinion as it is represented by those who actually vote. The effect is to make voters more conservative on many issues than the population as a whole, though the more educated electorate might be more liberal on some noneconomic questions.[9] However, the distortion may not be too great when considered in terms of the choice between candidates. On one hand, the variation in participation tends to aid the Republican party, as their identifiers are the most likely to turn out in an election. However, it appears that nonvoters seem to react to short-term forces in the same way that independent voters do and that they

[6] Stanley Kelley, Jr., Richard E. Ayres, and William G. Bowen, "Registration and Voting: Putting First Things First," *American Political Science Review*, 61 (1967), 359–79.

[7] William G. Andrews, "American Voting Participation," *Western Political Quarterly*, 19 (1963), 639–54.

[8] These and following generalizations are confirmed by a number of sources, many of which are summarized in Lester W. Milbrath, *Political Participation: How and Why Do People Get Involved in Politics?* (Chicago: Rand McNally, 1965), chap. 5.

[9] Sidney Verba and Norman H. Nie, *Participation in America: Political Democracy and Social Equality* (New York: Harper and Row, 1972), chaps. 15 and 16.

would generally have voted for the winning candidate for president.[10] Thus, in terms of general presidential elections, the fact that not everyone votes does not necessarily affect the outcome, though it could. In low turnout local elections, however, the distortion may be considerable.

VOTING BEHAVIOR:
THE STATIC FACTORS

The key question to be dealt with in this chapter is that of the individual voter: Does he communicate any policy preferences through his vote? Many would argue that the answer is generally a negative one. There is considerable evidence that a good part of voting behavior can be explained by reference to static factors (i.e., constant or habitual patterns of thought that bear little or no relationship to the actual issues before the electorate). In this section we shall examine the extent to which these static factors predominate and their implications.

Party Identification. As was pointed out in Chapter 10, most people identify with one political party, and this exercises a great effect upon their votes.[11] Overall, party identification is an extremely good predictor of voting behavior. The extent to which party identifiers adhere to their party in a particular election will depend upon the strength and direction of the short-term forces, of course. In an election in which one party did much better than the normal vote would indicate, only a tiny fraction of its identifiers would be likely to deviate. Party identifiers are very likely to report always voting for their party in past elections, and only a minority in most elections are likely to split their ticket for candidates of different parties. This tendency toward party regularity is even stronger for those elections below the presidential office, where the candidates and issues are much less visible to the average voter. In 1958 (a year that saw more short-term deviation in congressional voting than normally), 84 percent of all of the votes for congressional candidates were cast by party identifiers voting in line with their established loyalties; only 16 percent were attributable to independents or defectors.[12] Clearly, party identification has an independent effect upon voting behavior that cannot be entirely explained by reference to other variables.

[10] This observation is based upon inspection of those responses to the Survey Research Center's election surveys that ascertain the preferences of nonvoters.

[11] Generalizations in this section are mainly drawn from Angus Campbell *et al.*, *The American Voter* (New York: John Wiley, 1960), chap. 6.

[12] Donald E. Stokes and Warren Miller, "Party Government and the Salience of Congress," in Angus Campbell *et al.*, *Elections and the Political Order* (New York: John Wiley, 1966), p. 197.

Party identification also exercises an indirect effect upon voting, for it greatly influences perceptions and evaluations of candidates and issues. The authors of *The American Voter* found that there was a high degree of relationship between party identification and the attitudes expressed both toward presidential candidates and toward the parties on a number of different dimensions. This effect is quite in line with our understanding of the functional nature of opinion formation. If an individual has an established party loyalty, then one would expect that he would react to new candidates of his party favorably and would react unfavorably toward those of the opponents. Thus, party identification—because of its dual role—is of crucial relevance in explaining why many people vote the way they do.[13]

The tendency to form opinions and vote in accordance with one's party identification does not necessarily mean that issue preferences play no part in voting. It is conceivable that voters might be operating on the basis of some overall ideology that would lead to support for one party. Or perhaps expressed identification is simply a reflection of preferences in that year and is itself a result, rather than a cause, of current evaluations. Neither of these alternative explanations seems to find much support in the real world. We know that only a small part of the public can qualify as ideological by even the loosest of criteria. Party identification seems to flow, not from political beliefs, but from the process of political socialization in childhood. As was pointed out in Chapter 4, most people have the same party loyalties as their parents and they acquire these during childhood. Party identification also does not fluctuate as rapidly as do attitudes toward candidates and issues. It is estimated that only 2 percent of the individuals in the American electorate change their party identification each year.[14] Hence, this most important source of the voting choice is a static factor that, for most people, is often a result of influences bearing no relevance to contemporary political questions.

Social Correlates.   Much the same sort of conclusion is reached if we examine the effects of social correlates on voting behavior. There are definite patterns of social groupings that have an effect on party identification and therefore on voting. Democratic identifiers are more likely to be of lower status, Catholic, Jewish, and black; Republicans, the opposite. To be sure, there is a touch of issue-relatedness in these patterns. The parties have traditionally favored different

[13] The direct and indirect effects of party identification were demonstrated by Arthur S. Goldberg's causal model presented in Chapter 8.

[14] William H. Flanigan, *Political Behavior of the American Electorate*, 2nd ed. (Boston: Allyn and Bacon, 1972), p. 48.

economic groups, so that it might be considered rational for the businessman to be a Republican and for the blue-collar worker to be a Democrat. It also seems reasonable to conclude that black voters have far more reason to support Democratic candidates than Republicans. But many of these social patterns lack any contemporary relevance. The political cleavage between Catholics and Protestants has its roots in events of the last century. In fact, religious issues today very rarely become sources of partisan disagreement.[15] The 1960 presidential election showed the greatest degree of religious polarization, but here the issue was purely symbolic and had nothing to do with the policies overtly advocated by either candidate.

The lack of relevance to current public issues is even more true of the subcultural variations in political behavior. The effect of historically developed patterns of partisan support has often been counter to issue preferences. The South remained solidly Democratic long after the candidates of that party ceased to represent many of its interests. And while that habit has been broken in the last decade, the Democratic party still dominates at the state and local levels in the South. Thus, the distribution of party loyalties bears only a slight resemblance to the distribution of public opinion. If social correlates are viewed as constant influences on voting behavior, people seem to be communicating relatively little to government through their votes.

Change in the Electorate? Any national election in the United States is apt to be decided by the way in which those who consider themselves to be "independents" generally vote, for they hold the balance of power between the two parties. One might therefore argue that these people who are not committed to a party must be choosing on the basis of their reaction to alternatives posed by the candidates and that the results of elections are consequently likely to reflect public concern. Such a conclusion, however, has generally not been accepted because of what we have known about the independent voter. Contrary to the stereotype of independents as public-spirited citizens voting for the "best man" or "on the issues," it has appeared that these nonidentifiers actually have less knowledge than do stronger partisans. As *The American Voter* concludes, independents "have somewhat poorer knowledge of the issues, their image of the candidates is fainter, their interest in the campaign is less, their concern over the outcome is relatively slight, and their choice between competing candidates . . . seems much less to spring from discoverable evaluations of the elements of national politics." [16] In-

[15] There are public policy questions involving religious disagreement, such as aid to parochial schools and abortion, but political parties generally do not take opposing stands on them.

[16] Campbell *et al.*, *The American Voter*, p. 143.

dependents in America have apparently included mostly those people who simply have not been interested enough in politics to develop any commitment.

More recent analyses have suggested that this negative evaluation may not be quite accurate. There has been a slight tendency toward an increase in the relative number of nonidentifiers, and this seems to include a substantial number of younger and well-educated voters. Flanigan's conclusion, drawing on data through the late 1960s, is that there is really little difference in the amount of knowledge and political competence of partisans and independents.[17] DeVries and Tarrance argue that rather than focusing on self-proclaimed independents, one should look at that part of the electorate who will split their ticket for candidates of differing parties.[18] This group of ticket-splitters, a somewhat different set of individuals than the nonidentifiers, comprises a substantial part of the American electorate, and appears to be somewhat more educated and aware than the average voter. There is certainly an increase in the tendency of Americans to not simply vote a straight party slate.[19] The difference in support for the parties at the congressional and presidential levels in the last several years is unprecedented in American history. Hence, it can be argued that voters are responding to something other than traditional constant factors in their voting choice, for they are reacting differently to candidates for different offices. However, this greater volatility seems to be limited to the most visible offices—president, senator, governor—while straight-ticket party line voting is more likely to be the rule for congressional and other state and local offices. In short, voters may be indicating that they can achieve sufficient knowledge and interest to select candidates in accordance with their policy preferences, but they have not yet proved that they regularly do so.[20]

VOTING BEHAVIOR: ISSUE CONTENT

While static, nonissue causes of voting choice account for a portion of the results of elections, they are only a part of the story. As explained

[17] Flanigan, *Political Behavior*, pp. 47–48.

[18] Walter DeVries and Lance Tarrance, Jr., *The Ticket-Splitter: A New Force in American Politics* (Grand Rapids, Mich.: William B. Eerdmans Publishing Co., 1972).

[19] Walter Dean Burnham, *Critical Elections and the Mainsprings of American Politics* (New York: W. W. Norton, 1970), pp. 106–09.

[20] Even ticket-splitting for an office may not prove that votes reflect policy preferences. In 1970, Michigan voters moved against the tide to reelect Governor Milliken, yet they also voted contrary to his position on three major referenda. DeVries and Tarrance, *The Ticket-Splitter*, p. 101.

in Chapter 10, there are also short-term forces that cause deviations from expected voting patterns. We shall be concerned in this section with the extent to which these short-term forces include preferences on issues.

It has been suggested that three things are necessary before issues could play a role in voting behavior: (a) the voter would have to be aware of the issue; (b) he would have to have some preference on it; and (c) he would have to perceive some difference between the positions of the parties or candidates on that issue.[21] On most of the important issues analyzed in *The American Voter,* six out of ten people met the first two criteria of knowledge and preference. However, the third criterion, perceived party difference, eliminated approximately half of these, leaving only one-third to one-fourth of the voters as capable of voting on the basis of most issues. Hence, the conclusion might be drawn that issues play little role in presidential voting. There are two complicating factors, furthermore. First, one must recognize that not all issues are salient to everyone. A particular voter might be highly informed on a few issues of interest to him and disregard those about which he does not care. Secondly, the criterion of perceived difference depends not only on the voter, but on the parties and candidates themselves. If there is little or no difference between the electoral choices, then one can hardly expect the average citizen to discern a contrast. It can be argued that the politics of the 1950s probably did not offer much in the way of dramatic policy alternatives. Pomper has analyzed survey data from 1952 to 1968 and found that there has been a definite increase in the perception of party difference by the public and in the degree of consensus as to the positions of the parties, the greatest change coming with the "critical" election of 1964.[22] As the political system offers clearer choices to the voters, therefore, they are able to respond with a greater degree of responsibility.

"The Responsible Electorate."   One problem that keeps popping up as one tries to assess whether voters are expressing their preferences is that of party identification. It is easy to demonstrate that there is a definite, though imperfect, tendency for the voting decision to be consistent with opinions. To take only one example, 84 percent of those who were in favor of medicare voted for Johnson in 1964, while 63 percent of those opposed voted for Goldwater.[23] However, this seeming display of issue voting is complicated by the fact that

[21] Campbell, *et al., The American Voter,* pp. 169–83.
[22] Gerald M. Pomper, "From Confusion to Clarity: Issues and American Voters, 1956–1968," *American Political Science Review,* 66 (1972), 415–28.
[23] Computed by the author from results of the Survey Research Center's 1964 election study.

most of those who favored the policy were Democratic identifiers and presumably would have voted for Johnson anyway. The question is whether issue preferences exercise an independent effect upon voting behavior, or whether they too are just a consequence of party loyalty.

One notable attempt to deal with this problem is Key's *The Responsible Electorate*.[24] Taking the "perverse and unorthodox" view that "voters are not fools," Key uses survey results over a twenty-year period to attempt to illustrate the issue-related character of American voting. His method of excluding the effect of party identification is to focus on those voters who reported switching their party choice from one election to the next and then to look at their opinions on important issues of the time. In almost every case he was able to find, there appeared a definite tendency for switchers to hold opinions consistent with their change. Since those voters who do switch are usually the less involved independents, in whom one would have less confidence, Key is inclined to conclude that voters do respond to their issue preferences and that the electorate does, therefore, behave in a responsible manner. While this finding increases our respect for voters, it really cannot be regarded as conclusive. One problem is that these "switchers" represent only a minority of the total electorate, albeit a critically important one. Another is that many of the issues for which data were available, particularly after the Roosevelt years, were phrased in terms of reactions to presidents or parties per se (e.g., "which political party . . . do you think is better for people like yourself . . . ?") and therefore do not necessarily tap actual preferences on substantive policy questions. Still, this and other evidence does make the point that voters, whether strong party identifiers or complete independents, do generally vote for those candidates who favor the same policies as those who vote for them.

The Perception of Issues.   Much of the problem with gauging the extent of issue-oriented voting lies fundamentally with the perception voters have of what issues are important and how candidates stand on them. Research has begun to inquire into this problem. An analysis by RePass of open-ended questions allowing voters in the 1964 election to state those issues of greatest concern to them is particularly instructive.[25] On those issues of greatest salience to the voters, most perceived a party difference. There was, of course, some

[24] V. O. Key, Jr., *The Responsible Electorate: Rationality in Presidential Voting, 1936–1960* (Cambridge: Harvard University Press, 1966).

[25] David E. RePass, "Issue Salience and Party Choice," *American Political Science Review*, 65 (1971), 389–400.

evidence of distortion showing that the voter tended to perceive "his" party as agreeing with him, but this distortion was relatively low on the most salient issues. When the relationship between party identification, issue opinion, and voting choice was examined, it was found that "salient issues had almost as much weight as party identification in predicting voting choice." [26] In the analysis of presidential voting in 1972 performed by Miller and his colleagues, it was found that the relative proximity between the voter's own position and that which he attributed to the candidates on a range of issues exercised at least as much effect upon voting as did party identification and social characteristics.[27]

When we take into account the perceptions of individuals, our conclusion on the role of opinions in the electoral process is much like that for the question of the rationality of public opinion in general. If we allow for the subjectively interpreted information that voters have internalized, then we must conclude that their votes do reflect their preferences. In those cases in which there is a conflict between the dictates of established party loyalty and perceived candidate position, there is a definite tendency to vote in accordance with the issues.[28] (Most voters, however, do not face this conflict.) At a purely individual level, then, there is substantial reason to believe that voters are communicating their preferences to government, at least in presidential elections. But if we choose to look to the level of the political system, our conclusions may not be so sanguine. Given the tendency of political candidates and parties to obscure their differences, voters may easily misperceive the alternatives. The issues viewed as salient by the individual voter may not be those of real substantive importance to the nation's future.

ISSUES AND LONG-TERM FORCES

Let us return to the question of the constant, long-term forces in American voting behavior. As noted earlier, there is a strong interrelationship between party loyalty and position on a number of basic issues. Undoubtedly, social characteristics, particularly economic status, have helped to establish and maintain these regularities. On one hand, it has been argued that habitual patterns mean

[26] *Ibid.*, p. 400. The candidate-image variable had an even greater weight. This conclusion is based upon a multiple regression analysis in which the effect of each variable on voting is controlled for the other two.

[27] Arthur H. Miller *et al.*, "A Majority Party in Disarray: Policy Polarization in the 1972 Election," paper delivered at the American Political Science Association, September 4–8, 1973, New Orleans, pp. 67–69.

[28] Campbell *et al.*, *The American Voter*, p. 142, and RePass, "Issue Salience," pp. 399–400.

less issue-oriented voting, for if a voter is reacting to the past, his response may be irrelevant to the present. Yet this is not necessarily so, for many important issues are present over whole generations. In the United States, the economic dimension of politics seems to qualify as one of these important issues. As Campbell and his colleagues found, Americans generally held stereotypes of the Republican party as the friend of business and the Democratic party as the representative of the working man.[29] While these are oversimplifications, they do offer a relatively valid basis for predicting the actions of the two political parties in office. Thus, at a very gross level, voting along party lines may allow many partisans to express their preferences on some general issues.

The fact that election results are a composite of long-term and short-term forces illustrates this point. Boyd's normal vote analysis of the 1968 election demonstrates how certain issues reflect the long-term force of established party identification and how other issues cause short-term deviations from the expected vote. Among the issues with the greatest relationship to party identification were the traditional economic ones of medical care and aid to education. More topical issues such as race and Vietnam policy were important in creating the short-term deviations in voting.[30] Voters may therefore be expressing their policy preferences both when they hold to an established party loyalty and when they deviate from it.

One can also make an argument for the meaningful nature of elections by viewing them from a greater historical perspective. The established alignments of political parties along issue and social cleavages eventually develop strains which become so severe that an electoral upheaval occurs. Such realignments take place particularly in conjunction with the "critical elections" discussed in Chapter 10. In these critical elections, old issues are settled and the broad outlines of policy are set for succeeding decades. In 1860, the issue of slavery and union was electorally resolved; in 1932, the fundamental question of whether government should take an active role in insuring domestic welfare was answered by the voters. In these elections, the voters speak, and do so with great effect. From this standpoint, elections do determine policy for the future. Yet such elections seem to occur only once in a generation, too infrequently for all but the most patient advocates of democracy.

[29] Campbell *et al.*, *The American Voter*, pp. 44–59.
[30] Richard W. Boyd, "Popular Control of Public Policy: A Normal Vote Analysis of the 1968 Election," *American Political Science Review*, 66 (1972), 448. This mode of analysis was previously presented in Chapter 10. Two issues ranked at the top of both the long-term and short-term forces: assessment of the Johnson administration and reaction to the power of the federal government.

THE RELEVANCE OF ELECTIONS:
SOME CONCLUSIONS

We have examined a considerable amount of evidence on voting behavior in America and its possible effect on linking opinions with policy. Some general conclusions may now be offered. While the American voter is certainly not inclined to view politics in terms of an ideological political philosophy, and sometimes sees nothing more than the party label, his political world is far from devoid of policy content. His votes are generally consistent with his preferences for those issues which he feels are important and on which he can see some alternative between the candidates. Such issues are most often those that directly concern the routine of everyday life, whether in terms of economic issues or fearful reaction to social upheavals. His reaction to government will be particularly sensitive to what government has done in the past. Voters who lack any degree of sophistication about the political world can still evaluate whether or not incumbents have run things to their liking. As we have noted before, the public deals in results, rather than means.

The role of party identification in affecting voting behavior should not be underestimated, but neither should its effect be overestimated. American voters are quite willing to vote against their party if they are displeased. In four of the last six presidential elections, the minority Republican party has been the victor, in three of these by comfortable margins. As Pomper says, voters are "meddling partisans." [31] They react to real events and conditions in the political world and, though usually leaving policy choices up to their elected officials, occasionally put their hands in to discipline leaders who have been unsuccessful. Party loyalty may cloud evaluations of politicians and parties to some extent, but reality has a way of breaking through the perceptual screen.

In sum then, voters exercise a high degree of control over the broadest outlines of public policy. They do not make choices between alternative means of accomplishing specific goals. Even if they were geared to do so, the political system would have difficulty in responding. It is hard for any winner of an election to validly claim a mandate for all of his proposals, for different voters have chosen him for a variety of reasons, some of which may have nothing to do with the policies he advocates. The electoral process is a meaningful mechanism for increasing the degree of democracy in the political system. This is particularly true for presidential elections, where alternatives are highly visible to the electorate. We know much less about voting for lower offices, but the evidence seems to

---

[31] Pomper, *Elections in America*, pp. 92–98.

be that the degree of popular control through the electoral process would have to be somewhat less.

While elections do communicate some public preferences to government, they do so incompletely and imperfectly. As we have seen, this is partially a result of the characteristic pattern of mass behavior. The fault is not entirely that of the average citizen, however. As we have seen in this chapter, there are questions to be raised also about the role of political parties and about the extent to which public officials are willing to take public opinion into account in the decision-making process. These institutional considerations will be explored in the succeeding chapters of this book.

Political Parties: Are They Responsible?

15

As became clear in the last chapter, one cannot understand the electoral process in the United States without taking account of the role of political parties. Identification with these organizations forms a basic frame of political reference for a large part of the population, and the vast majority of elected officials are chosen as representatives of one of the two major parties. Since parties play such an obvious role in the linkage between the mass public and its government, their effects must be investigated.

Parties are not only important from this practical standpoint. It can also be argued that they have the potential for increasing democratic responsiveness to popular wishes. Given that direct democracy is not feasible for a populous and complex society, some form of representative government is necessary.[1] Political parties may offer a means for insuring that those representatives do reflect public opinion. This potential of parties gives rise to the idealized theory discussed below, as well as to frequent criticism of American parties for not fulfilling that function adequately. It is this representative role of political parties on which we shall concentrate. Parties may fulfill other social requisites, such as providing an outlet for political tensions or acting as channels of upward mobility for individuals, but we shall not go into these. Our concern will be with empirically evaluating the extent to which political parties in America act as a meaningful linkage between public opinion and public policy.

RESPONSIBLE PARTY GOVERNMENT MODEL

There is a long tradition in American political thought that compares the actual state of political parties with an ideal. Different authors over the last century have varied in the particular requirements they

[1] See Austin Ranney and Willmoore Kendall, *Democracy and the American Party System* (New York: Harcourt, Brace, 1956), chap. 3, for a complete discussion of this point.

would assign to parties, but there is a considerable consensus as to what should be included in this ideal of responsible party government.[2] The assumptions of the model are as follows:

1. Political parties will adopt clear and distinct positions on major issues, thus offering a clear set of alternatives to the voter.

2. There will be sufficient discipline within each party that candidates and elected officials will adhere to the established policy positions of the party.

3. As a consequence of the preceding assumptions, the winning party will put all of its promises into effect, while the losers will not be able to enact their programs.

Additionally, there are often implicit assumptions that (a) voters will select parties on the basis of their proposed programs and that (b) parties will be internally democratic in their decision-making processes. Such a model, it seems clear, would offer an opportunity for a high degree of democracy within a large and complex political system, for voters would be choosing between alternative sets of policies and they would be guaranteed receiving the program of the party that they had put into office. Such a system would not be perfectly democratic, for a party might receive a majority even though the public did not favor some of its particular proposals. Still, it does suggest a way in which a representative government could very closely approximate a direct democracy and still be practical.

Nor is this theory only a fanciful flight of the political imagination. To a great extent, it was developed from observation of the operation of parties in Great Britain. The British system, as it has developed over the last century, does not perfectly duplicate this ideal, but it generally functions along these lines. Advocates of more responsible parties could also point to the systems of a number of European countries as producing ideological parties that would fit the model, though the instability engendered by ideological parties in some multiparty systems makes the model seem less ideal. In short, it is conceivable that parties could function along the lines suggested by the responsible-party-government model.

While many have argued that parties *should* follow this respon-

[2] The leading analysis and critique of these theories is Austin Ranney, *The Doctrine of Responsible Party Government: Its Origins and Present State* (Urbana: University of Illinois Press, 1962). The trend of advocacy of this position may have reached its zenith with the publication of a report by a committee of the American Political Science Association, "Toward a More Responsible Two-Party System," *American Political Science Review*, 44, no. 3, pt. 2 (1950). For an analysis and critique of that report, see Evron M. Kirkpatrick, " 'Toward a More Responsible Two-Party System': Political Science, Policy Science, or Pseudo-Science?," *American Political Science Review*, 65 (1971), 965–90.

sible-party-government model, no one has ever suggested that American parties actually do work this way. From James Bryce's observation half a century ago that the American parties resembled two differently labeled bottles, both of them empty, to George Wallace's assertion that there is not a "dime's worth of difference" between Republicans and Democrats, observers of all persuasions have customarily castigated the parties for a lack of attention to policy. It is argued that they do not offer alternatives on issues nor do they keep the promises they make. American parties, it is popularly believed, are concerned solely with winning elections as an end in itself and are not involved with policy, except as reference to it might prove useful in hoodwinking an unsuspecting voter. Hence, many would conclude that while parties in the United States might serve some useful functions of encouraging alternation in office, they contribute little to increasing public input into government.

This image of American parties as lacking in meaningful issue content is widely held both by the mass public and by students of politics. Yet, as we have seen repeatedly in the study of public opinion, one must be wary of accepting conventional judgments without empirical scrutiny. Accordingly, we shall examine the nature and role of American parties, largely in the context of the responsible-party-government model, though recognizing that there could be other ways in which parties could act as a linkage between people and policy.

TENDENCIES TOWARD RESPONSIBILITY IN AMERICAN PARTIES

Is There a Difference Between the Parties?   Is there any more difference between Republicans and Democrats than their names and some historical symbols? The cynic might answer that there is not, for both usually express a generally "centrist" political philosophy and neither advocates radical change in any direction. If one takes a less wide perspective, however, he can see that there are some significant differences within that center of the political spectrum which have distinguished the two parties over the years. There are several sorts of evidence for this conclusion.

As we know from earlier discussions of party identification and voting, the parties have different coalitions of individuals and interests from which they derive support. The Democratic coalition includes more Catholics, blue-collar workers, blacks, residents of large cities, and (at least below the presidential level of politics) southerners. Republicans are more likely to be Protestants, residents of suburbs and smaller communities, and white-collar employees.

Some of these concentrations may be only historical artifacts while others are related to more contemporary issues. In either case, their existence has an effect upon policy. Party support and party policy are mutually reinforcing. The party seeks to respond to those who elect it, those voters thereby receiving more reason to give their support, and the circle continues. This tendency is reinforced by organized interest groups as they give financial and organizational backing to one party over the other. Labor unions almost always back Democratic candidates; business groups usually fall into the Republican camp. And the sympathies of elected officials is as one would expect. Thus, to the extent that these politically relevant cleavages reflect different preferences on certain kinds of policies, so do the parties.

This source of difference between the two parties is borne out by the opinions of those who comprise the formal organization of the political parties. McClosky and his colleagues surveyed the attitudes of delegates to the Republican and Democratic national conventions and compared the patterns of preferences to those of ordinary identifiers with the party in the mass public.[3] The results indicated that delegates diverged even more in their beliefs than did the rank-and-file party identifiers. In other words, there was a much greater liberal-conservative gap between Democratic and Republican leaders than was the case for Democratic and Republican voters. The tendency toward ideological consistency was the greatest on those issues of most direct concern to the party coalitions, such as taxation, regulation of business, labor-management relations, and federal spending for social welfare purposes. On issues not so related to the interests of groups supporting the parties, such as foreign affairs, party regularity was relatively less. This same sort of liberal-conservative division between leaders of the two parties is also confirmed by Eldersveld's study of local party officials in Detroit.[4] The conclusion to be drawn from these studies is that the notion of an ideologically divided electorate whose preferences are glossed over by pragmatic activists is probably not accurate. It must be noted that these data refer only to the personal preferences of party leaders, not to their official pronouncements or to their actions. We shall deal with the public effects of leadership perspectives presently.

Party Platforms.   One of the problems in trying to evaluate the policy role of American parties is finding out what, if anything, is the

[3] Herbert McClosky, Paul J. Hoffman, and Rosemary O'Hara, "Issue Conflict and Consensus Among Party Leaders and Followers," *American Political Science Review*, 54 (1960), 406–27.

[4] Samuel J. Eldersveld, *Political Parties: A Behavioral Analysis* (Chicago: Rand McNally, 1968), chap. 8.

"official" position of a party on an issue. The only authoritative statement on policy that the party ever makes as an organization is the platform adopted at the national convention every four years. These statements of policy enjoy, to say the least, a very dubious reputation in the conventional wisdom. Most commentators, if they mention platforms at all, assume that they mean little in the first place and are not remembered after election day.

National party platforms might have retained this image had not Pomper systematically analyzed their provisions and results.[5] In analyzing platforms of both parties from 1944 through 1964, he finds that they are more than just generalities and "hot air." Almost half of the statements in the platforms were "pledges of future action" (i.e., promises of what the party would do if elected). Most of the rest of the platform consisted of evaluations of past actions by the party and its opponent—meaningful content in light of the tendency of many voters to evaluate governmental performance retrospectively. Pomper's conclusion is that national party platforms are meaningful and "rational" documents, both for the parties to campaign on and for voters to judge.

These data, however, deal only with the content of platforms and not with what happens to their promises. But Pomper takes the second step and analyzes the pledges of future action with respect to their eventual enactment. Promises may be kept in several ways, ranging from legislation completely fulfilling the pledge, through promises kept by presidential action alone involving partial fulfillment, to the keeping of a promise not to do something by not doing it. Considering all of these varieties of fulfillment together, Pomper's data reveal that 72 percent of all platform promises over this twentyyear period were kept.[6] An additional 18 percent were brought up for congressional consideration but failed to pass. Thus, the popular notion that campaign platform promises are generally forgotten is erroneous nine out of ten times.

The contrast here between the conventional image and political reality is sufficiently striking that one might be tempted to conclude that American parties do meet the explicit criteria of the responsibleparty-government model after all. Such a conclusion, however, would ignore some highly relevant details. First, that figure of almost three-fourths fulfillment of the promises includes those made by the party that lost the election. Even though the voters in 1964 rejected the Republican presidential candidate and his party rather substantially, some 40 percent of the Republican platform pledges in that

[5] Gerald M. Pomper, *Elections in America: Control and Influence in Democratic Politics* (New York: Dodd, Mead, 1968), chaps. 7 and 8.
[6] *Ibid.*, p. 186.

year were kept in some way.[7] The nature of the policy-making process in the United States is such that political minorities can sometimes achieve their goals, while winning parties are never able to reach all of theirs. Even when the electorate seemingly makes a strong statement of their preferences and the parties are aligned in accordance with those views, the response in terms of policy decisions will be imperfect.

A related problem is that a considerable number of promises are made by both parties. About one-third of all pledges, according to Pomper, were bipartisan in nature. Over half of the promises were made by one party alone, with the opposition making no commitment on the subject, leaving only a tenth of the cases that were situations in which there was a direct conflict between the parties.[8] Thus, the first norm of the responsible party theory is violated, for it is relatively rare for the Republican and Democratic parties to offer precise and conflicting alternatives on future policies to the voters. No matter how meaningful the promises of the party platform or how faithfully these are kept, one would still be reluctant to cite this as a significant linkage between voters and policies, for the simple reason that few voters ever see a platform.[9] No doubt, some of the content reaches the public through news reporting and candidate statements, but there is little to suggest that platform pledges are a significant influence on anyone's voting choice. The content of platforms occasionally becomes a visible issue in itself, as in the debates over the Vietnam plank at the Democratic convention of 1968, but the provisions of platforms usually remain as anonymous as the committees that labor over them.

To a great extent, American campaign platforms reflect the nature of the parties themselves. On the domestic economic dimension, which is the source of much of the organized support for parties, one is apt to encounter a number of conflicting or at least competing policy proposals. One party, for instance, may include a promise calculated to retain the support of a particular minority interest that is included in its coalition, while the opposition ignores the subject. On issues of less immediate interest to the voters and less aligned with political cleavages, such as foreign policy, bipartisan promises are

[7] *Ibid.*

[8] *Ibid.*, p. 194.

[9] As the author found from personal observation, the Republican party in Indiana received only two hundred copies of the 1968 platform for the whole state, hardly enough to inform over two million voters. For those who do desire to read past platforms, they are reproduced in Kirk H. Porter and Donald Bruce Johnson, *National Party Platforms: 1840–1968*, 4th ed. (Urbana: University of Illinois Press, 1970). Platforms are reprinted at the time of their adoption in the *Weekly Report* published by Congressional Quarterly, Inc., and by some other news sources.

the most common.[10] American parties therefore do have a degree of responsibility, for they divide on some important issues and these promises are kept for the most part. While this pattern is far from the idealized responsible-party-government model, it does refute the notion that parties in the United States are unconcerned about policy questions. This degree of responsibility, however, seems to occur somewhat apart from the attention paid to the parties by the public. Hence, we must inquire into the role of parties within the workings of the governmental process.

Parties in Government. What effect does political party have, once a candidate has achieved office? This question is most easily answered with reference to legislative bodies, for the availability of data on the U.S. Congress has led it to be probably the most intensively studied political institution in the world.[11] Consider the requisites of the responsible-party-government model. According to this model, legislative voting would have only one pattern: all of the majority party voting in one way and all of the minority members voting against them. Such is the case in the British House of Commons, where strict party unity is customarily maintained on all issues, except for a few deemed so unimportant that individual members are allowed to vote in accordance with their personal preferences.

What is expected under this ideal system is almost a rarity in the United States. A "party-line vote" can be operationally defined as one in which at least 90 percent of one party votes in opposition to at least 90 percent of the opposition party. If this measure is used, then one finds less than 10 percent of congressional decisions being made on a strict party basis, and this proportion has apparently been decreasing over the last half-century.[12] If one were to take a much weaker definition, that of a party vote as being one on which a bare majority of one party oppose a majority of the other, then still less than half of all votes in recent sessions of Congress can be accounted

[10] Pomper found a high degree of bipartisan unity on civil rights pledges through 1964, but this trend does not appear to have continued in the last two presidential election years.

[11] There are so many important works on congressional behavior that we shall note only a few summaries. Short, analytical compilations may be found in Ralph K. Huitt and Robert L. Peabody, *Congress: Two Decades of Analysis* (New York: Harper and Row, 1969), pp. 3–73, and in W. Wayne Shannon, *Party, Constituency and Congressional Voting: A Study of Legislative Behavior in the United States House of Representatives* (Baton Rouge: Louisiana State University Press, 1968), chaps. 1 and 2. Two leading texts on the subject are William Keefe and Morris Ogul, *The American Legislative Process*, 3rd ed. (Englewood Cliffs, N.J.: Prentice-Hall, 1973), and Malcolm E. Jewell and Samuel C. Patterson, *The Legislative Process in the United States*, 2nd ed. (New York: Random House, 1972).

[12] Julius Turner, *Party and Constituency: Pressures on Congress*, revised by Edward V. Schneier, Jr. (Baltimore: Johns Hopkins Press, 1970), p. 17.

for.[13] It is clear that legislative decision making in the United States is simply not conducted along the neat party lines envisioned by those who would wish parties to govern.

This does not mean that party affiliation is irrelevant to congressional behavior. On the contrary, a number of analyses have shown that *party is the single best predictor of how a congressman will vote* on the whole spectrum of bills. Over 90 percent of all nonunanimous votes show some statistically significant party difference.[14] This influence of party varies, of course, depending on the nature of the policy in question. Three types of situations seem to produce the greatest degree of party difference. First, there are occasional questions that relate to the advantage or disadvantage of one party as an organization. The question of methods and regulation of campaign financing and spending in recent years offers a well-known example.[15] Second and more important, the influence of the president tends to bring out partisan tendencies. On those issues on which the chief executive has taken a stand, he is customarily supported by most of his own party and by only a minority of the opposition.[16] This cleavage particularly appears on domestic, as opposed to foreign, issues. Finally, the parties in Congress divide most clearly on those questions that tap their fundamental sources of group support: questions of domestic economic and social welfare policy. This is shown in the "ratings" of individual congressmen calculated by various interest groups, the best known being that of the AFL-CIO's Committee on Political Education.[17] These customarily show a sharp contrast between the liberalism or conservatism of members of the two parties—but it is ideology defined in terms of the interests of particular groups, whether labor unions, business, farmers, or whatever. On other types of issues, party is of little or no consequence, and other factors are dominant. On questions of race, constituency opinions are apt to be the most important, and votes will largely fall along regional lines. Some issues are so narrow that the prime input may come from one or a few organized groups whose interests are particularly touched. Finally, a congressman will typically ignore any sort of external pressures if he perceives that the welfare of his own district would be affected by a proposed policy. Thus, party plays a mixed

[13] *Ibid.*

[14] *Ibid.*, pp. 35–36.

[15] The history of this issue is presented in Robert L. Peabody *et al.*, *To Enact a Law: Congress and Campaign Financing* (New York: Praeger, 1972).

[16] See, for example, the data presented in *Congressional Roll Call: A Chronology and Analysis of Votes in the House and Senate: 91st Congress, First Session* (Washington: Congressional Quarterly Service, 1970), pp. 16–18.

[17] The ratings by a number of these groups are included in Michael Barone, Grant Ujifusa, and Douglas Matthews, *The Almanac of American Politics* (Boston: Gambit, 1973).

role: important (though not all-powerful) on some issues, minor or lacking on others.

Consistent with the frequency of defection from party in the U.S. Congress is the lack of party discipline. Unlike Great Britain, where an M.P. may lose his party's nomination for failing to support the leadership on a particular issue, American congressmen may do so with impunity. The few cases in which anything approaching disciplinary actions were even attempted are rare events. Franklin Roosevelt attempted to use his tremendous prestige to "purge" a few anti-New Deal Democrats from the party, but with mixed results. In 1970, in a senatorial contest in New York, the Nixon administration came out at the last minute for Conservative party candidate James Buckley over liberal Republican Senator Charles Goodell, with success, but only because of the peculiarities of a three-way race. After the 1964 election, two Mississippi Democrats lost their seniority as a penalty for having supported Goldwater. But other congressmen have failed to support their party's nominee and suffered no such sanctions. A few more historical examples might be found, but they represent infrequent exceptions to the general lack of discipline. True, failure to go along with the party on a regular basis might lead to some informal sanctions and lack of cooperation by other congressional members of the party. However, the functioning of the seniority system has rewarded some southern Democrats who have been far from the mainstream of their party by placing them in powerful committee chairmanships. Party regularity in the Congress is a matter of *loyalty* to the party, rather than fear of discipline, and the party is only one of many competing sources of influence.

In summary, American parties deviate quite far from the ideal of issue-oriented, well-disciplined, policy-making organizations. They divide on some issues, though quite imperfectly, and have little or no impact on others. There are differences between the parties on some policy questions, but the parties do not offer meaningful alternatives on many important issues. Furthermore, the lack of any systematic application of sanctions for failure to support the party position means that even when alternatives have been offered, that alternative preferred by the electoral majority may not triumph. Parties would seem to aid in the linking of public opinion and public policy in the United States, but by no means guarantee it.

WHY THE PARTIES ARE NOT MORE RESPONSIBLE

In spite of almost a century of critical commentary by countless writers (including Woodrow Wilson), the American party system has made little progress toward the ideal of responsible party government. To attribute this lack of progress completely to the lack of vision by political leaders would be incorrect. To be sure, there is an inertia factor in this case, as always in human behavior. Those who hold positions of power have succeeded within the system as it is and therefore fail to see cogent reasons for change, particularly when that change would lessen their own independence and power. But there are also some very fundamental characteristics of the political structure and the mass public that have worked against the development of ideological and disciplined parties.

Clearly, the constitutional structure of the United States works against the notion of party government. The fact of a separation of powers between the legislative and executive branches removes the stimulus for party regularity found in parliamentary systems. American congressmen might be less willing to disregard the wishes of the president if defeating him meant new elections. The other innovation of the American constitution—federalism—also has an impact. The characteristic pattern of decentralization of authority that has developed in the governmental sector is also true of the party organization. The power in American parties is found at the state and local levels of the organization, while the national committees and chairpersons exercise almost no power over them or over elected officials. It is instructive to note that the title of the major study of national party organization is *Politics Without Power*.[18]

Some historical and cultural factors also seem to be related to the nature of American parties. It is important to remember that American parties are perhaps the oldest in the world, having developed into full-blown organizations many years before those in Britain. Unlike many European parties that were established in the early twentieth century as an outgrowth of socialist and labor movements, American parties developed first *within government*, created as a means for increasing the chances of incumbents for reelection. Hence, the extragovernmental, mass membership type of organization has never exercised the control over American elected officials that it has over continental officials. Another factor, both historical and cultural in nature, is the great degree of heterogeneity within the United States, representing a variegated collection of ethnic, religious, and racial groups, regional variations, etc. Given that there are only two major parties in the United States, it would be difficult for them under these circumstances to maintain a high degree of consistency and discipline. As a result, American parties have always been broad coalitions of disparate groups. Throughout much of our history, the main source of political cleavage has been sectionalism,

[18] Cornelius P. Cotter and Bernard C. Hennessy, *Politics Without Power: The National Party Committees* (New York: Atherton Press, 1964).

thus allowing the parties to vary their positions within particular regions.

All of the foregoing represent some basic reasons why American parties are what they are. It is at least conceivable that changes in leadership perspectives, formal structure of government, and historical evolution might alter the situation so that parties might be able to better resemble the responsible-party-government model. However, there would still remain a final obstacle: the public itself. Some characteristics of public opinion and mass political behavior are inconsistent with this goal of more issue-oriented and disciplined parties. As we now know quite well, Americans are not prone to thinking along consistent ideological lines across a range of issues. Parties will hardly prosper therefore by taking positions on the basis of ideological purity. It might be objected that there is no great evidence that the inhabitants of nations with more responsible party systems, such as Britain, are any more enamored of political philosophy. This may be true, but there is an important difference. Unlike most European systems, the United States has never developed a sense of social class sufficiently strong to serve as a surrogate for ideological awareness, and therefore also as the basis for responsible parties. Other sources of cleavage, such as religion, might have served at one time, but their political relevance seems to have been diminishing. The racial cleavage alone might qualify, but the numerical distribution of the races is sufficiently uneven to preclude that as a basis for two competing parties. Hence, the United States seems to lack the psychological and social basis for two parties that would always offer ideological alternatives on all issues.

The nature of the mass public also poses some practical limitations on any attempt to reform parties along these idealized lines. First, while Americans have firm attachments to political parties, they are also somewhat suspicious of them. As a result, the public is quite wary of any attempts to concentrate power within the hands of the party organization. As Dennis has found, Americans support the party system of the status quo and would resist attempts to make it more ideological and disciplined.[19] Secondly, it is doubtful that even if popular notions of proper ideological alignments changed, the electorate would be prepared to exercise the necessary discipline. As Stokes and Miller found, probably less than half of the electorate knows which party is presently in control of Congress, information that would seem vital to an evaluation of the party's record.[20] Furthermore, they point out that less than half of the voters they studied

[19] Jack Dennis, "Support for the Party System by the Mass Public," *American Political Science Review*, 69 (1966), 600–15.

[20] Donald E. Stokes and Warren E. Miller, "Party Government and the Salience of Congress," *Public Opinion Quarterly*, 26 (1962), 531–46.

knew anything about the two candidates running for Congress in their district and that most of what was known was not politically relevant. If one knows nothing of the legislative record of a congressional candidate, then he can hardly be expected to discipline that candidate for failing to support the party. Assuming that nominations in the United States will continue to be made through local primaries, it is hard to conceive of any regular imposition of party discipline. As Stokes and Miller conclude, "what the public knows about the legislative records of the parties and individual congressional candidates is a principal reason for the departure of American practice from an idealized conception of party government." [21]

DOWNS'S ECONOMIC ALTERNATIVE MODEL

The responsible-party-government model, emphasizing contrasts in ideology and policy between competing political parties, developed out of a tradition of normative criticism of the American system. As we have seen, it is only of limited applicability as an explanatory device for the actual role of parties in the United States. An approach to the same problem that is very different in both method and substance is that pursued by Downs in *An Economic Theory of Democracy*.[22] His basic approach is (a) to use the method of economics for making some abstract assumptions about the real world and (b) to look at the logical consequences of those assumptions. His model rests upon two postulates about the political world:

1. Political parties are concerned with maximizing votes in order to win elections, rather than with ideological purity.

2. Voters will vote for that party which is the least distant from them ideologically.[23]

If these two statements are true, it is possible to predict the behavior of political parties and the response of voters to them. Figure 15-1 depicts the working of this theory. The baseline represents some sort of ideological spectrum from liberal to conservative. (Downs suggests that the question of government involvement in the economy may be the most basic dimension.) Individual voters are distributed across this scale in their personal preferences, the frequency at different points being indicated by the height of the curve.[24] There is

---

[21] *Ibid.*, p. 545.

[22] Anthony Downs, *An Economic Theory of Democracy* (New York: Harper and Row, 1957).

[23] Our statement of these principles and the following discussion of the Downsian theory are somewhat simplified and neglect a number of qualifications and variations.

[24] As depicted here, we are assuming a normal sort of distribution, with most of the voters in the middle. If some additional assumptions are made (e.g., that there can

Figure 15-1
The Economic Model of Parties and Voters

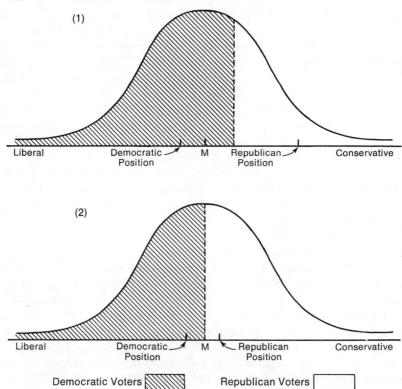

Democratic Voters ⧄   Republican Voters ▢

a hypothetical midpoint (M), which is the point dividing the population ideologically into equal halves. Political parties also must take
some position along this scale.

Given the assumptions cited earlier, we can predict what will happen. In the case shown in (1), the Republican party has taken a position toward the conservative end of the scale, while the Democratic
party is only slightly left of center. Since voters will vote for the
party closest to their own views, the parties will automatically get
the votes of all of those who are more extreme than they are, Republicans receiving the votes of those from the conservative side and
Democrats, those from the liberal. But what of the voters in between? Since we are assuming that they will vote for the closest
party, we can calculate the point of equal distance between the two
partisan positions, as indicated by the broken line. Everyone to the

only be two parties), then the model will achieve the same outcome, regardless of the
shape of the distribution.

left of the line should vote Democratic; everyone to the right, Republican. In this case, a Democratic majority is assured, as they have everyone on the liberal side of M and some of the moderates on the conservative half of the scale.

Let us recall the first assumption, that politicians are more interested in winning elections than in holding onto their ideologies. That being the case, the Republican party will not remain in the minority position created by (1). The logical thing for them is to move closer to the center point. Since the Democrats would not benefit by a shift to the left, they too will remain close to the center. The result will be the situation in (2), in which both parties are very close to the center of public opinion and therefore will receive approximately equal numbers of votes. The Downsian model thus predicts that political parties will not offer greatly divergent alternatives on issues, but will tend to converge in their policy positions at the median point of popular preferences.

Like any formal model, this one is not perfectly applicable to reality. Voters do not behave exactly as Downs assumes. Nor are party leaders always perfectly rational and devoid of any commitment to their goals. Yet, the political system seems to reflect the operation of a model like this fairly well. First, although voters are influenced by other factors, such as party identification, in addition to their ideological perceptions, these perceptions do play a part in the voting choice, as we saw in Chapter 14. This would be particularly true for independent voters—and it is their division that determines the outcome of most national elections in the United States. Secondly, political leaders, particularly in the United States, usually do attempt to choose candidates and take positions that they think would win elections. While in their own personal preferences they may divide more clearly in ideology than the mass public, this does not mean that they will not disregard their own views in order to maximize the fortunes of the party.[25] The Downsian model seems to explain very well the behavior of the electorate in several recent presidential elections. In 1964, the situation appears to have resembled that in (1): candidate Goldwater took a decidedly conservative position, while incumbent Johnson generally seemed to be close to the center, and the election results were as the model would predict. In 1968, the Republican party and candidate were careful to avoid any appearance of ideological extremism and the election was a very close one. In 1972, it

[25] A study of party officials in Indiana found that ideology was a much less important motivation and seen as a much less salient party goal than was winning elections and some other objectives, and this lack of emphasis on ideology was more true of higher officials than of precinct committeemen. Alan D. Monroe, "Political Party Activism: Causes and Consequences" (unpublished Ph.D. dissertation, Department of Political Science, Indiana University, 1971), pp. 91–94.

seems clear that McGovern was perceived by the voters as being quite far to the liberal side, while the incumbent occupied the center. Again, the result was as expected. The Downsian model offers a theoretical justification for Scammon and Wattenberg's advice that "The winning coalition in America is the one that holds the center ground on an attitudinal battlefield." [26]

If, as seems to be the case, American parties represent this "economic" theory much more than they do the responsible party ideal, what are the implications for the question of democracy? In a real sense, the notion of parties adjusting their ideologies to fit the distribution of public opinion does represent a linkage between the public and government. In essence, what Downs is saying is that parties are attempting to give the people what they want. Assuming that they follow through on the policies they advocate, then a degree of democracy results, just as it would in an ideal party government model. The difference is that both parties are going "where the votes are," rather than presenting two alternatives for decision.

For some issues, this process would seem to be the most responsive to public opinion. On those issues where most of the public does fall generally in the middle, there would be no particular virtue in offering two widely separated alternatives, neither of which would really please the majority. Thus, on many issues, particularly those of a substantive domestic nature (such as spending for social welfare), the tendency of American parties to promise similar or identical programs is exactly what needs to be done to reflect public opinion. On other types of issues, particularly those involving symbolic conflicts, the response is not so successful. If half the population is strongly in favor of an action and the other half violently opposed, then the middle ground may please no one. As we have noted before, the response of the parties and elected officials is typically to try to avoid such issues altogether. We come back again to a generalization that has appeared several times in this chapter: American parties do a fairly successful job in acting as a linkage between public opinion and public policy on the traditional economic dimension. Beyond this, their contribution is greatly reduced. Those individuals who have well-developed and intense ideological preferences may not approve of the inevitable centrism of American politics, but articulate as they may be, the system does not respond to their wishes. Such is democracy.

[26] Richard M. Scammon and Ben J. Wattenberg, *The Real Majority* (New York: Coward-McCann, 1970), p. 80.

Public Officials: Are They Responsive?

16

In the preceding chapters, we have investigated the role of two mechanisms—elections and parties—that ought to make those in governmental positions responsive to the public. In this final chapter, we shall focus directly on the officials themselves and inquire as to the degree to which they respond to public opinion and why. In part because of the availability of research on legislators and in part because the norms of democratic theory say that legislative bodies should be the great receptors of popular wishes, we shall concentrate upon the behavior of legislators.

There are competing notions, both in theory and practice, about how a legislator ought to make his decisions. Should he be a *delegate* who attempts to do what he believes his constituents desire? Or should he act as a *trustee* and work for those policies that he thinks will be best for the people, whether they favor them or not? [1] (There are alternative roles, most notably that of the party loyalist in a responsible party system, but this is not very applicable to the American system.) A number of studies have sought to find out how American legislators see themselves in terms of these roles. Wahlke and his colleagues found that "trustees" far outnumbered "delegates" in four state legislatures.[2] Davidson reports that slightly more U.S. congressmen consider themselves to be "trustees" than "delegates," though half of all his respondents fall into a "politico" category that combines elements of both.[3] A related question is whether the legislator sees his job as representing only his own district or the interests of the whole political system. Both the Davidson and Wahlke studies found more representatives oriented toward their own districts than to the whole state or nation.[4] Not surprisingly, the more competitive

[1] These role types are explained in John C. Wahlke *et al.*, *The Legislative System: Explorations in Legislative Behavior* (New York: John Wiley, 1962), pp. 272–80.

[2] *Ibid.*, p. 281.

[3] Roger H. Davidson, *The Role of the Congressman* (New York: Western Publishing Co., 1969), p. 117.

[4] *Ibid.*, p. 122, and Wahlke *et al.*, p. 292.

the local district was, the more likely the orientation was to be toward it.

Data such as these are valuable, but these self-perceptions cannot fully answer the question of whether or not public officials really respond to public opinion. The questions that must be resolved are these: How much does the legislator actually respond to his perceptions of public preference? How correct are his perceptions? How does this process vary across different types of issues? These are complex questions of fact and interpretation, and we shall suggest some empirical findings relevant to them below.

EVIDENCE OF RESPONSIVENESS IN CONGRESSIONAL DECISION MAKING

Informal descriptions of congressional behavior by legislators themselves and by other observers generally indicate that most congressmen seem to worry about the opinions and interests of their districts. If a representative perceives that a proposed policy would favorably or unfavorably affect his district—and therefore his chances for re-election—this consideration will often outweigh any ties of party loyalty or personal friendship. In fact, members may sometimes be urged by party leaders to go against the party to protect their own interests.[5] Most commonly, these district considerations will involve the economic interests of the area, for these are the most visible and the most likely to be communicated to the legislator by local interest groups. More difficult is the task of responding to the opinions of the general public. The chief source of knowledge about public opinion is the mail received. Letters from constituents are, of course, a poor means of measuring mass sentiment, and most legislators seem to be aware of this fact. This is particularly true when there is a large volume of mail on a single subject that has been generated through the efforts of organized interest groups. Such correspondence is easily identifiable and its import is appropriately discounted. The most precise way of measuring opinions would be scientific survey research. However, national surveys offer little clue about particular districts, and it would be extremely costly for the congressman himself to conduct them for his locality. Surveys are being increasingly used by legislators, but usually in the context of election campaigns, rather than for purposes of policy making. The other alternative is conducting "polls" by means of ballots mailed out to be returned by the voters. A majority of congressmen surveyed do use such a technique, often sending them to most or all of the households in the dis-

[5] E.g., the incident reported in Joseph W. Martin, Jr., *My First Fifty Years in Politics* (New York: McGraw-Hill, 1960), p. 183.

trict.[6] This technique, even if objectively applied, suffers from much the same problem as relying on spontaneous letters, as only a small proportion of the voters will return the ballot. Actually, this technique could better be classified as a method of communication from the congressman to his constituents, rather than from the voters to their representative.[7] All of this suggests that congressmen are concerned about the preferences of the public, but that their knowledge of them is not necessarily going to be accurate. A significant proportion of congressional activities on behalf of the voters deals with rendering services and assistance to individuals (e.g., aiding in clearing bureaucratic red tape). Regardless of the merits of this "errand boy" function, it is not really relevant to the question we are considering here.

A more systematic way of seeing the impact of constituency opinion on legislative behavior is to examine the variation in legislative voting among representatives from different types of districts. Since opinions in the mass public vary according to demographic attributes on many issues, one would expect the distribution of opinions within districts to follow these same lines. A number of studies have shown that the makeup of the district has a definite correlation with roll-call voting across a range of issues.[8] This impact is in addition to the effect of the representative's political party; the choice of a congressman from a particular party is also an indication of constituency preference on issues. Of the various constituency characteristics, the urban or rural nature of the district tends to have the greatest effect across the board. Racial and ethnic distributions have an effect more limited to specific issues. One might hypothesize that congressmen from more competitive districts will be more likely to deviate from party lines in accordance with the character of their district; analysis shows that this tendency is only a slight one and is not conclusively demonstrated.[9] Thus, there is some tentative evidence here of responsiveness to constituencies. This evidence, however, assumes that public opinion in different kinds of districts is as one would

[6] John S. Saloma III, *Congress and the New Politics* (Boston: Little, Brown, 1969), p. 175.

[7] For some findings on the use and misuse of postcard polls by legislators, see Walter Wilcox, "The Congressional Poll—and Non-Poll," in *Political Opinion and Behavior: Essays and Studies*, eds. Edward C. Dreyer and Walter A. Rosenbaum, 2nd ed. (Belmont, Calif.: Wadsworth, 1970), pp. 527–36.

[8] E.g., Julius Turner, *Party and Constituency: Pressures on Congress*, revised by Edward V. Scheier, Jr. (Baltimore: Johns Hopkins Press, 1970), chaps. 4 and 5; W. Wayne Shannon, *Party, Constituency, and Congressional Voting: A Study of Legislative Behavior in the United States House of Representatives* (Baton Rouge: Louisiana State University Press, 1968), chap. 7; and Donald R. Matthews, *U.S. Senators and Their World* (New York: Random House, 1960), pp. 230–39.

[9] Shannon, *Party, Constituency, and Congressional Voting*, chap. 8.

think that it logically should be. Such assumptions are always dangerous.

There is one piece of empirical analysis that directly measures the relevant elements of the representation process. In a study of the 1958 elections, Miller and Stokes broke down their national sample into subsamples representing one hundred and sixteen congressional districts.[10] There was thus a direct measurement of the opinions of voters in those districts on several issue dimensions. They also conducted interviews with the congressmen from these districts with particular reference to their own views on these same issue dimensions and their perception of constituency opinion. Finally, roll-call votes on each issue dimension were scaled and analyzed to measure the actual voting behavior of the congressmen. Three types of issues were investigated: domestic social welfare policies, foreign involvement, and civil rights.

On the social welfare and foreign affairs dimensions, there was relatively little relationship between the congressman and his constituency. There was a tendency for his perceptions to be correct, but only a very slight one. There was also only a weak relationship between the representative's own preferences and those of the voters. In the civil rights dimension, however, there was a high degree of correspondence between the four elements. In other words, congressional perception of constituency opinion on civil rights was correct; it accorded with the congressman's own views; and both were highly related to the way in which he voted on relevant legislation. Figure 16-1 shows a causal model based on this same data that was tested by Cnudde and McCrone.[11] Thus, on the issue of civil rights, there was an impressive linkage between constituency opinion and representative behavior. The greatest part of that linkage, moreover, can be ascribed to the path from constituency opinions through perception by the representative, including the effect of perception on the congressman's own opinions.[12]

This analysis has some implications for the role of public opinion in affecting policy decisions:

1. Public opinion can have a very direct impact on decisions, as it did in civil rights.

[10] Warren E. Miller and Donald E. Stokes, "Constituency Influence in Congress," *American Political Science Review*, 57 (1963), 45–52. They offer a statistical explanation for the validity of relying on a limited number of cases as a measure of opinion within each district.

[11] Charles F. Cnudde and Donald J. McCrone, "The Linkage Between Constituency Attitudes and Congressional Voting Behavior: A Causal Model," *American Political Science Review*, 60 (1966), 66–72.

[12] *Ibid.*

Figure 16-1.
A Causal Model of Constituency Influence on Civil Rights

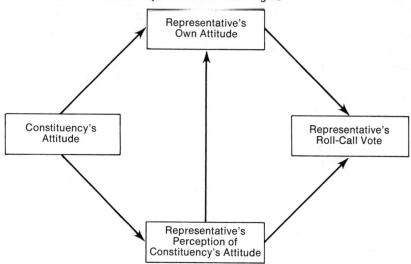

Source: Charles F. Cnudde and Donald J. McCrone, "The Linkage Between Constituency Attitudes and Congressional Voting Behavior: A Causal Model," *American Political Science Review*, 60 (1966), 69.

2. The representative's *perception* of public opinion is the crucial factor, influencing his own beliefs as well as directly affecting his voting.

3. There was no direct linkage between constituency attitudes and those of the congressman aside from that arrived at through perception. This suggests that responsiveness is not simply a matter of officials holding the same values as their constituents.

4. The fact that the relationships for issue areas other than civil rights were much weaker suggests that popular inputs will be influential on those issues that are of a symbolic nature and therefore produce intense popular feelings.

The lesson of empirical study, then, is that congressmen do respond to their constituents' preferences as these are perceived. On an occasional issue such as race, these preferences are likely to be strong and the response direct. On most other issues, however, the public input is much weaker. This allows for distorted assessments of popular feelings; it also encourages responsiveness to organized minorities, rather than to the public as a whole. We shall investigate both possibilities in the next two sections.

THE PROBLEM OF INTEREST GROUPS

We have thus far ignored the role of organized interest groups in communicating public desires to government. Many who would doubt the efficacy of direct control by the mass public see groups as the main channel for popular inputs. In fact, this notion has become a dominant theory in American political science during the last two decades. This body of thought, largely synonymous with the "pluralist" interpretation of American politics, has argued that not only do interest groups influence public policy, they do so in a manner that makes policy consistent with the preferences and interests of the mass public.[13] Reduced to its essentials, this argument makes the following points:

1. Most people belong to organized groups with common political interests.

2. By influencing government, groups cause government to follow policies that benefit their members.

3. Because there are so many different competing groups, no one set of interests can dominate over the interests of the majority. Other factors, such as overlapping memberships and the possibility of potential groups being established, also keep the power of groups within reasonable limits.

4. Therefore, the policies that result from the influence of groups will be those that promote the public interest.

To attempt a complete analysis and evaluation of this argument would fill several volumes. We shall here attempt merely to point out some relevant facets of the role that interest groups play in communicating opinions to government.

Few observers would quarrel with the notion that interest groups do exercise a significant effect upon government policy. To understand this effect, however, it is important also to understand the characteristic nature of the process of lobbying. (Here again, we shall confine our attention to congressional decision making, though inter-

[13] The most influential work in this tradition is David B. Truman, *The Governmental Process: Political Interests and Public Opinion* (New York: Alfred A. Knopf, 1951). Other important statements in this tradition include Robert A. Dahl, *Who Governs? Democracy and Power in an American City* (New Haven: Yale University Press, 1961), and Arnold M. Rose, *The Power Structure: Political Process in American Society* (New York: Oxford University Press, 1967). Basic disagreement with the pluralist position has come mainly from sociologists, who see the system as far less democratic than the pluralist theory would indicate. The most influential source here is C. Wright Mills, *The Power Elite* (New York: Oxford University Press, 1956), and more recently, G. William Domhoff, *Who Rules America?* (Englewood Cliffs, N.J.: Prentice-Hall, 1967), and *The Higher Circles: The Governing Class in America* (New York: Random House, 1970).

est groups also lobby the executive and judicial branches, albeit with different methods.) First of all, contrary to the popular stereotype, lobbying does not (with rare exceptions) involve bribery; to make offers of cash is actually a very foolish technique for an interest group to attempt. Rather, the lobbyist must establish a relationship of *trust* with the legislator, and this usually involves dealings over a period of years.[14] Among the more effective means of building friendship and acquiring influence is to supply the congressman with research materials concerning legislation. Many congressmen argue that this is an important function of interest groups, for it allows them to deal on slightly more even terms with the federal bureaucracy, which comes equipped with vast staffs and mounds of information. Perhaps the most useful approach of all for the lobbyist is to convince the legislator that his policy goals will benefit the congressman's own constituents. In this way, the legislator can feel that he is responding, not to some selfish group, but working for the benefit of those who will be reelecting him. Thus, interest groups with a widely dispersed clientele, such as farmers, are the most likely to be successful in dealing with Congress. On the other hand, techniques identified as "pressure" usually are less successful. Interest groups that threaten to defeat an incumbent for reelection usually cannot carry out that threat—and the congressman knows it; for if they could, they would not have needed to make the threat in the first place. To a great extent, interest groups deal with their friends, with those legislators already somewhat predisposed to favor their goals, and avoid stirring up those who will probably be opposed.

To the extent that the above description is a correct one, it may remove some of the inherent apprehension created by the specter of interest group activity. However, there are some flaws in the argument that interest groups act to further the public interest.[15] First, the system of interest groups that has developed does a poor job of representation. Significant segments of the population do not belong to any strong group that effectively represents their interests before government.[16] This is particularly a problem for those who need the

[14] This description of the relationship between congressmen and interest groups is based upon a number of sources, including Matthews, *U.S. Senators*, chap. 8; Truman, *Governmental Process;* Raymond A. Bauer, Ithiel de Sola Pool, and Lewis Anthony Dexter, *American Business and Public Policy: The Politics of Foreign Trade* (New York: Atherton Press, 1963); and Lester W. Milbrath, *The Washington Lobbyists* (Chicago: Rand McNally, 1963).

[15] Many of the following points are pungently made in E. E. Schattschneider, *The Semi-Sovereign People: A Realist's View of Democracy in America* (New York: Holt, Rinehart, and Winston, 1960), chap. 2.

[16] For a summary of findings on membership in organizations, see Constance Smith and Anne Freedman, *Voluntary Associations: Perspectives on the Literature* (Cambridge: Harvard University Press, 1972), pp. 117–29.

help of government the most—the poor. Additionally, there is the problem of certain types of important interests in the society which tend to be left out of the picture. These are the interests that are so broad that they affect everyone and therefore are of special interest to no one. The interests of consumers, taxpayers, and of the environment would fall into this category. While it is rational for a few manufacturers to work to avoid product safety regulations from being passed, it is not worth the while of an average consumer to go to any significant effort to work for those regulations. In the past the task of representing these broad interests has been largely ignored; today, "public interest" lobbies are emerging, but lack the resources of their opponents. And even where there are organized groups on both sides of the question, their effectiveness is apt to be disproportionate to their numerical strength. Any influence that a tiny, but powerful, interest group (e.g., oil well owners) exerts will be out of proportion to its size in the population.

There are some other problems with representation through interest groups. One assumption that can be attacked is that they will indeed represent the preference of their members. Interest groups are not noted for being internally democratic, for they are typically dominated by their leadership, which acts to promote its own control of the organization, rather than the goals of the members.[17] This is particularly true of those groups that attract large memberships because of some sort of individual benefits (e.g., insurance policies), but then use the resources of the group to further particular policy goals with which the membership may not necessarily agree.[18] Finally, let us point out that even major groups with different interests often do not compete. Rather, they concentrate on the segment of policy of direct concern to their own interests; thus, potentially countervailing forces do not oppose each other. The conclusion that the effect of interest groups is to promote the common good in a quasi-democratic manner is therefore a very questionable one. Interest groups do represent some parts of the public and do further their interests, but to the probable detriment of the public as a whole.

The arguments we have advanced here are intended to refute the pluralist position that interest groups promote democracy.[19] While

[17] This tendency is the "iron law of oligarchy," first stated by Robert Michels, *Political Parties*, trans. Eden and Cedar Paul (New York: Dover Publications, 1959). First published in 1915.

[18] This phenomenon of interest group membership on the basis of individual or "selective" benefits is discussed in Mancur Olson, *The Logic of Collective Action* (Cambridge: Harvard University Press, 1965), pp. 132–41.

[19] The fact that the author rejects the pluralist interpretation of the role of interest groups does not mean that he accepts the "power elite" assumption of many critics of pluralism. The critical comments here on interest groups are consistent with the posi-

there are many points of fact that could be argued, the basic disagreement may be really a philosophical one. The pluralist position
conceives of the public in terms of a number of smaller publics with
different interests. This is in distinction to the concept we advanced
in the first chapter of the public as including everyone in the society
and weighting all preferences equally in the determination of "public opinion." Viewing the situation in our terms, the conclusion must
be drawn that interest groups generally represent only minority segments of the total public and that governmental responsiveness to
groups is, on balance, contrary to democracy.

SUBJECTIVITY IN ELITE PERCEPTIONS

The key to understanding the way in which political elites who hold
decision-making positions respond to various inputs lies in the fact
that these individuals are subject to the same psychological phenomena as people in general. Attitudes fulfill functions for decision
makers, just as for the man in the street, and they will therefore exercise the same kinds of psychological mechanisms to interpret and
screen out information. The costs of distorted perceptions may be
higher for those who are intimately involved in the political process,
and they may therefore hold a more accurate view of the world. But
subjectivity in evaluating stimuli still plays a crucial role.

This fact of subjectivity appears in the way that a congressman
views interest groups. Those groups that agree with him will tend to
be perceived as made up of public-spirited citizens; those that would
change his mind are perceived as selfish interests using "pressure." [20] Since congressmen usually only hear from those interest
groups with which they are already in agreement, there is not much
difficulty in deciding how to respond. The effects of subjectivity also
affect responsiveness to other sources of influence. In the absence of
any reliable measure of opinions in the district, the legislator can
easily feel that the people probably agree with him, or would if they
knew all of the facts. Even the more pressing stimulus of party can
conceivably be forced into the mold of existing beliefs. The southern
Democrat can rationalize that his segregationist beliefs represent the
true position of the Democratic party, its current subversion notwithstanding, just as the liberal Republican can view himself as representing the true progressive character of Republicanism. Thus, the
personal values held by a legislator exercise a powerful effect upon

---

tion taken by Theodore J. Lowi, *The End of Liberalism: Ideology, Policy, and the
Crisis of Public Authority* (New York: W. W. Norton, 1969).

[20] Lewis Anthony Dexter, "The Representative and His District," *Human Organization*, 15 (1957), 2–13.

his behavior, for they determine, in part, what he will perceive as legitimate influences on his actions. The political world of official decision makers is not nearly as homogeneous as that of the average man, but psychological functioning can greatly reduce the problem of hard decisions between competing stimuli.

This tendency toward subjectivity also has another implication, and one that would seem to increase responsiveness to the public. In actual fact, most legislators need to give little concern to the wishes of their constituents in order to be reelected. Most congressmen come from relatively safe congressional districts, and the odds that they will be defeated by a challenger are quite small. Furthermore, the public pays so little attention to most of the actions of their congressmen that they can generally vote as they please without affecting their image back home. There are exceptions—a southern congressman a few years ago could not afford to be even a moderate on civil rights—but these are few.[21] Why, then, do these officials bother to worry at all about opinions in the district, assuming that their concern is not purely out of a love for theoretical democracy?

The answer seems to lie in the fact that their perceptions are often inaccurate. Kingdon, interviewing a number of congressional and state candidates in Wisconsin, found that those who had won elections were likely to ascribe their victories to their own personal qualities and to the issues they advocated.[22] Losers were perhaps more realistic in attributing election outcomes to party fortunes and other variables beyond their control. Winners were therefore more likely to feel that the voters were possessed of high interest and intelligence, while losers were less laudatory. (Kingdon calls this the "congratulation-rationalization" effect.) Hence, those who win office may tend to have a higher regard for the capabilities of the electorate than an objective appraisal would indicate. The same implication is found in the way that candidates perceived the probable closeness of their elections. Kingdon found that almost half of those candidates who won or lost by decisive margins had been unsure of whether or not they would win.[23] Thus, politicians may often pay closer attention to what they feel are the wishes and interests of their constituents than objective political reality would demand.

"THE ATTENTIVE PUBLIC"

Thus far, we have a rather mixed bag of assessments about the responsiveness of government to the public. We see a tendency toward

[21] Miller and Stokes, "Constituency Influence," p. 371.

[22] John W. Kingdon, *Candidates for Office: Beliefs and Strategies* (New York: Random House, 1968), pp. 20–43.

[23] *Ibid.*, pp. 87–89.

clear linkage on a few, visible issues, and more nebulous relationships on most others. We see that congressmen, for various reasons, try to represent public opinion, but that their perception of it is often clouded. Much of the problem rests with the public itself, for on many issues of substantive importance but low salience, most of the public lacks the knowledge and interest to have opinions. Or if there are preferences, they are not communicated to government in any dependable fashion. What if we were to focus on that part of the public which does have information, hold opinions, and occasionally communicates with government?

This approach is taken by Devine in *The Attentive Public*.[24] He first of all analyzes survey data on a number of variables in order to determine which individuals fall into this category. Using the components of attention to political campaigns, newspapers, magazines, conversations about politics, and general political attentiveness, he is able to select the fourth of the population that most nearly represents the attentive public. This group is much more likely than the public as a whole to vote and to hold opinions on issues. It is a group that is somewhat biased in favor of higher education and economic status, but also includes substantial proportions of lower-class individuals.[25]

Devine then investigates the relationship between the opinions of this attentive group and actual policy decisions by government as compared to the opinions of the less attentive and the nonattentive. Using a number of policy areas—such as foreign aid, medicare, and civil rights—he finds that there is a parallel between the course of actual policy and the opinions of the attentive group, but not with those of the remainder of the public.[26] Furthermore, a policy change was likely to occur when a majority of the attentive public favored it, rather than a majority of the general public. Thus, it would appear that public policy tends to follow the preferences of those who pay the most attention to government. This sort of data, of course, does not necessarily prove that the attentive public causes policy change. The results, however, would be consistent with that conclusion.

Assuming that government does respond more to the attentive public, what are the implications of that fact? First of all, it is not very surprising, for policy makers can hardly respond as readily to that part of the public which holds fewer and less intense opinions and is silent about them. On all but the most visible issues, it will only be this minority that is at all interested in influencing government. In a strict sense, it may seem undemocratic that a fourth of the

---

[24] Donald J. Devine, *The Attentive Public: Polyarchical Democracy* (Chicago: Rand McNally, 1970).
[25] *Ibid.*, p. 64.
[26] *Ibid.*, pp. 65–92.

population should exercise more influence than the remainder. Yet it must be remembered that anyone can become a member of the attentive public. Lack of minimal education or extremely low income makes it more difficult to be highly informed or to correspond with public officials or to take part in political campaigns, but it does not make it impossible. The attentive public represents that segment of the population which views politics as sufficiently salient to take an interest in it. And if government should respond to this substantial and open segment of the population, that would seem considerably more democratic than responsiveness to any interest group.

PUBLIC OPINION AND POLICY MAKING: SOME CONCLUSIONS

In trying to draw together the material from the last three chapters on the role of elections, parties, and elite perceptions in linking public opinion to public policy, one conclusion seems inescapable: the extent of the influence of public opinion and the linkage through which it will have an impact depend on the kinds of issue that are involved. Let us offer some generalizations on that conclusion (realizing that these are oversimplifications that really ought to have appended qualifications too numerous to mention).

1. The influence of the public through the electoral process is basically one of voicing approval or disapproval of the results of government under the incumbents. To some extent, it may indicate a desire for more or less liberalism in domestic social welfare programs.

2. The role of political parties seems to be a dual one: (a) they innovate and implement in the area of domestic social welfare legislation, and (b) they follow the majority of the public in moving to the Left or Right in terms of general orientations toward policy.

3. Elected officials will respond directly to public opinion on a rare and visible issue where public opinion is very clear. On many other issues, on which neither public nor party offers much input, they will necessarily respond to organized interest groups.

Thus, the public has a number of channels of input, should it care to use them. There are numerous imperfections in the system that cause a lack of responsiveness. Some are a result of the way in which the formal structure of government has developed (e.g., a decentralization and lack of authority that allows minorities to block majorities). Others stem from the history and culture of the society (e.g., a party system and cleavage structure not well equipped to mobilize political support for issues). Some of the blame must be placed upon the public itself for a lack of attentiveness. The conclusion as to whether the United States is therefore "undemocratic" or not will depend upon the subjective judgments of the reader, particularly upon how upset he is at the failures of the system to respond to his perception of public opinion on particular issues. One thing seems clear: when a majority of Americans not only agree on a preference, but also feel intensely about it, government will respond.

Postscript to Part IV
AMERICAN DEMOCRACY AND PUBLIC OPINION

This book opened with a discussion of democracy and posed some questions about the nature and role of public opinion on it. Let us offer a few more summary comments on the subject.

One striking generalization that emerges from an empirical study of the mass public is that public opinion is typically a weak force. On many issues of substantive importance, considerable proportions of the public lack specific preferences. Additionally, the weak ideological interrelationship between opinions on different types of issues makes it hard to mobilize active support for majority positions. The problem comes down largely to one of low salience of politics to the mass public. The political world, furthermore, is such that intense minorities can often triumph over casually interested majorities. Thus, despite all of the valid criticisms that one can make about the structure of the political system and the behavior of its leaders, the greatest obstacle to majority rule is the individuals who make up the majority.

Our study of substantive patterns of opinion also suggests that the question of whether or not a higher degree of democracy would be desirable should be considered. Advocates of civil liberties, particularly, might have doubts as to whether they would want public policy to follow public opinion. Also, the tendency of the mass public to favor contradictory policies and goals would render a system that responded perfectly to public opinion unworkable. To know that the public would simultaneously desire lower taxes, more government spending for certain purposes, and no inflation hardly gives useful direction to a political decision maker. The operation of the political system contains a number of mechanisms that frustrate majority rule—at least temporarily—but there is also merit in those mechanisms for those who value humane and effective government.

While public opinion has its weak and unpleasant sides, these should not be overemphasized. One can point out many cases in which the public has been more progressive or reasonable than its leaders and their policies. And if the public customarily slumbers through the turmoil of public affairs, it also is occasionally roused to action. In the long run, the public almost always gets its way.

Index